Principles
of Victory

Also compiled by
Louis Gifford Parkhurst, Jr.,
PRINCIPLES OF PRAYER
from the writings of
Charles Finney

Charles G. Finney

Principles of Victory

Great themes from Romans by one of America's foremost evangelists and Bible teachers

Compiled & Edited by
Louis Gifford Parkhurst, Jr.

BETHANY HOUSE PUBLISHERS
Minneapolis, Minnesota 55438
A Division of Bethany Fellowship, Inc.

Published by Bethany House Publishers,
A Division of Bethany Fellowship, Inc.
6820 Auto Club Road, Minneapolis, Minnesota 55438

Printed in the United States of America

Library of Congress Cataloging in Publication Data

Finney, Charles Grandison, 1792-1875.
   Principles of victory.

   Bibliography: p.
   1. Bible. N.T. Romans—Sermons. 2. Sermons,
American. I. Parkhurst, Louis Gifford, 1946-
II. Title.
BS2665.4.F56   1981   227'.106   81-15464
ISBN 0-87123-471-8   AACR2

REV. CHARLES G. FINNEY.

CHARLES G. FINNEY was America's foremost evangelist. Over half a million people were converted under his ministry in an age that offered neither amplifiers nor mass communication as tools. Harvard Professor Perry Miller affirmed that "Finney led America out of the eighteenth century." As a theologian, he is best known for his "Revival Lectures" and his "Systematic Theology."

LOUIS GIFFORD PARKHURST, JR., is pastor of First Christian Church of Rochester, Minnesota. He garnered a B.A. and an M.A. from the University of Oklahoma and an M.Div. degree from Princeton Theological Seminary. Before his ordination he was a graduate assistant in philosophy at the University of Oklahoma. He is married and the father of two young children. His first book in this series is entitled *Principles of Prayer*.

ACKNOWLEDGMENTS

By way of personal tribute, I owe much to Gordon Olson of the Bible Research Fellowship, Inc., for the gracious loaning of some materials on Finney, for his own books, and for his taped lectures. His warm friendship, advice, and devotion to Jesus Christ were beyond measure to me personally in completing this project. I must also thank Francis Schaeffer of the L'Abri Fellowship Foundation. His books and counsel convinced me that without any doubt the Bible is true and without error in all that it affirms, and Christianity has the only sufficient answers to the great questions of life and to the real problems of our world. Finally, I thank Harry Conn for his encouragement, and his suggestions, during the initial stages of this book. More than any others, these men have convinced me of the reasonableness of Christianity, and they have inspired in me a deeper love for our God and Saviour.

To two librarian friends, Ardis Sawyer, Librarian of the Minnesota Bible College, and Jack Key, Librarian of the Mayo Clinic, both of Rochester, Minnesota, I owe a special thanks for materials and advice. I also wish to acknowledge the assistance of Speer Library, Princeton Theological Seminary, Princeton, New Jersey. And I thank W. E. Bigglestone, Archivist, of the Oberlin College Archives, Oberlin, Ohio, for some special pictures relating to Finney as a preacher, and for other assistance and materials.

I wish also to thank Carol Johnson, managing editor of Bethany House Publishers, for her desire to make Finney's works more accessible to the many thousands who seek to know more about him and know his theology better for the sake of presenting an intelligent Gospel to those struggling for a reasonable and Spirit-filled life. Her kindness and encouragement and sincere concern to publish attractive and well-designed books has made it a real joy for me to compile these sermons and provide an analysis of Finney as the greatest American preacher of the nineteenth century.

Finally, I wish to thank Judy Bonadore for her careful typing of portions of this manuscript. And, I appreciate more than I can repay the faithful members of First Christian Church, who have struggled with me as I have tried to clarify my theological and biblical positions in the light of what I was learning from Charles Finney about the truth of the Gospel. This project would never have been completed apart from my family, who still loved me and encouraged me during my most frustrating moments with Finney's sermons.

For the sake of His Kingdom,

L. G. Parkhurst, Jr.
First Christian Church
Rochester, Minnesota
January 13, 1981

CONTENTS

HOW TO PREACH SO AS TO CONVERT NOBODY

1. Let your supreme motive be popularity rather than salvation.
2. Study to please your congregation and to make a reputation rather than to please God.
3. Take up popular, passing and sensational themes to draw the crowd, and avoid the essential doctrines of salvation.
4. Denounce sin in the abstract, but pass lightly over sins that prevail in your congregation.
5. Preach on the loveliness of virtue and the glory of heaven, but not on the sinfulness of sin.
6. Reprove the sins of the absent, but make those who are present pleased with themselves, so that they will enjoy the sermon and not go away with their feelings hurt.
7. Make the impression on worldly church members that God is too good to send anyone to hell, even if there is a hell.
8. Preach the universal Fatherhood of God and brotherhood of man so as to show that no second birth is really needed.

Charles G. Finney

CHARLES FINNEY: PREACHER

Charles G. Finney was the greatest preacher and theologian of the nineteenth century. He stood head and shoulders above his peers by excelling in every field of Christian endeavor: in preaching, in teaching, in debating, in formulating a relevant and biblical theological system, in evangelism, and in ecumenical relationships. From the time of his dramatic conversion in 1821 to his death in 1875, Finney traveled as an evangelist and revivalist in the United States and England, served in settled pastorates, taught as a professor of systematic theology, promoted social activism, published his sermons and wrote books on revival and theology, and later served as President of Oberlin College. If Jonathan Edwards was the outstanding theologian of the eighteenth century, surely Charles Finney deserves that distinction for the nineteenth. Both men expressed the evangelical Christian faith with such intellectual integrity and power that they dramatically changed and shaped the subsequent course of American religious and social history. We can only hope to remedy the problem Jeremy Rifkin and Ted Howard described in their book, *The Emerging Order,* when they wrote of Charles Finney, "It's ironic that so few Americans today have any knowledge of this man, who, more than any other single individual of the nineteenth century, was responsible for sparking the abolitionist and feminist drives, the demand for increased education and the development of voluntary associations in the United States."[1] Even as his sermons were the first introduction most of his contemporaries had to him and to the doctrines he preached, so this new edition of his collected sermons and Bible lectures on Paul's "Letter to the Romans" may introduce modern Americans and Internationals to this biblical expositor and theologian.

We cannot overemphasize the impact of Charles Finney, the preacher. Nor can we neglect his sermons in any study of nineteenth-century preaching. For no American preacher of that time had a greater or longer lasting impact than did Finney. But more importantly, those of us who call ourselves "Twentieth-Century Christians" need to consider and appropriate for our lives and our nation Finney's deep concern and expression for God's honor, God's will, and God's Kingdom. We need to possess Finney's ability to show love and compassion for his fellowman, because this enabled him to apply the Bible to the world and change it. Over 500,000 persons professed conversion during the revival that began with Finney's conversion and subsequent preaching. It is estimated that during the year 1857-58, about 100,000 persons became Christians as either the direct or indirect result of his preaching, teaching, and writing. According to actual research, 85% of those professing conversion to Christ during Finney's meetings remained true to their commitment; whereas, 70% of those professing conversion at the meetings of D. L. Moody became backsliders. Finney had the admirable ability to impress on people through his preaching the necessity of continued holy living. As a preacher, his outstanding results were due primarily to the logical presentation of the truth in God's Word, to the work and influence of the Holy Spirit (for which he prayed so fervently), and to his loving and compassionate sermon delivery.

Finney's legal background had a decided influence upon his theology and preaching. He preached as a lawyer for a verdict. While practicing law, he was impressed by the frequent references to the Mosaic Law as the source and authority for much English and American law, and so he purchased the first Bible he ever owned in order to more closely study the references in context. Literally with lawbooks in one hand and the Bible in the other, Finney became convinced that the Bible was truly the Word of God. He came to recognize that since Christianity was true, he had an obligation to choose between the Christian faith and the pursuit of a worldly life. After his remarkable conversion, he put his lawbooks aside, picked up his Bible, and determined to plead the cause of Jesus Christ. In his subsequent preaching and writing, the unmistakable sound of the lawyer concerned about logical presentation and moral government is everywhere present. In his autobiography, he wrote that effective discourses lead to action, and the "language is in point, direct, and simple . . . sentences are short, cogent, and powerful. The appeal is made for action."[2] Early in his ministry the so-called learned ministry disdained his style, but the masses loved it because "he just talked to them." And with the masses he consistently won his case.

Finney's conversion experience was accompanied by a great outpouring of the Holy Spirit into his life. In the course of his preaching, he recognized how crucial prayer and the Holy Spirit were to any success from the pulpit. He said that if he lost the spirit of grace and supplication, then his preaching was without power. He discovered the truth of the gospel without the influence of the Holy Spirit would only harden the sinner in his rebellion against God. From some unpublished additional handwritten material in his autobiography, Finney wrote: "I found myself having more or less power in preaching, and in personal labors for souls, just in proportion as I had the spirit of prevailing prayer. I have found that unless I kept myself and have been kept in such relations to God as to have daily and hourly access to Him in prayer, my efforts to win souls were abortive; but that when I could prevail with God in prayer, I could prevail with man in preaching, exhortation, and conversation."[3] Finney also made the observation that "Without the direct teaching of the Holy Spirit, a man will never make much progress in preaching the Gospel. The fact is, unless he can preach the Gospel as an experience, present religion to mankind as a matter of consciousness, his speculations and theories will come far short of preaching the Gospel."[4]

Some of the sermons in this edition will read coldly logical, but bathed in prayer they were, and still are, powerful in their grasp and presentation of biblical truths. One purpose of this introduction is to make Finney, the preacher, known; then we can see beyond what may read coldly to the warmth of a loving and vibrant personality. All of the sermons and lectures are notes taken as verbatum as possible while Finney was preaching, and then carefully checked by him for accuracy of thought and expression, but none represent the hour and a half that Finney often preached. Each has been edited to contemporary standards without impairing their oratorical uniqueness.

The *manner* in which these sermons were delivered cannot be captured adequately on the printed page, but if we can learn about Finney's style we can appreciate them more. Finney recognized the importance of how things are said: "Very much, in this as in everything else, depends on the spirit in which it is said. If the people see that it is said in the spirit of love, with a yearning desire to do them good; if they cannot call it an ebullition of personal animosity, but if they see, and cannot deny that it is telling the truth in love; that it is coming right home to them to save them individually, there are very few that will continue to resent it."[5]

In analyzing his preaching during one revival, he wrote: "Everyone was out at the meeting; and the Lord let me loose upon them in a wonderful manner. My preaching seemed to them to be something new. Indeed, it seemed to myself as if I could rain hail and love upon them at the same time; or in other words, that I could rain upon them hail, in love. It seemed as if my love to God, in view of the abuse which they heaped upon Him, sharpened up my mind to the most intense agony. I felt like rebuking them with all my heart, and yet with a compassion which they could not mistake. I never knew that they accused me of severity; although I think I never spoke with more severity, perhaps, in my life. But the labors of this day were effectual to the conviction of the great mass of the population."[6]

Many others appreciated these fine qualities of character, discernment, and preaching skill in Charles Finney. In his biography of Finney, G. F. Wright has recorded several citations from people who had heard Finney preach on various occasions and from those who knew him well. They attributed his preaching success to the quality of his logical presentation, to his concern for the honor of God, and to his overwhelmingly tenderhearted compassion. Dr. Joseph P. Thompson, one of Finney's successors at the Broadway Tabernacle, New York City, on the last Sunday he himself occupied that great pulpit in April 1857, gave a lasting tribute to Finney and his preaching: "Mr. Finney's method of preaching was peculiar. Gifted with fine powers of analysis which were early disciplined in the study of law, he has, also, the constructive faculty in a high degree; so that he can at once dissect an error or sophism, analyze a complex feeling, motive, or action, and build a logical argument with cummulative force. With these he combines a vivid imagination, and the power of graphic description. Nor, with the seeming sharpness and severity of his logic and the terrors which his fancy portrays, is he wanting in tenderness of feeling. His experimental knowledge of divine truth is deep and thorough, and his knowledge of the workings of the human mind under that truth is extended and philosophical. Hence his preaching searches the conscience, convinces the judgment, and stirs the will either to assent or to rebellion. His elocution, though unstudied and so sometimes inelegant, is yet strangely effective; and in the proper mood of an assembly, a pause, a gesture, an emphasis, an inflection, an exclamation, will produce the highest oratorical effects. The conviction of sincerity attends his words; the force of an earnest mind goes with his logic.

"His sermons in the Tabernacle were unwritten, and were usually preached from a brief lying before him. But though extempore in their dress, they were not unstudied as to their matter or their form. In yonder study, the first pastor of the Tabernacle had a huge slate, upon which he would sketch an outline of a sermon, as an architect sketches his plan, the painter his groups. This done, he would betake himself to prayer, or pace the room in earnest thought. By and by, perhaps the whole plan would be effaced, and another substituted for it; or the first would be recast in the vigorous mould of a mind kindled by prayer, till it came forth glowing with the fire of the Holy Ghost. Then he was ready for the pulpit, and therefore God was with him in the pulpit."[7]

Mr. Wright, his biographer, who was well acquainted with Finney at Oberlin, also has observed: "We cannot understand the success of Finney's labors . . . without keeping in mind the intensity of his religious convictions and the great tenderness of his heart. [In] his . . . sermon . . . from the text, 'Ye generation of vipers, how can ye escape the damnation of hell?' [Matthew 23:33] . . . the words of rebuke were not those of one who loved denunciation: they were rather like the faithful probing of the surgeon who knows full well the gravity of the case. When his words of rebuke had accomplished their design, he then with tears set forth the promises of Christ."[8]

It is important for us to know of Finney the man and the preacher, and we have considered his character, style, and impact. But he would have had few enduring results if his theology had been warped or unbiblical. He marshalled biblical truth in a helpful way to lead many to what he termed "hopeful conversion," and to "fire up" his lukewarm Christian brethren so they too might become fellow co-workers with God in His Kingdom. In his *Autobiography,* he took great care to underscore the doctrines he preached at the different revivals, and how the people responded to what he consistently preached. The following doctrinal summary is a good representation of several you will find as you read his *Autobiography:* "The doctrines preached in promoting that revival [1825] were those I have preached everywhere: The total, moral, voluntary depravity of unregenerate man; the necessity of a radical change of heart, through the truth, by the agency of the Holy Spirit; the divinity and humanity of our Lord Jesus Christ; His vicarious atonement, equal to the wants of all mankind; the gift, divinity and agency of the Holy Spirit; repentance, faith, justification by faith, sanctification by faith; persistence in holiness as a condition of salvation—indeed all the distinctive doctrines of the Gospel were stated and set forth with as much clearness, and point, and power as were possible to me under the circumstances. A great spirit of prayer prevailed."[9]

Gordon Olson, who for almost 50 years has studied and analyzed Finney's theology and methodology to make it more accessible to us in a contemporary way through his Bible Research Fellowship, has highlighted seven key points in Finney's preaching which I will endeavor to summarize. First, Finney insisted that salvation was the complete transformation of the entire personality in relationship with God. A condition of salvation was giving up all sin in repentance.

Second, transformation of personality involved a change from a state of selfishness to an active, energetic love for God and one's fellowman.

Third, people were taught exactly what salvation and its requirements were, and they were given time (under the influence of the Holy Spirit and the truth of the gospel) to "seek God for themselves until they had a direct consciousness of an intelligent meeting with God, with a full assurance that they had confessed all the sins that they could think of and had been gloriously forgiven through a committal of faith in the atoning death of Christ."[10]

Fourth, Finney preached that sin was always a voluntary action, a wrong action of our wills, and was to be distinguished from physical depravity. Sinners needed a moral change rather than a constitutional (physical) change to be saved.

Fifth, he stressed that the understanding had to be reached or true lasting conversion would not take place. A man of great feeling, imagination, and emotion, he was ever vigilant to regulate any emotional excesses at his meetings.

Sixth, he insisted that much prayer and the work of the Holy Spirit were essential in presenting the truth to the mind.

Seventh, when attacked or condemned, Finney refused to retaliate or condemn or enter into any controversy, since this would inhibit, if not destroy, any revival then in progress.

With these doctrinal beliefs and methods *used consistently* in his revival preaching, it is no wonder that one of his early adversaries, Lyman Beecher, had to admit finally with warm admiration when comparing Finney to the revivalist Nettleton that, "Nettleton 'set snares' for sinners, but Finney rode them down with a cavalry charge."[11] W. H. Harding, who revised and edited an edition of Finney's *Lectures on Revivals of Religion,* wrote of him: "He was for mobilizing every unit of the forces of God and inspiring them afresh with a sense of the urgency and expectancy and self-abandonment of apostolic days. Moreover, his personality was such as to constitute him a chief force in any arena of thought or action, and *his spirit and words showed truly Pauline.* He mingled his reproofs with his tears, as he championed the cause of the slave, gave some smiting exposition of holy doctrine, or stopped suddenly, in a searching appeal, to describe his visions of the Coming Kingdom or the solemn dealings of the Lord God with his soul. He inevitably became one of the most conspicuous figures in the world's religious life, but no touch of unreality came upon him: he remained the soul of humility."[12]

Principles of Victory is a new collection of Finney's sermons and lectures on Paul's "Letter to the Romans," many of which have been out of print for many years and scattered in various volumes. Finney published more sermons on Paul's Romans than on any other book in the Bible. The principles in these chapters illustrate the decidedly "Pauline" cast of his mind and expound the doctrines he consistently preached. Furthermore, one cannot help but notice the recurring theme of Christ bringing us victory over all life's problems; and particularly victory over sin and the power of sin that threatens to undo us.

Finney preached on many of the most important verses and chapters from Romans, and these sermons represent some of his best overall. Some readers will want to turn immediately to the sermons on the crucial verses such as the sermons on Romans 1:18 or Romans 7. Others will want to rush to read "Sanctification by Faith," "Total Depravity," or "On the Atonement." Some will want to read through the sermons while they study Romans and make comparisons with a good commentary; and still others will draw conclusions as they think of what Luther, or Calvin, or Lloyd-Jones said on the same text.

Perhaps one of the most interesting sermons, from a sociological/ theological point of view, discusses the role of women in the 1830's and the parallels between the woman's role and Christ as the husband of the Church. Reading *Principles of Victory* and Finney's *Autobiography* should be two of your best introductions to Finney's life and thought in the primary sources. Both could be read to discover the biblical and spiritual mold of Finney's mind before tackling his famous *Systematic Theology.*

Finney sought in all of his sermons to produce wholehearted Christians. In this respect, each of his sermons and lectures on Romans can challenge and encourage us. We would do well to remember and heed, therefore, these words of Gordon Olson's, and apply them to our study of Finney's principles: "God never intended that men should set their minds to devise great theological speculations, but rather that they should occupy their minds with the simple Biblical revelations concern-

ing the Godhead and Gospel relationships. Each sincere servant of
Christ faces the sifting process as he seeks to discern God's mind and
message. In this the anointing of the Holy Spirit has been promised (I
John 2:27), in fulfillment of the Saviour's words (John 16:12-15). We
have before us one [Finney] of the noblest of our race, whose method of
approach to God and truth cannot be improved upon. We have every
testimony of his sincerity and humility, and of the extreme fertility of
his mind in logical processes. We also have recorded on the pages of
world history what happened when the conclusions he arrived at were
proclaimed. This by no stretch of the imagination could have occurred
apart from Divine approval and energy. Each inquirer for truth must decide the source of this message which moved multitudes of the most intelligent citizens of our land and of the world."[13]

L. G. Parkhurst, Jr.

References and Notes

1. Jeremy Rifkin with Ted Howard, *The Emerging Order* (New York: G. P. Put-
   nam's Sons, 1979), p. 143.
2. Charles G. Finney, *An Autobiography* (Old Tappan: Fleming H. Revell Co.,
   n.d.), p. 90: see also pp. 94-96. Helen Wessel has done a fine job of condensing
   Finney's Autobiography: *The Autobiography Of Charles G. Finney* (Minneapolis: Bethany Fellowship, Inc., 1977). A brief biography has been written by
   Basil Miller, *Charles Finney* (Minneapolis: Bethany Fellowship, Inc., n.d.)
   This was the official biography of Finney prepared in 1942 for the Sesquicen-
   tennial Conference in Chicago.
3. Excerpted from a paper by Gordon C. Olson, *"Quotations From the Writings
   and Experiences of Revivalist Charles G. Finney" (Reinforcing the Investigation on "What Will Bring Spiritual Revival")* published by the Bible Research Fellowship, Inc., 2624 Hawthorne Street, Franklin Park, Illinois,
   60131, 1967, revised 1977, p. 3. For much insight into why Finney's prayers
   were so effective in his preaching and evangelistic efforts see: Charles G. Finney, *Principles of Prayer,* edited by Louis Gifford Parkhurst, Jr. (Minneapolis: Bethany Fellowship, Inc.,1980).
4. *An Autobiography*, pp. 55, 56.
5. *Ibid.*, p. 92.
6. *Ibid.*, pp. 100, 101.
7. G. F. Wright, *Charles Grandison Finney* (Boston and New York: Houghton,
   Mifflin and Company, 1891), pp. 302-304.
8. *Ibid.*, pp. 35, 36.
9. *An Autobiography*, pp. 134, 135.
10. *"Quotations,"* p. 7.
11. C. G. Finney, *Revivals Of Religion*, edited by William H. Harding (London:
    Morgan and Scott, Ld., 1913), p. xi: see also pp. 217-249; "How to Preach the
    Gospel." Fleming H. Revell currently still prints this book, without the in-

troduction by Harding. Donald Dayton has compiled Finney's "Letters on Revival" from *The Oberlin Evangelist* in Charles G. Finney, *Reflections on Revival* (Minneapolis: Bethany Fellowship, Inc., 1979). The highlights of Finney's *Lectures on Revival* have been printed in book form: *Finney on Revival*, arranged by E. E. Shelhamer (Minneapolis: Bethany Fellowship, Inc., n.d.)

12. *Ibid.*, p. xi. The italics are my own.

13. *"Quotations,"* p. 11. Another very excellent analysis of Charles Finney as preacher and revivalist is in *Finney Lives On* by V. Raymond Edman (Minneapolis: Bethany Fellowship, Inc., 1951, 1971). The inspirational book *Deeper Experiences of Famous Christians* by James Gilchrist Lawson (Anderson, Indiana: The Warner Press, 1911, fourth printing 1978) has a good chapter on Finney and the author states, "The writer is inclined to regard Charles G. Finney as the greatest evangelist and theologian since the days of the apostles. . . . Finney's *Systematic Theology* is probably the greatest work on theology outside the Scriptures," p. 175. Finney's *The Heart of Truth* and *Systematic Theology* are also available from Bethany Fellowship, Inc., in 1976 reprints, and I suggest reading the former before the latter.

LETTER TO A YOUNG SEMINARIAN
ON PREACHING

The following letter from Charles G. Finney, addressed to his young friend Brainerd in 1828, indicates Finney's passionate concern for good preaching and the Christian character and spirit of prayer which must authenticate it.

"Your letter came duly to hand, and afforded me much pleasure. I seize a moment in which to mention a thing or two.

"First, be careful, amid the various specimens of public speaking which are constantly before you, not to become a copyist. Be *Brainerd*, or you will be *nobody*. I have seen many young men spoiled by setting up a model and attempting to fashion themselves after it. In this they fail. In the attempt, however, they *spoil themselves* by losing themselves under their borrowed manner, and often, to observing eyes, render themselves very ridiculous and disgusting.

"Be careful not to let yourself to be criticised out of a natural and colloquial style of communication. I cannot speak of Andover particularly as to style and manner, but I am certain that much that is called pulpit eloquence at the present day is mere bosh and noise and foppery. I have the greatest confidence in the piety and theology of Andover, but there are three principal defects in the specimens which I have seen from there. Their young men are not half enough in earnest. A hearer would be very apt to catch the impression that they were performing a professional *duty*. This makes infidels, however logically they may reason. Unless they appear to believe their own message, it would be a miracle if others believed it. They are too stiff; there is not enough of nature in their manner. They are not colloquial enough. Their style is too elevated, their periods too round; too much dress and drapery and millinery and verbiage about their preaching. They are, or seem to be, afraid of being called vulgar. They are not understood by the multitudes.

"I do not mean that these things are peculiar to Andover; they are the common defects of most theological students. The more I preach and the more I hear others preach, the more I am impressed with the conviction that a prominent reason why preaching produces so little effect, is because it is not understood. Young men are often afraid and ashamed of using common words. From this error stand off wide, keep clear, or you make a shipwreck of your usefulness.

"The remark is often made to me, 'I never understood preaching until I heard you.' Don't think by this that I mean to make myself a standard. By no means. I only advert to the fact, that if a man would be understood he must dare to be called vulgar.

"There is another thing, however, of infinite importance to a divinity student. I mean a spirit of *prayer*. I am convinced that nothing in the whole Christian religion is so difficult, and so, rarely attained, as a praying heart.[1] Without this you are as weak as weakness itself. With it you are irresistible. This would be thought to be a strange remark by some, and to savor strongly of fanaticism. But I tell you, before the Millennium comes the church will have to turn over a new leaf, and have to take a new lesson on the subject of prayer. You remember this! When I think how almost certain you are to lose what of the praying spirit you ever had, and come out of the Seminary very wise, but very dry, and go about your work without unction and life and spirituality, I am distressed, and could I raise my voice with sufficient strength, you would hear me cry, 'Beware! Lay down your books and pray!' Frequent seasons of secret prayer are, in my mind, wholly indispensable to the keeping up of an intercourse with God.

"Let me say again and again, if you lose your spirit of prayer you will do nothing, or next to nothing, though you had the intellectual endowments of an angel. If you lose your spirituality you had better stop and break off in the midst of your preparations, and repent and turn to God, or go about some other employment, for I cannot contemplate a more loathsome and abominable object than an earthly minded minister. The blessed Lord deliver and preserve his dear church from the guidance and influence of men who know not what it is to pray."[2]

References and Notes

1. See particularly the Introduction and pages 86, 87 of Charles G. Finney, *Principles of Prayer*, compiled and edited by Louis Gifford Parkhurst, Jr. (Minneapolis, Minnesota: Bethany Fellowship, Inc., 1980).
2. This letter was taken from "Charles G. Finney's Common Sense," *The Christian Standard*, December 21, 1878, pp. 11, 12.

FINNEY'S SUCCESSFUL PREACHING
IN ENGLAND

Charles Finney made two preaching tours of England and Scotland at the invitation of several ministers who had read his revival lectures. While these were being conducted, somewhat regular reports on their reception were printed in *The Oberlin Evangelist*. The following is an extract from the August 15, 1860, edition, Volume XXII:

"A small weekly sheet is published in London, called *The Revival*—a weekly summary of events connected with the present revival of religion. It has nearly finished its second year. From this sheet we extract the following statements, under the head of *Manchester*. They will show our readers how Pres. Finney and wife have been laboring during the spring months and early summer, and with what manifest tokens of blessing from the Lord.

"We are especially interested to observe the same class of results there which we have so often known to attend Pres. Finney's labors in this country—great searchings of heart, a deep sense of sin, confessions, restitutions, and peace of mind only *after* thorough repentance, and then through faith in the blood of the Lamb. We could wish that the revivals of just the past two years in this country had the same characteristics more generally and more deeply."

The Revival

" 'After a three month's stay at Bolton, during which period hundreds were converted to God, the distinguished American evangelist, the Rev. C. G. Finney, and his devoted wife, were induced to visit Manchester. They were invited by a few ministers who had long lamented the coldness and deadness of the churches, the comparative rarity of conversions, and the vast numbers of non-worshippers around, and who had earnestly prayed for a general and genuine Revival.

" 'Mr. and Mrs. Finney began their labors at the latter end of last

April. Since that time Mr. Finney has preached twice on the Sabbath, and four times during the week. Mrs. Finney has held meetings five times a week, for females exclusively, has addressed "mothers" every Thursday, and unmarried females every Friday afternoon.

" 'The season has, in some respects, been very unfavorable to revival work. Trade has been brisk. The working and middle classes have been employed until a late hour. Many of the higher classes are out of town. Above all, *Whitsuntide*, with its peculiar associations in Manchester, as a season of Sunday-school festivity, has been a sad drawback; yet, in spite of all hindrances, much good has been done; and seeds are sown every day, which will spring forth and bear much fruit.

" 'Mr. Finney is well known in America and England. His preaching is marked by strong peculiarities. It is highly argumentative—keenly logical—yet, being composed of good strong Saxon, is intelligible to the common people. Boldness, verging to severity, is one of its characteristics. Unpalatable truths are urged with a fearless courage. Human responsibility and the obligation of everyone to repent and believe the gospel are handled with a master's grasp. Professors are not suffered to hide beneath the covert of mere formalism, or an orthodox creed. Masks, pretexts, subterfuges of all sorts, are exposed; and the selfish, the worldly, the cowardly, the inconsistent, are driven from their retreats. Then comes the gospel, with its full and free antidote to despair; its gracious invitations to the penitent; its pardon and peace for the believing. Mr. F. is sixty-eight years of age, and has been a laborious worker in the cause of God forty years; yet he preaches with wonderful energy six times every week, and after every service holds meetings for anxious inquirers. The meetings for inquiry have been attended variably as to numbers; but, altogether, some hundreds of anxious souls have been gathered on these occasions. Many striking instances of conversion have occurred. Many backsliders have been reclaimed. Many professors have been quickened with new life. Selection is difficult. A respectable man and his wife, sitting near each other one evening, were almost at the same moment melted down into penitence. That night the husband prayed really for the first time for many years; and they have both continued to manifest the sincerity of their repentance and faith in Christ. A man who, for twenty years, never entered a place of worship, who has been an awful drunkard, and given up as hopeless by his friends, was converted to God last week; and his family can hardly believe their own eyes when they witness the change that has taken place in him. The writer noticed this man the other evening listening attentively to the truth of the gospel, while his face was wet with tears. A large number of the inquirers are men. One, who had been a Roman Catholic, and who came into chapel in his working clothes, was convinced and converted to God. The joy and gladness expressed by all who have yielded themselves to Christ are wonderful to see. Rich and poor are all alike proving the power of truth. Cases of restitution are not uncommon. Merchants, tradesmen, servants who have robbed employers, have confessed and restored what they had dishonestly obtained. Nor are children wanting to complete the picture. Two little boys, last evening, were among the lingering inquirers; and, after manifestation of deep emotion, yielded themselves to Christ. Those two lads will never forget till their dying day the prayer which the venerable man of God, in simple, touching, melting words, offered on their behalf, as he knelt at their side and commended them to the care of Jesus.

" 'Mrs. Finney's meetings have also produced a considerable effect. They have had a salutary and blessed influence on many a wife and mother: many have stirred up to pray for themselves; and their husbands and children have seen, in several instances already, the answer to their prayers. The work is thus going on. If ministers and people will only co-operate, throwing aside sectarian prejudice, the Revival will spread, and glorious triumphs of the gospel will be seen "not many days hence." ' "

The Broadway Tabernacle

The Broadway Tabernacle in New York City was designed and built by Finney in 1835. The building was 100 feet square, the walls were plain brick, and it had no exterior adornment. He planned this interior to seat 2,500 people, with arrangements to seat an additional 1,500. No listener was more than 80 feet from the speaker; and therefore anyone could hear Finney with ease. His study was located under the choir loft. The cost of the building was $65,000. This photo was furnished through the courtesy of the Oberlin College Archives.

The Oberlin Congregational Church

This is the Congregational Church Finney served as pastor in Oberlin, Ohio, from 1837 to 1872; and where he preached on Sundays and on Thursday afternoons. His Thursday sermons were teaching sermons that relied heavily upon his classroom method. The Oberlin College students believed these Thursday afternoon sermons were indispensable to their education; therefore most of the 20,000 students who passed through Oberlin during Finney's lifetime would have heard him preach here. Finney died August 16, 1875, and a simple inscription was placed on the pulpit of the church: "From this pulpit for many years Charles G. Finney presented to this community and to the world the unsearchable riches of Christ." This photo was taken about 1870 when Finney was pastor, and was furnished for reproduction here through the courtesy of the Oberlin College Archives.

1

THE WRATH OF GOD AGAINST THOSE WHO WITHSTAND HIS TRUTH*
Romans 1:18

"For the wrath of God is revealed from heaven against all ungodliness and un-righteousness of men who hold the truth in unrighteousness."

These words in their context show that the apostle has his eye espe-cially on those who, not having a written revelation from God, might yet know Him in His works of nature. Paul's view is that God's invisible at-tributes are apparent to the human mind, because they are revealed by the things He has made. In and by means of these works, we may learn of His eternal power and His real divinity. Hence all men have some means of knowing the great truths that pertain to God, our infinite Cre-ator. And hence God may, with the utmost propriety, hold men respon-sible for accepting this truth reverently, and rendering to their Creator the homage due. If they withhold their homage, they are utterly without excuse.

In discussing the subject presented in our text, let us inquire:

I. *What is the true idea of unrighteousness?*

Beyond question, unrighteousness is at least the negation of righ-teousness, and may imply more or less positive wickedness. Here the question will arise, *What is righteousness?* To which I answer, "right-ness"—*moral* rightness, the original term being used in regard to mate-rial things to denote what is straight; as, for example, a straight line. Unrighteousness, the opposite of this, must mean what is morally crooked, distorted—not in harmony with the rightness of God's law. To denote *sin*, the Scriptures employ some terms which properly signify a

---

Sermons on the Way of Salvation, pp. 187-202.

negation, or utter absense of what should be. Some theologians have maintained that the true idea of sin is simply *negative*, supposing sin to consist in *not* doing and *not* being what one ought to do and to be. This idea is strongly implied in our text. Sin is, indeed, a neglect to do known duty and a refusal to comply with known obligation. Inasmuch as love is required always and of all men, not loving must be a state of real disobedience. Suffice it, then, to say, that unrighteousness is an omission—a known omission—a refusal to *be* what we should, and to *do* what we should. Of course sin is only and wholly voluntary. The mind's refusal to obey God is a matter of its own free choice.

II. *What is implied in "holding the truth in unrighteousness"?*

The original term "hold" means to hold back, to restrain. The idea is that a person restrains the legitimate influence of the truth, and will not let it have its proper sway over his will.

The human mind is so constituted that truth is its natural stimulus. This stimulus of truth would, if not restrained and held back, lead the mind naturally to obey God. A person holds back the truth through his own unrighteousness, when, for selfish reasons, he overrules and restrains truth's natural influence, and will not allow it to take possession and hold sway over his mind.

III. *What is intended by "the wrath of God revealed from heaven"?* and *Why is it thus revealed against all such unrighteousness?* The obvious sense is that God, manifesting himself from heaven, has revealed His high and just displeasure against all restraining of the truth and withstanding of its influence.

Before I proceed to show why this is, I must be permitted to come very near to some of you whom I see before me this day, and talk to you in great frankness and faithfulness. I do not charge you with having been outwardly immoral, but you *have restrained the truth; you have withstood its influence.* You are therefore the very persons against whom the wrath of God is said to be revealed. This is true of every one of you who has not given himself up to the influence of truth. You have restrained that natural influence; therefore, against *you* God has revealed His wrath.

God's wrath is a terrible thing. The wrath of a king is terrible; how much more so is the wrath of *God*! Ah, who can stand before Him when once He shall arise in His wrath to avenge His truth and His own glorious name!

Why does God's wrath wax hot against this sin? Comprehensively, the reason is this: withstanding the truth is resisting God's revealed claims of love and obedience; and is therefore, the *whole of sin*. All is comprised in it. This is the very essence—the true idea of sin; it is *deliberate, intelligent, and intentional rebellion against God*. There can be no obligation until your conscience affirms it to you. The conscience cannot affirm obligation until there is some knowledge of God revealed to the mind; but when this knowledge is revealed, then conscience must and will affirm obligation. The more conscience is developed, the more it unfolds, the more strongly it affirms your obligation to obey God. Suppose a person were created asleep. Until he awakes, there could be in his mind no knowledge of God—not one idea of God; and consequently, no sense of obligation to obey Him. But as soon as the moral functions of the reason and the conscience create a sense of obligation, then the mind is brought to a decision. It must then either choose to obey or to disobey God. It must elect either to take God's law as its rule of duty or to reject it.

The alternative of rejecting God makes it necessary to hold back the truth and to withstand its claims. We might almost say that these processes are substantially identical—resisting the natural influence of God's truth on the mind and withstanding the known claims of God. When you know the truth concerning God, the great question being whether or not you will obey it, if your heart says, "No!" you do of course resist the claims of truth: you hold it back through your own unrighteousness.

The very apprehending of moral truth concerning God renders it impossible to be indifferent. Once you see God's claims, you cannot avoid acting upon them in one way or another. To stop after you know your duty and hold your minds aloof from obedience is to be just as wicked as you can be. You disown your whole obligation towards God and practically say unto Him, "Depart from me, for I desire not the knowledge of your ways." Is not this just to be as wicked as you can be; to disobey light you may have at the time? What more wicked thing could you do?

Let us look at this matter a little farther. Holding back the truth through unrighteousness implies the total rejection of the moral law as a rule of duty. This must be the case: when light concerning the meaning of this law comes before some, they repel it and resist its claims and virtually say, "That law is no rule of duty to me." Thus resisting the influence of truth, they practically deny all obligations to God. Truth comes before their minds, they perceive their obligation, but they withhold their minds from its sway.

You may probably have observed that some persons seem to have no sense of any other obligation except that created by human law. Legal obligation can reach them, but not moral. They will not pay an honest debt unless it appears that the strong hand of the law can take hold of them. Others have no concern for any claims except those that serve their business reputation. Take away their fear of losing their reputation; remove all the inducements to do right, except those that pertain to moral obligation, and see if they will ever do anything.

Now such men practically reject and deny God's rights altogether, and, equally so, their own obligations to God. Their conduct put into words would read: "I have some respect for human law and some fear of human penalty; but, for God's law or penalty, I care nothing!"

It is easy to see that to hold back the truth in this manner is the perfection of wickedness. Suppose a man refrains from sinning only because of his obligations to human laws: he shows that he fears human penalties only and has no fear of God.

Again, holding the truth in unrighteousness settles all questions regarding moral character. You may know the man with unerring certainty. His position is taken; his course is fixed; as to moral obligation, he cares nothing. Moral obligation does not decide his course at all. He becomes totally dishonest. This settles the question of his character. Until he reveres God's authority, there is not a particle of moral goodness in him. He does not act with even common honesty. Of course his moral character towards God is formed and is easily known. If he had any moral honesty, the perceived fact of his own moral obligation would influence his mind. But we see it does not at all; he shuts down the gate on all the claims of truth and will not allow them to sway his will. Hence it must be that his heart is fully committed to wickedness.

The wrath of God is revealed from heaven against all who thus hold back the truth, because this attitude of the will shows that you are reckless of your obligations towards God. It shows that with you a moral claim on your heart and conscience means nothing. If you restrain the truth from influencing your mind, this very fact proves that *you do not mean to serve God.* Some of you know that you are not doing what you know to be your duty. You are conscious that the presence of known duty does not move you. You have not done one act of obedience to God's claims because they are God's. Again, not only does this settle the question of moral character—which is of itself a good reason for God's wrath—but it also settles the question of *moral relations.* It shows that your moral character is altogether corrupt and wrong; it also shows that, in regard to moral relations, you are really God's enemy. From the moment you resist the claims of moral truth, God must regard you as His enemy and not by any means as His obedient subject. Not in any figurative sense, but in its most literal sense, *you are His enemy;* and therefore, He must be highly displeased with you. If He were not, His own conscience would condemn Him. You must know that it must be His duty to reveal to you this displeasure. Since He must feel it, He ought to be open and honest with you. You could not, in reason, wish Him to be otherwise. All of you who know moral truth, yet obey it not; who admit obligation which yet you refuse to obey, you are the men who hold the truth in unrighteousness. Let this be settled in every one of your minds, that if you restrain the influence of any truth known concerning God and your duty, then *against you* is His wrath revealed from heaven.

IV. We must next inquire, *Wherein and how is this wrath revealed?*

Perhaps some of you are already making this inquiry. Moralists tend to say, "We do not see any wrath coming. If we are as good as those who profess religion, why shall we not be saved as well as they?"

Wherein then is God's wrath revealed against this great wickedness?

1. Your conscience affirms that God must be displeased with you. It certifies to you beforehand that you are guilty, and that God cannot accept you.

2. The remorse which will sometimes visit such sinners yet more con-

firms God's displeasure. True, the feeling of remorse belongs to the sensibility; however, it does give admonitory warning. Its voice must be accounted as the voice of God in the human soul. He who made that sensibility so that it will sometimes recoil under a sense of guilt, and turn back to consume the life and joy of the soul, did not make it a *lie*. It is strange that any should suppose this remorse to be itself the punishment threatened of God against sin, and the whole of it. Far from it! This is not that punishment which God has threatened; it is only a premonition of it.

The very fears which people feel are often to be taken as an indication that the thing they dread is a reality. Why is it that men in their sins are so often greatly afraid to die? It is no other than a trumpet-tone of the voice of God sounding up from the depths of their very nature. How can they overlook the fact that these grim forebodings of coming doom are indeed a revelation of wrath made in the very nature God has given them!

God makes another revelation of His wrath in His juridical abandonment of sinners. God manifests His despair of doing anything more for their salvation when He manifestly withdraws His Spirit and gives them over to hopeless abandonment. By withdrawing His Spirit, He leaves them in great moral blindness. They may have been able to see and to discriminate spiritual things somewhat before, but, after God forsakes them, they seem almost utterly void of this power. Everything is dark; all is confused. When the light of the Holy Spirit is withdrawn, it is practically vain for the sinner himself, or for his sympathizing friends, to expect his salvation. This mental darkness over all spiritual things is God's curse on their rejection of truth, and significantly forebodes their speedy doom.

Analogous to this is the indication given in a moral paralysis of the conscience. Strangely it seems to have lost its sensibility; its ready tact in moral discrimination is gone; its perceptions seem unaccountably obtuse, and the tone of its voice waxes feeble and almost inaudible. Practically, one might almost as well have no conscience at all. What does this paralysis of conscience indicate? Plainly, that God has abandoned that soul. The conscience so long overborne by a perverse will gives way and God ceases to sustain its vitality.

It is painful to see how persons in this condition strain their endeavors, but such debility comes down upon them. They become indifferent; diverting influences are so potent that they drop their endeavors, powerless. Once their conscience had some activity; truth fell on their mind with appreciable force and they were aware of resisting it; but, by-and-by, there ensued a state of moral feeling in which the mind was no longer conscious of refusing; indeed, it seemed scarcely conscious of anything whatever. They have restrained the influence of truth until their conscience has mainly suspended its functions. Like the drunkard, who has lost all perception of the moral wrong of intemperance and who has brought this insensibility on himself by incessant violations of his better judgment, so the sinner has refused to hear the truth until the truth now refuses to move him. What is the meaning of this strange phenomenon? It is one of the ways in which God reveals His indignation at man's great wickedness.

An ungodly student put on the intellectual race-course alongside of his classmates soon becomes ambitious and jealous. At first he will probably have some sense of this sin, but he soon loses this sense and passes on as if unconscious of any sin. What is this but a revelation of God's displeasure?

Again, this wrath against those who hold back the truth in unrighteousness is abundantly revealed in God's Word. Think of what Christ said to the hypocritical scribes and Pharisees: "Fill ye up, then, the measure of your fathers." What did He mean by that? Their fathers had filled their cup of sin till God could bear with them no longer, and then He filled up His cup of wrath and poured it forth on the nation and *"there was no remedy."* So Christ intimates it shall be with the scribes and Pharisees. And what is this but to reveal His wrath against them for holding back the truth through unrighteousness?

Again, He lets such sinners *die in their sins.* Observe how, step by step, God gave them one revelation after another of His wrath against their sin; remorse, moral blindness, decay of moral sensibility, and the plain assertions of His Word. All these failing, He gives them up to some strong delusion; that they may believe a lie. God himself says, "For this cause God shall send them strong delusion, that they should believe a lie, that they all might be damned who believed not the truth, but had pleasure in unrighteousness." It is painfully instructive to study the workings of modern delusions, especially spiritualism, and to notice how it has come in following the track of those great revivals that blessed our country a few years ago. Do not I know scores of persons who passed through those revivals unblessed, and now they are mad with this delusion? They saw the glory of God in those scenes of revival power; but they turned away, and now they are mad under their idols and crazy under their delusions. God has given them up to die in their sins, and it will be *an awful death*! Draw near them gently, and ask a few kind questions; you will soon see that they make no just moral discriminations. All is dark which needs to be light, ere they can find the gate of life.

Remarks

1. You may notice the exact difference between saints and sinners, including among sinners all professors of religion who are not in an obedient state of mind. The exact difference is this: saints have adopted God's will as their law of activity, the rule that shall govern all their life and all their heart. You reveal to them God's will; this settles all further controversy. The very opposite of this is true of the sinner. With him, the fact of God's supposed will has no such influence at all; usually no influence of any sort, unless it be to excite his opposition. Again, the Chris-

tian, instead of restraining the influence of truth acts up to his convictions. If the question of *oughtness* is settled, all is settled. Suppose I go to Deacon A. or Deacon B. and I say, "I want you to do a certain thing; I think you must give so much of your money to this object." He replies, "I don't know about that; my money costs me great labor and pains." But I resume, and say, "Let us look calmly at this question"; and then I proceed to show him that the thing I ask of him is, beyond a doubt, his *duty* to God and to man. He interposes at once, "You need not say another word; that is enough. If it is my duty to Christ and to His people. I ask no more." But the sinner is not moved so. He knows his duty beforehand, but he has long ignored its claims on him. You must appeal to his selfish interests if you would reach his heart. With the Christian, you need not appeal to his hopes or his fears. You only need show his duty to God. The sinner you can hope to move only by appeals to his interests. The reason for this is that his adopted course of life is to serve his own interests, nothing higher.

2. With sinners the question of religion is one of loss and gain. But with Christians, it is only a question of right and duty towards God. This makes truth to him all important and duty imperative. But the sinner only asks, "What shall I gain? or What shall I lose?" It is wholly a question of danger. Indeed, so true is this, that ministers often assume that the only availing motive with a sinner must be an appeal to his hopes and fears. They have for the most part dropped any consideration of *right* between the sinner and God. They seem to have forgotten that when they stop short of the idea of right, and appeal only to the sinner's selfishness, their influence tends to make *spurious converts*. For if men enter upon the Christian life only for *gain* in the line of their hopes and fears, you must keep up the influence of these considerations, and must expect to work upon these only; that is, you must expect to have selfish Christians and a selfish church. If you say to them, "This is duty," they will reply, "What have we ever cared for *duty*? We were never converted to the doctrine of doing our duty. We became Christians at all, only for the sake of promoting our own interests, and we have nothing to do in the Christian life on any other motive."

Now observe, they may modify this language a little if it seems too repugnant to the general convictions of decent people; but nonetheless, this is their real meaning. They modify its language only on the same general principle of making everything subservient to self.

3. Again, we see how great a mistake is made by those selfish Christians who say, "I am honest towards my fellowmen. Is not this a proof of piety?"

What do you mean by "honest"? Are you really honest towards God? Do you regard God's rights as much as you wish Him to regard yours? But perhaps you ask, as many do, "What is my crime?" I answer: "Is it not enough for you to do nothing, really *nothing,* towards obedience to God? Is it not something serious that you refuse to do God's will and hold back the claims of His truth? What's the use of talking about your *morality*, while you disregard the greatest of all moral claims and obligations—those that bind you to love and obey God? What can it avail you to say perpetually, 'Am I not moral and decent towards men?' "

Why is God not satisfied with this?

4. You who think you are almost as good as Christians; in fact, it is much nearer the truth to say that you are almost as bad as devils! Indeed you are fully as bad, except you do not know as much; and therefore, cannot be so wicked. You say, "We are kind to each other. " So are devils. Their common purpose to war against God compels them to act in concert. They went in concert into the man possessed with a legion of devils as we learn in the gospel history. Very likely they are as kind towards each other, in their league against God and goodness as you are towards your neighbors. Selfish men have small ground to compliment themselves on being kind and good to each other, while they withstand God; since, in both these respects, they are only like devils in hell.

5. And now, my impenitent hearers, what do you say? Putting your conduct towards God into plain language, it would run thus: "Thou, Lord, callest on me to repent; I shall refuse. Thou dost strive to enforce my obligation to repent by various truths; I hold back those truths from their legitimate influence on my mind. Thou dost insist on my submission to thy authority; I shall do no such thing."

This, you will see, is only translating your current life and bearing towards God into plain words. If you were really to lift your face toward heaven and utter these words, it would be blasphemy. What do you think of it *now*? Do you not admit, and often assert, that actions speak louder than words? Do they not also speak more *truthfully*?

6. To those of you who are businessmen, let me make this appeal. What would you think of men who should treat you as you treat God? You take your account to your customer and you say to him, "This account, sir, has been lying a long time past due; will you be so good as to settle it? You cannot deny that it is a fair account of value received, and I understand you have abundant means to pay it." He very coldly refuses. You suggest the propriety of his giving some reasons for this refusal; and he tells you it is a fine time to get large interest on his money, and he therefore finds it more profitable to loan it out than to pay his debts. That is all. He is only selfish; all there is of it is simply this, that he cares for his own interests supremely, and cares little or nothing for yours when the two classes of interests—his and yours—come into competition.

When you shall treat God as well as you want your creditors to treat you, then you may hold up your head as, so far, an honest man; but, so long as you do the very thing towards God which you condemn as infinitely mean from your fellowmen towards yourself, you have little ground for self-complacent pride.

All this would be true and forcible, even if God were no greater, no better, and had no higher and no more sacred rights than your own. How much more, then, are they weighty beyond expression, since God is so much greater, better, and holier than mortals!

2

ON THE ATONEMENT*
Romans 3:25, 26

" . . . how that Christ died for our sins according to the Scriptures" (I Cor. 15:3).

"For he hath made him to be sin for us, who knew no sin; that we might be made the righteousness of God in him" (II Cor. 5:21).

"But God commendeth his love toward us, in that while we were yet sinners, Christ died for us" (Rom. 5:8).

"The Lord is well pleased for his righteousness' sake: he will magnify the law and make it honorable" (Isa. 42:21).

"Whom God hath set forth to be a propitiation, through faith in his blood, to declare his righteousness for the remission of sins that are past, through the forbearance of God. To declare, I say, at this time his righteousness: that he might be just and the justifier of him which believeth in Jesus" (Rom. 3:25, 26).

In this last passage, the apostle states with unusual fullness the theological and, I might even say, the philosophical design of Christ's mission to our world—that is, to set forth before created beings God's righteousness in forgiving sins. Here Christ is set forth as a propitiation that God may be just in forgiving sin, assuming that God could not have been just to the universe unless Christ had been first set forth as a sacrifice.

When we seriously consider the irresistible convictions of our own minds in regard to our relations to God and His government, we cannot but see that we are sinners and are lost beyond hope on the score of law and justice. The fact that we are grievous sinners against God is an ultimate fact of human consciousness; testified to by our irresistible convictions and no more to be denied than the fact that there is such a thing as *wrong*.

Sermons on Gospel Themes, pp. 204-214.

Now, if God be holy and good, it must be that He disapproves wrong-doing and will punish it. The penalty of His law is pronounced against it. Under this penalty, we stand condemned and have no relief save through some adequate atonement, satisfactory to God and safe to the interests of His Kingdom.

Thus far we may advance safely and on solid ground by the simple light of nature. If there were no Bible, we might know this much with absolute certainty. To this point even infidels are compelled to go.

Here then we are, under absolute and most righteous condemnation. Is there any way of escape? If so, it must be revealed to us in the Bible; for from any other source it cannot come. The Bible does profess to reveal a method of escape. This is the great burden of its message.

The Bible opens with a very brief allusion to the circumstances under which sin came into the world. Without being very detailed as to the *manner* in which sin entered, it is exceedingly full, clear and definite in its showing the *fact* of sin in the race. That God regards the race as being in sin and rebellion is made as plain as language can make it. It is worthy of notice that this fact and the connected fact of possible pardon are affirmed on the same authority—with the same sort of explicitness and clarity. These facts stand or fall together. Manifestly, God intended to impress on all minds these two great truths—first, that man is ruined by his own sin; secondly, that he may be saved through Jesus Christ. To deny the former is to gainsay both our own irresistible convictions and God's most explicit revealed testimony; to deny the latter is to shut the door, of our own free act and accord, against all hope of our own salvation.

The philosophical explanations of the reasons and governmental bearings of the atonement must not be confounded with the *fact* of an atonement. Men may be saved by the *fact* if they simply believe it, while they may know nothing about the philosophical explanation. The apostles did not make much account of the explanation, but they asserted the *fact* most earnestly, gave miracles as testimony to prove their authority from God, and so besought men to believe the fact and be saved. The fact, then, may be savingly believed, and yet the explanation be unknown. This has been the case, no doubt, with scores of thousands.

Yet, it is very useful to understand the reasons and governmental grounds of the atonement. It often serves to remove skepticism. It is very common for lawyers to reject the fact, until they come to see the reasons and governmental bearings of the atonement; this seen, they usually admit the fact. Many people need to see the governmental bearings, or else they will reject the fact. The reason why the fact is so often doubted is that the explanations given have been unsatisfactory. They have misrepresented God. No wonder men should reject them, and with them, the fact of any atonement at all.

The atonement is a governmental expedient to sustain law without the execution of its penalty on the sinner. Of course, it must always be a difficult thing in any government to sustain the authority of law, and respect due to it, without the execution of penalty. Yet God has accomplished it most perfectly.

A distinction must here be made between *public* and *retributive* justice.

Retributive justice visits on the head of the individual sinner a punishment corresponding to the nature of his offence. *Public justice* looks only toward the general good, and must do that which will secure the authority and influence of law.

Public justice may accept a substitute to inflicting the penalty on the individual sinner, provided it be equally effective to the support of law and the ensuring of obedience.

Public justice, then, may be satisfied in one of two ways: either by the full execution of the penalty; or by some substitute, which shall answer the ends of government at least equally well. When, therefore, we ask—What is necessary for the ends of public justice? The answer is:

1. *Not the literal execution of the penalty*; for if so, it must necessarily fall on the sinner and on no one else. Besides, it could be no gain to the universe for Christ to suffer the full and exact penalty due to every lost sinner who should be saved by Him. The amount of suffering being the same in the one case as in the other, where is the gain? And yet, further, if the administration of justice is to be retributive, then it cannot fall on Christ, and must fall on the sinner himself. If not retributive, the penalty certainly may be, as compared with that due the sinner, far different in kind and less in degree.

It has sometimes been said that Christ suffered all in degree and in kind what all the saved must else have suffered; but human reason revolts at this assumption, and certainly the Scriptures do not affirm it.

2. Some represent that God needs to be appeased, and to have His feelings conciliated. This is an egregious mistake. It utterly misrepresents God and misconceives the atonement.

3. It is no part of public justice that an innocent being should suffer penalty or punishment in the proper sense of these terms. Punishment implies crime—of which Christ had none. Christ, then, was not punished.

Let it be distinctly understood that the divine law originates in God's benevolence, and has no other than benevolent ends in view. It was revealed only and solely to promote the greatest possible good by means of obedience. Now, such a law can allow pardon provided an expression can be given which will equally secure obedience—making an equal revelation of the law-giver's firmness, integrity, and love. The law being perfect, and being most essential to the good of His creatures, God must not set aside its penalty without some equivalent influence to induce obedience.

The penalty was designed as a testimony to God's regard for the precept of His law and to His purpose to sustain it. An atonement, therefore, which should answer as a substitute for the infliction of this penalty, must be of such sort as to show God's regard for both the precept and penalty of His law. It must be adapted to enforce obedience. Its moral power must be in this respect equal to that of the infliction of the penalty on the sinner.

Consequently, we find that in the atonement God has expressed His high regard for His law and for obedience to it.

The design of executing the penalty of the law was to make a strong impression of the majesty, excellence, and utility of the law. Anything may answer as a substitute, which will as thoroughly demonstrate the mischief and odiousness of sin, God's hatred to it, and His determination to carry out His law in all its demands. Especially may the proposed substitute avail, if it shall also make a signal manifestation of God's love to sinners. This, the atonement, by the death of Christ, has most emphatically done.

Every act of rebellion denounces the law. Hence, before God can pardon rebellion, He must make such a demonstration of His attitude toward sin as shall thrill the heart of the created universe and make every ear tingle. Especially for the ends of the highest obedience, it was needful to make such demonstration as shall effectually secure the confidence and love of subjects toward their Lawgiver—such as shall show that He is no tyrant and that He seeks only the highest obedience and consequent happiness of His creatures. This done, God will be satisfied.

Now, what can be done to teach these lessons, and to impress them with great and everlasting emphasis on the universe?

God's testimony must be so given as to be well understood. Obviously, the testimony to be given must come from God, for it is *His* view of law, penalty, and substitute that needs to be revealed. Everyone must see that if He were to execute the penalty on the sinner, this would show at once His view of the value of the law. But, plainly, His view of the same thing must be shown with equal force by any proposed *substitute,* before He could accept it as such.

Again, in this transaction, the *precept* of the law must be accepted and honored both by God and by Jesus as Mediator. The latter, as the representative of the race, must honor the law by obeying it, and by publicly endorsing it—otherwise, the requisite homage cannot be shown to the divine law in the proposed atonement. This has been done.

Again, to make adequate provision for the exercise of mercy to the race, it is plainly essential that, in the person of their mediator, both the divine and the human should be united. God and man are both to be represented in the atonement; the divine Word represented the Godhead; the man Jesus represented the race to be redeemed. What the Bible thus asserts is verified in the history of Jesus; for He said and did things which could not have been said and done unless He had been man and equally could not have been said and done unless He were also God. On the one hand, too weak to carry His cross, through exhaustion of the human; and on the other, mighty to hush the tempest and to raise the dead through the plenitude of divine power. Thus God and man are both represented in Jesus Christ.

The thing to be done, then, required that Jesus Christ should honor the law and fully obey it; this He did. Standing *for* the sinner, he must, in an important sense, bear the curse of the law—not the literal penalty, but a vast amount of suffering, sufficient, in view of His relations to God and the universe, to make the needed demonstration of God's displeasure against sin, and yet of His love for both sinner and all His moral subjects. On the one hand, Jesus represented the race; on the other, He represented God. This is a most divine philosophy.

The sacrifice made on Calvary is to be understood as God's offering to public justice—God himself giving up His Son to death, and this Son pouring forth His life's blood in expiation for sin—thus throwing open the folding gates of mercy to a sinning, lost race. This must be regarded as manifesting His love to sinners. This is God's ransom provided for them. Look at the state of the case. The supreme Law-giver, and indeed the government of the universe, had been scouted by rebellion; of course there could be no pardon till this dishonor done to God and His law was thoroughly washed away. This is done by God's free-will offering of His own Son for these great sins.

This being all done for you, sinners, what do you think of it? What do you think of that appeal which Paul writes and God makes through him: "I beseech you, therefore, by the mercies of God, that you present your bodies a living sacrifice, holy, acceptable to God, which is your reasonable service." Think of those mercies. Think how Christ poured out His life for you. Suppose He were to appear in the midst of you today, and holding up His hands, dripping with blood, should say, "I beseech you by the mercies shown you by God, that you present your bodies a living sacrifice, holy, acceptable to God!" Would you not feel the force of His appeal that this is a *"reasonable* service"? Would not this love of Christ constrain you? What do you think of it? Didn't He die for all that they which live should not henceforth live unto themselves, but unto Him that loved them and gave himself for them? What do you say? Just as the uplifted ax would otherwise have fallen on your neck, He caught the blow on His own. You could have had no life if He had not died to save it; then what will you do? Will you have this offered mercy or reject it? Yield to Him the life He has in such mercy spared, or refuse to yield it?

Remarks

1. The governmental bearings of this scheme are perfectly apparent. The whole transaction tends powerfully to sustain God's law, and to reveal His love and even mercy to sinners. It shows that He is personally ready to forgive, and needs only to have such an arrangement made that He can do it safely with regard to His government. What could show His readiness to forgive more strikingly than this? See how carefully He guards against the abuse of pardon! Always ready to pardon, yet ever watchful over the great interests of obedience and happiness, lest they be imperiled by its freeness and fullness!

2. Why should it ever be thought incredible that God should devise

such a scheme of atonement? Is there anything in it that is unlike God or inconsistent with His revealed character? I doubt whether any moral agent can understand this system and yet think it incredible. Those who reject it as incredible must have failed to understand it.

3. The question might be asked: "Why did Christ die at all, if not *for us*?" He had never sinned; did not die on His own account as a sinner; nor did He die as the infants of our race do, with a moral nature yet undeveloped, and who yet belong to a sinning race. The only account to be given of His death is that He died not for himself, but for us.

It might also be asked: "Why did He die *so*?" See Him expiring between two thieves, and crushed down beneath a mountain weight of sorrow. Why was this? Other martyrs have died shouting. He died in anguish and grief, cast down and agonized beneath the hidings of His Father's face.

All nature seemed to sympathize with His griefs. Mark—the sun is clothed in darkness; the rocks are rent; the earth quakes beneath your feet; all nature is convulsed. Even a heathen philosopher exclaimed, "Surely the universe is coming to an end, or the Maker of the universe is dying!" Hark, that piercing cry; "My God, my God; why hast Thou forsaken Me?"

On the supposition of His dying as a Saviour for sinners, all is plain. He dies for the government of God, and must needs suffer these things to make a just expression of God's abhorrence of sin. While He stands in the place of guilty sinners, God must frown on Him and hide His face. This reveals both the spirit of God's government and His own infinite wisdom.

4. Some have impeached the atonement as likely to encourage sin. But such persons neglect the very important distinction between the proper use of a thing and its abuse. No doubt the best things in the universe may be abused, and by abuse be perverted to evil, and all the more by how much the better they are in their legitimate use.

Of the natural tendency of the atonement to good, it would seem that no man can rationally doubt. The tendency of manifesting such love, meekness, and self-sacrifice for us, is to make the sinner trust and love, and to make him bow before the cross with a broken and contrite heart. But many do abuse it; and the best things, abused, become the worst. The abuse of the atonement is the very reason why God sends sinners to hell. He says, "He that despised Moses' law, died without mercy under two or three witnesses; of how much sorer punishment, suppose you, shall he be thought worthy, who hath trodden under foot the Son of God, and counted the blood of the covenant an unholy thing, and hath done despite to the Spirit of grace?"

Hence, if any sinner will abuse atoning blood, and trample down the holy law, and the very idea of returning to God in penitence and love, God will ask of him; "Of how much sorer punishment shall he be thought worthy than he who despised Moses' law and fell beneath its vengeance?"

5. It is a matter of fact, that this manifestation of God in Christ does break the heart of sinners. It has subdued many hearts, and will thousands more. If they believe it and hold it as a reality, must it not subdue their heart to love and grief? Do not you think so? Certainly, if you saw it as it is, and felt the force of it in your heart, you would sob out on your very seat, break down and cry out; "Did Jesus love me so? And shall I love sin any more?" Ah, your heart would melt as thousands have been broken and melted in every age, when they have seen the love of Jesus as revealed on the cross. That beautiful hymn puts the case truthfully:

> "I saw One hanging on a tree,
>   In agony and blood;
> Who fixed His languid eyes on me,
>   As near the cross I stood."

But it was not the first look that fully broke his heart. It was only when:

> "A second look He gave which said,
>   I freely all forgive;
> This blood is for thy ransom paid—
>   I die that thou mayest live,"

that his whole heart broke, tears fell like rain, and he withheld no power of his being in the full consecration of his soul to this Saviour.

This is the genuine effect of the sinner's understanding the Gospel and giving Jesus Christ credit for His lovingkindness in dying for the lost. Faith thus breaks the stony heart. If this demonstration of God's love in Christ does not break your heart, nothing else will. If the death and love of Christ do not constrain you, nothing else can.

But if you do not look at it, and will not set your mind upon it, it will only work your ruin. To know this Gospel only enough to reject and disown it, can serve no other purpose except to make your guilt the greater, and your doom the more fearful.

6. Jesus was made a sin-offering for us. How beautifully this was illustrated under the Mosaic system! The victim was brought out to be slain; the blood was carried in and sprinkled on the mercy-seat. This mercy-seat was no other than the sacred cover or lid of the ark which contained the tables of the law and other sacred memorials of God's ancient mercies. There they were, in that deep recess—within which none might enter on pain of death, save the High Priest, and he only once a year, on the great day of atonement. On this eventful day, the sacred rites culminated to their highest solemnity. Two goats were brought forward upon which the High Priest laid his hands and confessed publicly his own sins and the sins of all the people. Then, one was driven far away into the wilderness, to signify how God removes our sins far as the east is from the west; the other was slain, and its blood borne by the High

Priest into the most holy place, and sprinkled there upon the mercy-seat beneath the cherubim. Meanwhile, the vast congregation stood without, confessing their sins, and expecting remission only through the shedding of blood. It was as if the whole world had been standing around the base of Calvary, confessing their sins, while Jesus bore His cross to the summit, to hang thereon, and bleed and die for the sins of men. How fitting that, while Christ is dying, we should be confessing!

Some of you may think it a great thing to go on a foreign mission. But Jesus has led the way. He left heaven on a foreign mission; came down to this more than heathen world, and no one ever faced such self-denial. Yet He fearlessly marched up without the least hesitation to meet the consequences. Never did He shrink from disgrace, from humiliation, or torture. And can you shrink from following the footsteps of such a leader? Is anything too much for you to suffer, while you follow in the lead of such a Captain of your salvation?*

---

*To pursue this governmental view of the atonement further, the editor recommends highly *The Atonement* by Albert Barnes, reprinted by Bethany Fellowship, Inc., in 1980. For a more contemporary treatment that follows the essential thought of Finney, see: *The Truth Shall Make You Free* by Gordon C. Olson (Bible Research Fellowship, Inc., 2624 Hawthorne, Franklin Park, Illinois 60131, copyright 1980).

3

SANCTIFICATION BY FAITH*
Romans 3:31

"Do we then make void the law through faith? God forbid; yea, we establish
the law."

The apostle had been proving that all mankind, both Jews and Gentiles, were in their sins, and refuting the doctrine so generally entertained by the Jews, that they were a holy people and saved by their
works. He showed that justification can never be by works, but by faith.
He then anticipates an objection, like this, "Are we to understand you as
teaching that the law of God is abrogated and set aside by this plan of
justification?" "By no means," says the apostle, "we rather establish
the law." In treating this subject, I design to pursue the following order:
  I. *Show that the gospel method of justification does not set aside or
  repeal the law.*
  II. *That it rather establishes the law by producing true obedience to
  it, and as the only means that does this.*
The greatest objection to the doctrine of Justification by Faith has
always been, that it is inconsistent with good morals, conniving at sin,
and opening the flood-gates of iniquity. It has been said, that to maintain that men are not to depend on their own good behavior for salvation, but are to be saved by faith in another, is calculated to make men
disregard good morals, and to encourage them to live in sin, depending
on Christ to justify them. Others have maintained that the gospel does
in fact release from obligation to obey the moral law, so that a more lax
morality is permitted under the gospel than was allowed under the law.
  I. *I am to show that the gospel method of justification does not set
aside the moral law.*

Lectures to Professing Christians (1880), pp. 307-319.

1. It cannot be that this method of justification sets aside the moral law, because the gospel everywhere enforces obedience to the law, and lays down the same standard of holiness.

Jesus Christ adopted the very words of the moral law: "Thou shalt love the Lord thy God with all thy heart, and with all thy soul, and with all thy mind, and with all thy strength, and thy neighbor as thyself."

2. The conditions of the gospel are designed to sustain the moral law.

The gospel requires repentance as the condition of salvation. What is repentance? The renunciation of sin. Man must repent of his breaches of the law of God, and return to obedience to the law. This is tantamount to a requirement of obedience.

3. The gospel maintains that the law is right.

If it did not maintain the law to its full extent, it might be said that Christ is the minister of sin.

4. By the gospel plan, the sanctions of the gospel are added to the sanctions of the law to enforce obedience to the law.

The apostle says, "He that despised Moses' law, died without mercy under two or three witnesses; of how much sorer punishment, suppose ye, shall he be thought worthy, who hath trodden under foot the Son of God, and hath counted the blood of the covenant, wherewith he was sanctified, an unholy thing, and hath done despite unto the spirit of grace?" Thus adding the awful sanctions of the gospel to those of the law to enforce obedience to the precepts of the law.

II. *I am to show that the doctrine of justification by faith produces sanctification by producing the only true obedience to the law.*

By this I mean, that when the mind understands this plan, and exercises faith in it, it naturally produces sanctification. Sanctification is holiness, and holiness is nothing but obedience to the law, consisting in love to God and love to man.

In support of the proposition that justification by faith produces true obedience to the law of God, my first position is that sanctification never can be produced among selfish or wicked beings by the law itself separate from the considerations of the gospel, or the motives connected with justification by faith.

The motives of the law did not restrain those beings from committing sin, and it is absurd to suppose the same motives can "reclaim" them from sin, when they have fallen under the power of selfishness, and when sin is a confirmed habit. The motives of the law can lose a part of their influence, when a being is once fallen. They even exert an opposite influence. The motives of the law, when viewed by a selfish mind, have a tendency to cause sin to abound. This is the experience of every sinner. When he sees the spirituality of the law, and does not see the motives of the gospel, it raises the pride of his heart, and hardens him in his rebellion. The case of the devil is an exhibition of what the law can do, with all its principles and sanctions, upon a wicked heart. He understands the law, sees its reasonableness, has experienced the blessedness of obedience, and knows full well that to return to obedience would restore his peace of mind. This he knows better than any sinner of our race, who never was holy, and yet it presents to his mind no such motives as to reclaim him, but on the contrary, drives him to a returnless distance from obedience.

When obedience to the law is held forth to the sinner as the condition of life; immediately, it sets him upon making self-righteous efforts. In almost every instance, the first effort of the awakened sinner is to obey the law. He thinks he must first make himself better, in some way, before he may embrace the gospel. He has no idea of the simplicity of the gospel plan of salvation by faith, offering eternal life as a mere gratuitous gift. Alarm the sinner with the penalty of the law, and he naturally, and by the very laws of his mind, sets himself to do better, to amend his life, and in some self-righteous manner obtain eternal life, under the influence of slavish fear. And the more the law presses him, the greater are his pharisaical efforts, while hope is left to him, that if he obeys he may be accepted. What else could you expect of him? He is purely selfish, and though he ought to submit at once to God, yet, as he does not understand the gospel terms of salvation, and his mind is of course first turned to the object of getting away from the danger of the penalty, he tries to get up to heaven some other way. I do not believe there is an instance in history of a man who has submitted to God until he has seen that salvation must be by faith, and that his own self-righteous strivings have no tendency to save him.

Again, if you undertake to produce holiness by legal motives, the very fear of failure has the effect of diverting attention from the objects of love, from God and Christ. The sinner is all the while compassing Mount Sinai, and taking heed to his footsteps, to see how near he comes to obedience, and how he can get into the spirit of heaven?

Again, the penalty of the law has no tendency to produce love in the first instance. It may increase love in those who already have it, when they contemplate it as an exhibition of God's infinite holiness. The angels in heaven, and good men on earth, contemplate its propriety and fitness, and see in it the expression of the good will of God to His creatures, and it appears amiable and lovely, and increases their delight in God and their confidence towards Him. But it is the reverse with the selfish man. He sees the penalty hanging over his own head, and no way of escape, and it is not in his mind to become enamored with the Being that holds the thunderbolt over his devoted head. From the nature of mind, he will flee from Him and not to Him. It seems never to have been dreamed of, by the inspired writers, that the law could sanctify men. The law is given to slay rather than to make alive, to cut off men's self-righteous hopes forever, and compel them to flee to Christ.

Again, sinners, under the naked law and irrespective of the gospel—I say, sinners, naturally and necessarily and of right under such circumstances, view God as an irreconcilable enemy. They are wholly selfish; and apart from the considerations of the gospel, they view God just as the devil views Him. No motive in the law can be exhibited to a selfish mind that will beget love. Can the influence of penalty do it?

A strange plan of reformation this; to send men to hell to reform them! Let them go on in sin and rebellion to the end of life, and then be punished until they become holy. I wonder why the devil has not become holy! He has suffered long enough; he has been in hell these thousands of years and he is no better than he was. The reason is that there is no gospel there, and no Holy Spirit to apply the truth, and the penalty only confirms his rebellion.

Again, the doctrine of justification can relieve these difficulties. It can produce, and has produced, real obedience to the precept of the law. *Justification by faith does not set aside the law as a rule of duty, but only sets aside the penalty of the law.* And the preaching of justification as a mere gratuity, bestowed on the simple act of faith, is the only way in which obedience to the law is ever brought about. This I shall now show from the following considerations.

1. It relieves the mind from the pressure of those considerations that naturally tend to confirm selfishness.

While the mind is looking only at the law, it only feels the influence of hope and fear perpetuating purely selfish efforts. But justification by faith annihilates this spirit of bondage. The apostle says, "We have not received the spirit of bondage again to fear." This plan of salvation begets love and gratitude to God, and leads the souls to taste the sweets of holiness.

2. It relieves the mind also from the necessity of making its own salvation its supreme object.

The believer in the gospel plan of salvation finds salvation full and complete, including both sanctification and eternal life already prepared; and instead of being driven to the life of a Pharisee in religion, of laborious and exhausting effort, he receives it as a free gift, a mere gratuity, and is now left free to exercise disinterested benevolence, and to live and labor for the salvation of others, leaving his own soul unreservedly to Christ.

3. The fact that God has provided and given him salvation as a gratuity is calculated to awaken in the believer a concern for others. When he sees them dying for the want of this salvation, he wants them to be brought to the knowledge of the truth and be saved. How far from every selfish motive are those influences! It exhibits God, not as the law exhibits Him as an irreconcilable enemy, but as a grieved and offended Father willing to be reconciled; nay, very desirous that His subjects should become reconciled to Him and live. This is calculated to beget His love! It exhibits God as making the greatest sacrifice to reconcile sinners to himself; and from no other motive than a pure and disinterested regard to their happiness. Try this in your own family. The law represents God as armed with wrath, and determined to punish the sinner, without hope or help. The gospel represents Him as offended; indeed, but yet so anxious they should return to Him that He has made

the greatest conceivable sacrifices out of pure disinterested love to His wandering children.

I once heard a father say that he had tried in his family to imitate the government of God, and when his child did wrong he reasoned with him and showed him his faults; and when he was fully convinced and confounded and condemned so that he had not a word to say, then the father asked him; "Do you deserve to be punished?" "Yes, sir. I know it." "Now if I were to let you go what influence would it have over the other children? Rather than do that I will take the punishment myself." So he laid the ferule on himself, and it had the most astonishing effect on the mind of the child.* He had never tried anything so perfectly subduing to the mind as this. And from the laws of mind, it must be so. It affects the mind in a manner entirely different from the naked law.

4. It brings the mind under an entire new set of influences and allows it to weigh the reasons for holiness, and decide accordingly.

Under the law, none but motives of hope and fear can operate on the sinner's mind. But under the gospel, the influence of hope and fear are set aside, and a new set of considerations presented with a view of God's entire character in all the attractions He can command. It gives the most heart-breaking, sin-subduing views of God. It presents Him to the senses in human nature. It exhibits His disinterestedness.** The way Satan prevailed against our first parents was by leading them to doubt God's disinterestedness. The gospel demonstrates the truth and corrects this lie. The law represents God as the inexorable enemy of the sinner, as securing happiness to all who perfectly obey, but thundering down wrath on all who disobey. The gospel reveals new features in God's character which were not known before. Doubtless, the gospel increases the love of all holy beings. It gives greater joy to the angels in heaven, greatly increasing their love and confidence and admiration, when they see God's amazing pity and forebearance towards the guilty. The law drove the devils to hell, and it drove Adam and Eve from Paradise. But, when the blessed spirits see the same holy God waiting on rebels, nay opening His own bosom, and giving His beloved Son for them, and taking such unwearied pains for thousands of years to save sinners, do you think it has no influence in strengthening the motives in their minds to obedience and love?

---

*A ferule was a flat stick with the inflicting end shaped like a pear. A hole was drilled in the center to raise blisters: the editor.

**To be "disinterested" is to be free of bias or self-interest; impartial. (Not to be confused with "uninterested" which means lack of interest or unconcerned.) "Disinterested Benevolence" is lovingkindness or a good act towards others, given without partiality or concern about recognition and reward. (This is a very good definition of Agape type love.) These definitions are taken from the excellent Glossary written by Harry Conn in *Finney's Systematic Theology* (Minneapolis: Bethany Fellowship, Inc., 1976), pp. 427-435.

The devil, who is a purely selfish being, is always accusing others of being selfish. He accused Job of this: "Doth Job fear God for nought?" To our first parents he accused God of being selfish, and that the only reason for His forbidding them to eat of the tree of knowledge was the fear that they might come to know as much as himself. The gospel shows what God is. If He were selfish, He would not take such pains to save those whom He might, with perfect ease, crush to hell. Nothing is so calculated to make selfish persons ashamed of their selfishness, except seeing disinterested benevolence in others. Hence the wicked are always trying to appear disinterested. Let the selfish individual, who has any heart, see true benevolence in others, and it is like coals of fire on his head. The wise men understood this, when Jesus said, "If thine enemy hunger, feed him; if he thirst, give him drink; for in so doing, thou shalt heap coals of fire on his head." Nothing is so calculated to cut down an enemy, and win him over, and make him a friend.

This is what the gospel does to sinners. It shows that notwithstanding all that they have done to God, God still exercises toward them disinterested love. When the sinner sees God stooping down from heaven to save him, and understands that it is indeed true, oh, how it melts and breaks down his heart and strikes a death-blow to selfishness and wins him over to unbounded confidence and holy love. God has so constituted the mind that it must necessarily do homage to virtue. It must do this as long as it retains the powers of moral agency. This is as true in hell as in heaven. The devil feels this. When an individual sees that God has no interested motives to condemn him, when he sees that God offers salvation as a mere gratuity, through faith, he cannot but feel admiration of God's benevolence. His selfishness is crushed. The law has done its work. He sees that all his selfish endeavors have done no good, and the next step is for his heart to go out in disinterested love.

Suppose a man were under sentence of death for rebellion and had tried many expedients to recommend himself to the government, but failed, because his efforts were all hollow-hearted and selfish. He sees that the government understands his motives, and that he is not really reconciled to the government. He knows himself that his motives were all hypocritical and selfish, moved by the hope of favor or the fear of wrath, and that the government is more and more incensed at his hypocrisy. Now let a paper be brought to him from the government offering him free pardon on the simple condition that he would receive it as mere gratuity, making no account of his own works—what influence will it have on his mind? The moment he finds the penalty set aside, and that he has no need to go to work by any self-righteous efforts, his mind is filled with admiration. Now, let it appear that the government has made the greatest sacrifices to procure this; his selfishness is slain, and he melts down like a child at his sovereign's feet, ready to obey the law because he loves his sovereign.

5. All true obedience turns on faith. Faith secures all the requisite influences to produce sanctification. Faith gives the doctrines of eternity

52

access to the mind and a hold on the heart. In this world the motives of time are addressed to the senses. The motives that influence the spirits of the just in heaven do not reach us through the senses. But when faith is exercised, the wall is broken down, and the vast realities of eternity act on the mind here with the same kind of influence that they have in eternity. Mind is mind, everywhere. And were it not for the darkness of unbelief, men would live here just as they do in the eternal world. Sinners here would rage and blaspheme just as they do in hell; and saints would love and obey and praise just as they do in heaven. Now, faith makes all these things realities. Faith swings the mind loose from the clogs of the world, and the mind beholds God, and apprehends His law and His love. In no other way *can* these motives take hold on the mind. What a mighty action must it have on the mind when it takes hold of the love of Christ! What a life-giving power when the pure motives of the gospel crowd into the mind and stir it up with energy divine! Every Christian knows that in proportion to the strength of his faith his mind is buoyant and active, and when his faith flags his soul is dark and listless. It is faith alone that places the things of time and eternity in their true comparison, and sets down the things of time and sense at their real value. It breaks up the delusions of the mind; the soul shakes itself from its errors and clogs, and it rises up in communion with God.

Remarks

1. It is as unphilosophical as it is unscriptural to attempt to convert and sanctify the minds of sinners without the motives of the gospel.

You may press the sinner with the law, and make him see his own character, the greatness and justice of God, and his ruined condition. But hide the motives of the gospel from his mind, and it is all in vain.

2. It is absurd to think that the offers of the gospel are calculated to beget selfish hope.

Some are afraid to throw out upon the sinner's mind all the character of God, and they try to make him submit to God by casting him down in despair. This is not only against the gospel, but it is absurd in itself. It is absurd to think that in order to destroy the selfishness of a sinner you must hide from him the knowledge of how much God loves and pities him, and how great sacrifices He has made to save him.

3. It is far from being true that sinners are in danger of getting false hopes if they are allowed to know the real compassion of God. While you hide this, it is impossible to give them any other than a false hope. Withholding from the sinner, who is writhing under conviction, the fact that God has provided salvation as a mere gratuity is the very way to confirm his selfishness. If he gets any hope, it must be a false one. To press him to submission by the law alone is to set him to build a self-righteous foundation.

4. So far as we can see, salvation by grace is the only possible way to reclaim selfish beings.

Suppose salvation were not altogether gratuitous, but some degree of good works were taken into the account, and for those good works in part we were justified. Insofar as this consideration is in the mind, there is a stimulus to selfishness. You must bring the sinner to see that he is entirely dependent on free grace, and that a full and complete justification is bestowed on the first act of faith, as a mere gratuity, and no part of it as an equivalent for anything he is to do. This alone dissolves the influence of selfishness and secures holy action.

5. If all this is true, sinners should be put in the fullest possible possession, and in the speediest manner, of the whole plan of salvation.

Sinners should be made to see the law, and their own guilt, and that they have no way to save themselves; and then the whole length and breadth and heighth and depth of the love of God should be opened. You will crush his selfishness, and subdue his soul in love to God. Do not be afraid, in conversing with sinners, to show the whole plan of salvation and to give the fullest possible exhibition of the infinite compassion of God. Show him that, notwithstanding his guilt, the Son of God is knocking at the door and beseeching him to be reconciled to God.

6. You see why so many convicted sinners continue so long compassing Mount Sinai with self-righteous efforts to save themselves by their own works.

How often do you find sinners trying to get more feeling, or waiting till they have made more prayers and made greater efforts, and expecting to recommend themselves to God in this way. Why is all this? The sinner needs to be driven off from this, and made to see that he is all the while looking for salvation under the law. He must be made to see that all this is superseded by the gospel offering him all he wants as a mere gratuity. He must hear Jesus saying, "You will not come *unto me* that you may have life: Oh, no, you are willing to pray, and go to meeting, and read the Bible, or anything, but come unto me. Sinner, this is the road; I am the way, and the truth, and the life. No man cometh to the Father but by me. I am the resurrection and the life. I am the light of the world. Here, sinner, is what you want. Instead of trying your self-righteous prayers and efforts, here is what you are looking for, only believe and you shall be saved."

7. You see why so many professors of religion are always in the dark.

They are looking at their sins; confining their observations to themselves and losing sight of the fact that they have only to take right hold of Jesus Christ and throw themselves upon Him and all is well.

8. The law is useful to convict men; but, as a matter of fact, it never breaks the heart. The gospel alone does that. The degree to which a convert is brokenhearted is in proportion to the degree of clearness with which he apprehends the gospel.

9. Converts, if you call them so, who entertain a hope under legal preaching, may have an intellectual approbation of the law, and a sort of dry zeal; but they never make mellow, brokenhearted Christians. If

they have not seen God in the attitude in which He is exhibited in the gospel, they are not such Christians as you will see sometimes with the tear trembling in their eye and their frames shaking with emotion at the name of Jesus.

10. Sinners under conviction, and professors in darkness, must be led right to Christ and made to take hold of the plan of salvation by faith. You cannot do them good in any other way.

4

GOD'S LOVE COMMENDED TO US*
Romans 5:8

"But God commendeth his love toward us, in that, while we were yet sinners, Christ died for us."

What is meant here by "commend"? To "recommend"—to set forth in a clear and strong light.

Towards whom is this love exercised? Towards *us*—towards all beings of our lost race. To each one of us He manifests this love. Is it not written: "God so loved the world that he gave his only begotten Son, that whosoever believeth in him should not perish, but have everlasting life"?

How does He commend this love? By giving His Son to die for us. By giving one who was a *Son* and a Son well-beloved. It is written that God "gave him a ransom for all"; and that "He tasted death for every man." We are not to suppose that He died for the sum total of mankind in such a sense that His death is not truly for each one in particular. It is a great mistake to suppose that Christ died for the race in general, and not for each one in particular. By this mistake, the gospel is likely to lose much of its practical power on our hearts. We need to apprehend it as Paul did, who said of Jesus Christ: "He loved *me* and gave himself *for me*." We need to make this personal application of Christ's death. No doubt this was the great secret of Paul's holy life, and of his great power in preaching the gospel. So we are to regard Jesus as having loved *us* personally and individually. Let us consider how much effort God has taken to make us feel that He cares for us personally. He has taken great effort in His providence and so also in His gospel. He would fain make us sin-

---

Sermons on Gospel Themes, pp. 307-318.

gle ourselves out from the masses and feel that His loving eye and heart were upon us individually.

For what end does He commend His love to us? Is it for personal ambition to make a display? Surely there can be no affectation in this. God is infinitely above all affectation. He must from His very nature act honestly. Of course He must have some good reason for this manifestation of His love. No doubt He seeks to prove to us the reality of His love. Feeling the most perfect love towards our lost race, He deemed it best to reveal this love and make it manifest, both to us and to all His creatures. And what could evince His love if this gift of His Son does not? Oh, how gloriously is love revealed in this great sacrifice! How this makes divine love stand out prominently before the universe! What else could He have done that would prove His love so effectually?

Again, He would show that His love is *unselfish*; for Jesus did not die for us as friends, but as enemies. It was *while* we were yet enemies that He died for us. On this point, Paul suggests that "scarcely for a righteous man will one die; yet peradventure for a *good* man, some would even dare to die." But our race were as far as possible from being *good*. Indeed, they were not even righteous, but were utterly wicked. For a very dear friend one might be willing to die. There have been soldiers who, to save the life of a beloved officer, have taken into their own bosom the shaft of death; but for one who is merely just and not so much as good, this sacrifice could scarcely be made. How much less for an enemy! Herein we may see how greatly "God commendeth his love to us, in that while we were yet enemies, Christ died for us."

Notice yet further, this love of God to us cannot be the love of esteem or complacency, because there is in us no ground for such a love. It can be no other than the love of unselfish benevolence. This love had been called in question. Satan had questioned it in Eden. He made bold to insinuate: "Hath your God indeed said, Ye shall not eat of every tree in the garden?" Why should He wish to debar you from such pleasure? So the old Serpent sought to cast suspicion on the benevolence of God. Hence there was the more reason why God should vindicate His love.

He would also commend the great strength of this love. We should think we gave evidence of strong love if we were to give our friend a great sum of money. But what is any sum of money compared with giving us a dear Son to die? Oh, surely it is surpassing love, beyond measure wonderful, that Jesus should not only labor and suffer, but should really *die*! Was ever love like this?

Again, God designed also to reveal the *moral character* of His love for men, and especially its justice. He could not show favors to the guilty until His government was made secure and His law was duly honored. Without this sacrifice, He knew it would not be safe to pardon. God must maintain the honor of His throne. He must show that He could never wink at sin. He felt the solemn necessity of giving a public rebuke of sin before the universe. This rebuke was the more expressive because Jesus himself was sinless. Of course it must be seen that in His death

God was not frowning on *His* sin, but on the sin of those whose sins He bore and in whose place He stood.

This shows God's abhorrence of sin since Jesus stood as our representative. While He stood in this position, God could not spare Him, but laid on Him the chastisement of our iniquities. Oh, what a rebuke of sin was that! How expressively did it show that God abhorred sin, yet loved the sinner! These were among the great objects in view—to beget in our souls the two-fold conviction of *His* love for us and of *our* sin against Him. He would make those convictions strong and abiding. So He sets forth Jesus crucified before our eyes—a far more expressive thing than any mere words. No *saying* that He loved us could approximate toward the strength and impressiveness of this manifestation. In no other way could He make it seem so much a reality—so touching and so overpowering. Thus He commends it to our regard. Thus He invites us to look at it. He tells us angels desire to look into it. He would have us weigh this great fact, examine all its bearings, until it shall come full upon our souls with its power to save. He commends it to us to be reciprocated, as if He would incite us to love Him who has so loved us. Of course He would have us understand this love, and appreciate it, that we may requite it with responsive love in return. It is an example for us that we may love our enemies and, much more, our brethren. Oh, when this love has taken its effect on our hearts, how deeply do we feel that we cannot hate anyone for whom Christ died? Then instead of selfishly thrusting our neighbor off, and grasping the good to which his claim is fully as great as ours, we love him with a love so deep and so pure that it cannot be in our heart to do him wrong.

It was thus a part of the divine purpose to show us what true love is. As one said in prayer: "We thank Thee, Father, that Thou hast given us Thy Son to teach us how to love." Yes, God would let us know that He himself *is love*, and hence that if we would be His children, we too must love Him and love one another. He would reveal His love so as to draw us into sympathy with himself and make us like Him. Do you not suppose that a thorough consideration of God's love, as manifested in Christ, does actually teach us what love is, and serve to draw our souls into such love? The question is often asked, *How shall I love?* The answer is given in this example: "Herein is love! Look at it and drink in its spirit. Man is prone to love himself supremely. But here is a totally different sort of love from that. This love commends itself in that while we were yet *sinners*, Christ died for us." How forcibly does this rebuke our selfishness! How much we need this lesson, to subdue our narrow selfishness and shame our unbelief!

How strange it is that men do not realize the love of God! The wife of a minister, who had herself labored in many revivals, said to me: "I never, till a few days since, knew that God is love." "What do you mean?" said I. "I mean that I never apprehended it in all its bearings before." Oh, I assure you, it is a great and blessed truth, and it is a great thing to see it as it is! When it becomes a reality to the soul, and you come under its powerful sympathy, then you will find the gospel indeed the power of God unto salvation. Paul prayed for his Ephesian converts that they might "be able to comprehend with all saints what is the breadth and length and depth and height; and to know the love of God that passeth knowledge, that they might be filled with all the fulness of God."

God sought, in thus commending His love to us, to subdue our slavish fear. Someone said, "When I was young, I was sensible of fearing God, but I knew I did not love Him. The instruction I received led me to fear, but not to love." So long as we think of God only as One to be feared not to be loved, there will be a prejudice against Him as more an enemy than a friend. Every sinner knows that he deserves to be hated of God. He sees plainly that God must have good reason to be displeased with him. The selfish sinner judges God from looking at himself. Knowing how he should feel toward one who had wronged him, he unconsciously infers that God must feel so toward every sinner. When he tries to pray, his heart won't; it is nothing but terror. He feels no attraction toward God, no real love. The child spirit comes before God, weeping indeed, but loving and trusting. Now the state of feeling which fears only, God would fain put away, and make us know that He loves us still. We must not regard Him as being altogether such as ourselves. He would undeceive us and make us realize that though He has "spoken against us, yet He does earnestly remember us still." He would have us interpret His dealings fairly and without prejudice. He sees how, when He thwarts men's plans, that they are bent on misunderstanding Him. They will think that He is reckless regarding their welfare, because they are blind to the precious truth that He shapes all His ways toward them in love and kindness. He would lead us to judge thus, that if God spared not His own Son, but gave Him up freely for us all, then He will much more give us all things else most freely.

Yet again, He would lead us to serve Him in love and not in bondage. He would draw us forth into the liberty of the sons of God. He loves to see the obedience of the heart. He would inspire love enough to make all of our service free and cheerful and full of joy. If you wish to make others love you, you must give them your love. Show your servants the love of your heart, so will you break their bondage, and make their service one of love. In this way God commends His love towards us in order to win our hearts to himself, and thus get us ready and fit to dwell forever in His eternal home. His ultimate aim is to save us from our sins that He may fill us forever with His own joy and peace.

Remarks

1. We see that saving faith must be the heart's belief of this great fact that God so loved us. Saving faith receives the death of Christ as an expression of God's love to us. No other sort of faith—no faith in anything else—wins our heart to love God. Saving faith saves us from our bondage and our prejudice against Him. It is this which makes it *saving*.

Any faith that leaves out this great truth must fail to save us. If any one element of faith is vital, it is this. Let any man doubt this fact of God's love in Christ, and I would not give much for all his religion. It is worthless.

2. The Old Testament system is full of this idea. All those bloody sacrifices are full of it. When the priest, in behalf of all the people, came forward and laid his hand on the head of the innocent victim and then confessed his sins and the sins of all, and then when this animal was slain and its blood poured out before the Lord, and He gave tokens that He accepted the offering, it was a solemn manifestation that God substituted for the sufferings due the sinner, the death of an innocent lamb. Throughout that ancient system, we find the same idea showing how God would have men see His love in the gift of His own dear Son.

3. One great reason why men find it so difficult to repent and submit to God is that they do not receive this great fact—do not accept it in simple faith. If they were to accept it and let it come home to their hearts, it would carry with it a power to subdue the heart to submission and to love.

4. One reason why young men are so afraid they shall be called into the ministry is their lack of confidence in this love. Oh, if they saw and believed this great love, surely they would not let eight hundred millions go down to hell in ignorance of this gospel! Oh, how it would agonize their heart that so many should go to their graves and to an eternal hell, and never know the love of Jesus to their perishing souls! And yet here is a young man for whom Christ has died who cannot bear to go and tell them they have a Saviour! What do you think of this magnanimity? How much is his heart like Christ's heart? Do you wonder that Paul could not hold his peace, but felt that he must go to the ends of the earth and preach the name of Jesus where it had never been known before? How deeply he felt that he must let the world know these glad tidings of great joy! How amazing that young men now can let the gospel die unknown and not go forth to bless the lost! Ah, did they ever taste its blessedness? Have they ever known its power? And do you solemnly intend to conceal it that it may never bless your dying brethren?

5. This matter of commending God's love is the strongest and most expressive He could employ. In no other way possible could He so forcibly demonstrate His great love to our race.

Hence, if this fails to subdue men's enmity, prejudice, and unbelief, what can avail? What methods shall He use after this proves unavailing? The Bible demands, "How shall we escape, if we neglect so great salvation?" Well may it make this appeal, for if this fails to win us, what can succeed?

6. If we had been His friends, there would have been no need of His dying for us. It was only because we were yet sinners that He died for us. How great, then, are the claims of this love on our hearts!

7. Sinners often think that if they are pious and good, then the Lord might love them. So they try to win His love by doing some good things.

They try in every such way to make God love them, and especially by mending their manners rather than their hearts. Alas, they seem not to know that the very fact of their being sunk so low in sin is moving God's heart to its very foundations! A sinless angel enjoys God's complacency, but not His pity; he is not an object of pity, and there is no call for it. The same is true of a good child. He receives the complacency of his parents, but not their compassion. But suppose this child becomes vicious. Then his parents mourn over his fall, and their compassion is moved. They look on him with pity and anxiety as they see him going down to the depth of vice, crime, and degradation. More and more as he sinks lower and lower in the filth and abominations of sin, they mourn over him; and as they see how changed he is, they stand in tears, saying: "Alas, this is our son, our once-honored son! But how fallen now! Our bowels are moved for him, and there is nothing we would not do or suffer, if we might save him!"

So the sinner's great degradation moves the compassions of his divine Father to their very depths. When the Lord passes by and sees him lying in his blood in the open field, He says, "That is my son! He bears the image of his Maker. Since I have spoken against him, I do earnestly remember him still; therefore, my bowels are troubled for him: I will surely have mercy upon him." Sinners should remember that the very fact of their being sinners is the thing that moves God's compassion and pity. Do you say, "I do not see how God can make it consistent with His holiness to pardon and love such a sinner as I am?" I can tell you how— *By giving His own Son to die in your stead!*

8. Christ died for us that He might save us, not *in*, but *from*, our sins. Then must it not grieve Him exceedingly that we should continue in sin? What do you think? Suppose you were to see Jesus face to face, and He were to show you those wounds in His hands and in His side, and were to say, "I died for you because I saw you lost beyond hope, and because I would save you from your sins; and now, will you repeat those sins again? Can you go on yet longer to sin against me?"

9. You may infer from our subject that Jesus must be willing to save you from wrath, if you truly repent and accept Him as Saviour. How can you doubt it? Having suffered unto death for this very purpose, surely it only remains for you to meet the conditions, and you are saved from wrath through Him.

10. You may infer that God, having spared not His Son, will also with Him freely give you all things else: grace enough to meet all your wants; the kind care of His providence; the love of His heart; everything you can need. To continue in sin in spite of such grace and love must be monstrous! It must grieve His heart exceedingly.

A friend of mine, who has charge of one hundred and fifty boys in a Reform School, is accustomed, when they misbehave, to put them for a time on bread and water. What do you think he does himself in some of these cases? *He goes and puts himself with them on bread and water!* The boys in the school see this, and they learn love of their superinten-

dent and father. Now, when tempted to crime, they must say to themselves: "If I do wrong, I shall have to live on bread and water; but the
worst of all my father will come and eat bread and water with me and for
my sake; and how can I bear that? How can I bear to have my father,
who loves me so well, confine himself to bread and water for my sake!"

So Jesus puts on himself pain and shame and death that you might
have joy and life—that you might be forgiven and saved from sinning;
and now will you go on to sin more? Have you no heart to appreciate His
dying love? *Can* you go on and sin yet more and nonetheless for all the
love shown you on Calvary?

You understand that Christ died to redeem you from sin. Suppose
your own eyes were to see Him face to face, and He should tell you all He
has done for you. "Sister," He says, "I died to save you from that sin;
will you do it again? Can you go on and sin just the same as if I had never
died for you?"

In that Reform School of which I spoke, the effects produced on even
the worst boys by the love shown them is really striking. The Superintendent had long insisted that he did not want locks and bars to confine
his boys. The Directors had said, "You must lock them in; if you don't
they will run away." On one occasion, the Superintendent was to be absent two weeks. A Director came to him urging that he must lock up the
boys before he left, for while he was absent, they would certainly run
away. The Superintendent replied, "I think not; I have confidence in
those boys." "But" responded the Director, "give us some guarantee.
Are you willing to pledge your city lot, conditioned that if they do run
away, the lot goes to the Reform School Fund?" After a little reflection,
he consented, "I will give you my lot—all the little property I have in the
world—if any of the boys run away while I am gone." Before he set off,
he called all the boys together; explained to them his pledge; asked
them to look at his dependent family, and then appealed to their honor
and their love for him. "Would you be willing to see me stripped of all
my property? I think I can trust you." He went; returned a little unexpectedly and late on one Saturday night. Scarce had he entered the
yard, when the word rang through the sleeping halls, "Our father has
come!" and almost in a moment they were there greeting him and
shouting, "We are all here! *We are all here!*"

Cannot Christ's love have as much power as that? Shall the love the
Reform School boys bear to their official father hold them to their place
during the long days and nights of his absence; and shall not Christ's
love to us restrain us from sinning? What do you say? Will you say thus?
"If Christ loves me so much, then it is plain He won't send me to hell,
and therefore I will go on and sin all I please." Do you say that? Then
there is not hope for you. The gospel that ought to save you can do nothing for you but sink you deeper in moral and eternal ruin. You are fully
bent to pervert it to your utter damnation! If those Reform School boys
had said thus, "Our Father loves us *so well*, he will eat bread and water
with us, and therefore we know he will not punish us to hurt us"; would

they not certainly bring a curse on themselves? Would not their reformation be utterly hopeless? So of the sinner who can make light of the Saviour's dying love. Oh, is it possible that when Jesus has died for you to save your soul from sin and from hell that you will sin again and yet again? Will you live on in sin only the more because He has loved you so much?

Think of this and make up your mind. "If Christ has died to redeem me from sin, then away with all sinning henceforth and forever! I forsake all my sins from this hour! I can afford to live or to die with my Redeemer; why not? So help me God. I have no more to do with sinning forever!"

5

DEATH TO SIN THROUGH CHRIST*
Romans 6:11

"Likewise reckon ye also yourselves to be dead indeed unto sin, but alive unto God through Jesus Christ our Lord."

The connection of this passage will help us to understand its meaning. Near the end of the previous chapter Paul had said, "The law entered that the offence might abound; but where sin abounded, grace did much more abound, that as sin hath reigned unto death, even so might grace reign through righteousness, unto eternal life, by Jesus Christ our Lord." He speaks here of sin as being a reigning principle or monarch, and of grace also as reigning. Then, in chapter 6, he proceeds: "What shall we say then? Shall we continue in sin that grace may abound? Likewise reckon ye also yourselves to be dead indeed unto sin, but alive unto God through Jesus Christ our Lord."

You observe here that Paul speaks of the man, the old sinner, as being *crucified with Christ*—so destroyed by the moral power of the Cross that he who was once a sinner shall no longer serve sin. When he speaks of our being planted or buried with Christ, we must of course understand him as employing figures of speech to teach the great truth that the *Gospel redeems the soul from sin. As* Christ died for sin, so by a general analogy we die to sin; while, on the other hand, as He rose to a new and infinitely glorious life, so the convert rises to a new and blessed life of purity and holiness.

But returning particularly to our text, let me say that the language used in our translation would seem to denote that our death to sin is precisely analogous to Christ's death for sin; but this is not the case. We are

---

Sermons on Gospel Themes, pp. 380-397.

dead to sin in the sense that it is no longer to be our master, implying that it has been in power over us. But sin never was in power over Jesus Christ—never was His master. Christ died to abolish its power over us—not to abolish any power of sin over himself, for it had none. The analogy between Christ's death in relation to sin and our dying to sin goes to this extent and no farther: He died for the sake of making an atonement for sin and for the sake of creating a moral power that should be effective to kill the love of sin in all hearts; but the Christian dies *unto* sin in the sense of being divorced from all sympathy with sin and emancipated from its control.

But I must proceed to remark upon the text itself, and shall inquire:

I. *What it is to be dead unto sin in the sense of the text.*
II. *What it is to be alive unto God.*
III. *What it is to reckon ourselves to be dead unto sin, but alive unto God through Jesus Christ our Lord.*
IV. *What it is to be alive unto God through Jesus Christ.*
V. *What is implied in the exhortation of our text.*

I. *Being dead to sin must obviously be the opposite of being dead in sin.* The latter must undeniably be a state of entire sinfulness—a state in which the soul is dead to all good through the power of sin over it. But right over against this, *to be dead to sin, must be to be indifferent to its attractions—beyond the reach of its influence—as fully removed from its influences as the dead are from the objects of sense in this world.* As he who is dead in the natural sense has nothing more to do with earthly things, so he who is dead to sin has nothing to do anymore with sin's attractions or with sinning itself.

II. *What is it to be alive unto God?* To be full of life for Him—to be altogether active and on the alert to do His will; to make our whole lives a perpetual offering to Him, constantly delivering up ourselves to Him and His service that we may glorify His name and subserve His interests.

III. *What is to reckon ourselves dead indeed unto sin?*

The word rendered *reckon* is sometimes rendered *account.* Abraham's faith was *accounted* unto him for righteousness. So, in this passage, reckon must mean—*believe, esteem* yourselves dead indeed unto sin. Account this to be the case. Regard this as truly your relation to sin; you are entirely dead to it; it shall have no more dominion over you.

A careful examination of the passages where this original word is used will show that this is its usual and natural sense. And this gives us the true idea of Gospel faith—embracing personally the salvation which is by faith in Jesus Christ. But more of this hereafter.

IV. *What is meant by reckoning yourselves alive indeed unto God through Jesus Christ?* Plainly this: you are to expect to be saved by Jesus Christ and to calculate on this salvation as your own. You are to esteem yourself as wholly dead to sin and as consequently brought into life and peace in Christ Jesus.

V. *What is implied in the exhortation of our text?*

That there is an adequate provision for this expectation, and for realizing these blessings in fact. For if there were no ground for realizing this, then the injunction would be most absurd. A precept requiring us to account ourselves dead indeed unto sin and alive unto God would be utterly untenable if there were no probability of the thing—if no provision were made for our coming into such relations to sin on the one hand and to God through Christ on the other. For if these blessings could not be reasonably expected, then there could be no rational ground for the expectation. If it were not reasonable to expect it, then to enjoin us to expect it would be palpably unreasonable. Who does not see that the very unjunction implies that there is a foundation laid and adequate provision made for the state required?

What is implied in complying with this injunction?

1. Believing such a thing to be possible. Believing it possible even that through Christ we may live in the required manner that we may avoid sin—desist from sinning—give it up and abandon it altogether and put it forever away. There can be no such thing as an intelligent compliance with this precept except as there shall underlie it this belief in its practicability. A state actually made practicable by adequate grace; adapted to the laws of mind and to the actual moral condition of lost men.

2. That we cease from all expectation of attaining this state of ourselves, and by our own independent, unaided efforts. There is no beginning to receive it by grace till we renounce all expectation of attaining it by natural works. It is only when empty of self that we begin to be filled of Christ.

3. A present willingness to be saved from sin. We must actually renounce all sin *as such*; that is, renounce sin because it is sin and for what it is. This position the mind must take: I can have nothing more to do with sinning, for God hates sin and I am to live henceforth and forever to please and glorify Him. My soul is committed with its utmost strength of purpose to this pleasing of God and doing His will.

4. It implies also an entire committal of your whole case to Jesus Christ, not only for present, but for all future salvation from sin. This is absolutely essential. It must always be the vital step—the cardinal act in this great work of salvation from sin.

5. It implies also the foreclosing of the mind against temptation, in such a sense that the mind truly expects to live a life purely devoted to God. This is the same sort of foreclosing of the mind which takes place under a faithful marriage contract. The Bible everywhere keeps this figure prominent. Christians are represented as the *bride* of Christ. They stand in a relation to Him which is closely analogous to that of a bride to her husband. Hence when they commit their whole hearts to Him, reposing their affections in Him and trusting Him for all good, their hearts are strongly foreclosed against temptation. The principle here involved we see illustrated in the merely human relation. When parties are sol-

emnly betrothed in mutual honest fidelity, there is no longer any thought of letting the eye rove or the heart go abroad for a fresh object of interest and love. The heart is fixed—willingly and by plighted faith *fixed*, and this fact shuts out the power of temptation almost entirely. It renders it comparatively an easy matter to keep the heart safely above the influence of temptation to apostasy. Before the sacred vows are taken, individuals may be excused for looking round and making any observations or inquiries; but never *after* the solemn vow is made. After the parties have become *one* by vow of marriage, never to be broken, there is to be no more question as to a better choice—no further thought about changing the relation or withdrawing the heart's affections. No wavering is admissible now; the pledge is made for *everlasting* faithfulness, settled once and forever! This is God's own illustration, and surely none need be more apt or more forcible. It shows how the Christian should look upon sin and upon all temptation to sin. He must say, "*Away from my heart forever!* I am married to Jesus Christ; how then can I look after other lovers? My mind is forever settled. It rests in the deep repose of one whose affections are plighted and fixed—to rove no more! Sin? I can think of yielding to its seductions no longer. I can not entertain the question for a moment. I can have nothing to do with sinning. My mind is settled—the question forever foreclosed, and I can no more admit the temptation to small sins than to great sins—no more consent to give my heart to worldly idols than to commit murder! I did not enter upon religion as upon an experiment, to see how I might like it—no more than a wife or husband take on themselves the marriage vow as an experiment. No; my whole soul has committed itself to Jesus Christ with as much expectation of being faithful forever as the most faithful husband and wife have of fulfilling their vows in all fidelity till death shall part them."

Christians in this state of mind no more expect to commit small sins than great sins. Hating all sin for its own sake and for its hatefulness to Christ, any sin, however small, is to them as murder. Hence if the heart is ever afterwards seduced and overcome by temptation, it is altogether contrary to their expectation and purpose; it was not embraced in their plan by any means, but was distinctly excluded; it was not deliberately indulged aforetime, but broke on them unexpectedly through the vantage ground of old habits or associations.

Again, the state of mind in question implies that the Christian knows where his great strength lies. He knows it does not lie in works of fasting, giving alms, making prayers, doing public duties or private duties—nothing of this sort; not even in resolutions or any self-originated efforts, but only in Christ received by faith. He no more expects spiritual life of himself apart from Christ, than a man in his senses would expect to fly by swinging his arms in the air. Deep in his soul lies the conviction that his whole strength lies in Christ alone.

When men are so enlightened as truly to apprehend this subject, then to expect less than this from Jesus Christ as the result of committing the whole soul to Him for full salvation is virtually to reject Him as a revealed Saviour. It does not honor Him for what He is; it does not honor the revelations He had made of himself in His word by accepting Him as there presented. For consider, what is the first element of this salvation? Not being saved from hell, but being saved from *sin*. Salvation from punishment is quite a secondary thing in every sense. It is only a *result* of being saved from sin, and not the prime element in the gospel salvation. Why was the infant Messiah to be called Jesus? Because He should *save His people from their sins.* And does the Bible anywhere teach any other or different view from this?

Remarks

1. This text alone, "Reckon yourselves to be dead indeed unto sin, but alive unto God through Jesus Christ," most entirely justifies the expectation of living without sin through all-abounding grace. If there were no other passage bearing on this point, this alone is adequate; and for a Christian to offer this only as a reason for such a hope in Him is to offer as good a reason as need be given. There are indeed many others that fully justify this expectation.

2. To teach that such an expectation is a dangerous error is to teach unbelief. What if the apostle had added to this injunction which requires us to account ourselves dead indeed unto sin, but alive unto God, this singular averment: "You let me warn you, nobody can rationally hope to be free from sin in this world. You must remember that to entertain such an expectation as God enjoins in this language is a dangerous error." What should be thought of this if it were attached to Rom. 6:11?

No man can deny that the passage treats of sanctification. The whole question is, "Shall Christians *continue in sin* after having been forgiven and accepted in their Redeemer?" Paul labors to show that they *should*, and of course that they *may* die to sin—even as Christ died for sin; and may also live a new, a spiritual life (through faith in His grace), even as Christ lives a higher and more glorious life.

Let me refer here to another passage, in which it is said, "Be not unequally yoked with unbelievers—what agreement hath the temple of God with idols? For ye are the temple of the living God. Wherefore come out from among them and be ye separate, saith the Lord, and touch not the unclean thing, and I will receive you, and will be a Father unto you and ye shall be my sons and daughters, saith the Lord Almighty." "Having, therefore, these promises, dearly beloved, let us cleanse ourselves from all filthiness of the flesh and of the spirit, perfecting holiness in the fear of God," 2 Cor. 6:11-18, and 7:1. This is a very remarkable passage. Note how precept and promise are intermingled, and how, finally, upon the basis of a most glorious promise, is founded the precept enjoining us to *perfect holiness*. Now what should we think of Paul and of the Divine Spirit who spake through Paul, if He had immediately subjoined, "Take care lest any of you should be led by these remarks to indulge the very dangerous and erroneous expectation that you can *perfect holiness,* or *cleanse yourselves from any sin,* either of flesh or spirit, in this world?" Would not this have been trifling with the intelligence and Christian sensibility of every reader of His words through all time? Should we not account it as substantially blasphemous?

It so happens that the Bible never gainsays its own teachings; but I ask—What if it had? What if the Bible had solemnly asserted, "No mere man, either of himself or by any grace received in this life, has ever kept or shall ever keep the commandments of God wholly, but doth daily break them in thought, word, and deed?"

To teach that such an expectation is dangerous is a great deal worse than no teaching at all. Far better to leave men to their own unaided reading of God's Word, for this could scarcely in any case so sadly mislead them, however inclined they might be to misapprehension. Dangerous to expect salvation from sin? Dangerous? What does this mean? What! *Dangerous to expect victory over any sin? If so what is the gospel worth?* What gospel have we that can be deemed *good news* at all?

Many indulge the very opposite expectation. Far from expecting any such thing as the apostle authorizes them to expect, they know they have no such expectation.

Of some yet more than this is true—they expect to count themselves always in sin. They depend on reckoning themselves, not dead indeed unto sin, but somewhat alive to it through all their mortal life, and in part alive to God through Jesus Christ. It follows as quite a thing of course that expecting no such thing as complete *victory over sin,* they will use no appropriate means, since *faith* stands foremost among those means, and faith must include at least a confidence that the thing sought is possible to be attained.

In this and the following chapters we have the essence of the good news of the gospel. Anyone who has been wounded and made sore by sin—its bitter shafts sinking deep into his moral being—one who has known its bitterness and felt the poison thereof drink up his spirit—such a one will see that there is glory in the idea of being delivered from sin. He will surely see that this deliverance is by far the greatest want of his soul, and that nothing can be compared with escaping from this body of sin and death. Look at Romans 7. There you will have the state of a man who is more than convinced, who is really *convicted.* It is one thing to be convinced, and yet a further stage of progress in the right direction to be convicted. This term implies the agency of another party. The criminal at the bar may be quite convinced of his guilt by the view that he was compelled to take of his own case; but his being *convicted* is a still further step, since the testimony and the jury *convict* him.

Some of you know what it is to see yourself a sinner, and yet the sight of the fact brings with it no smart—no sting; it does not cut deep into your very soul. On the other hand, some of you may know what it is to see your sins all armed like an armed man to pierce you through and through with daggers. Then you cry out as here, "O wretched man that I am! Who shall deliver me from the body of this death?" You feel a piercing sting as if your soul were filled with poison—with dark, rankling venom, diffusing through the depths of your soul the very agonies of hell! This is what I mean by being convicted; a state of mind beyond being merely convinced. The shafts and the smiting of sin seem really like the piercings of an arrow, as if arrows from the Almighty did really drink up your spirit. When you experience this, then you can understand what the good news of the gospel is. A remedy for such pangs must be good news beyond all contradiction. Then to know that the blood of Christ can save is indeed a cordial of life to the fainting soul.

Place a man in this state of cutting, piercing conviction, and then let him feel that there is actually no remedy, and he sinks under the iron shafts of despair. See his agony? Tell him there can never be any remedy for his guilty soul. You must lie there in your wailing and despair forever. Can any state of mind be more awful?

I remember a case that occurred in Reading, Pa., many years ago. There was a man of hard heart and iron frame, a strong, burly man, who had stood up against the revival as if he could shake off all the arrows of the Almighty, even as the Mastodon of which the tradition of the red man says, "He shook off all the arrows of the warriors from his brow and felt no harm." So he stood. But he had a praying wife and a praying sister, and they gathered their souls in the might of prayer close about him as a party of men would hem in a wild bull in a net. Soon it was apparent that an arrow from the quiver of the Almighty had pierced between the joints of his harness and had taken hold of his innermost heart. Oh, was not he in agony then! It was night—dark and intensely cold. It seemed that absolutely he could not live. They sent for me to come and see him. I went. While yet sixty rods from his house I heard his screams and wailings of woe. It made me feel awfully solemn—so like the echoes of the pit of hell! I reached the house: there he lay on the floor rolling in his agony and wailing, such as is rarely heard this side the pit of despair. Cold as the weather was, he sweat like rain, every part of his frame being in a most intense perspiration. Oh, his groans! And to see him gnaw his very tongue for pain—this could not but give one some idea of the doom of the damned. "Oh," said I, "if this be only conviction, *what is hell*?" But he could not bear to hear anything about sin; his conscience was already full of it, and had brought out the awful things of God's law so as to leave nothing more to be done in that direction. I could only put Christ before him, and just hold his mind to the view of Christ alone. This soon brought relief. But suppose I had nothing else to say but this, "Mr. B., there is no help possible for your case! You can wail on and wail on: no being in the universe can help you"? Need you say to him hell has no fire? Oh, he has fire enough in his burning soul already. It seems to him that no hell of fire can possibly be worse than this.

How perfectly chilling and horrible for persons to oppose the idea of expecting deliverance from sin, and yet talk calmly of going on in sin all the rest of their earthly days!

An elder, whom I knew, rose in meeting and told the Lord he had been living in sin thus far, and expected to go on in sin as long as he lived. He had sinned today and should doubtless sin tomorrow and so on—and yet he talked as calmly about it all as if it were foolish to make any ado, as well as impossible to make any attempt to change for the better. Talk of all this calmly—think of that! Quite calm about living along in sin all the rest of his days! How horrible! Suppose a wife should say to her husband, "I love you some, but you know I love many other men too, and I find it pleasant to indulge myself with them. You certainly must be aware that all women are frail creatures, and liable to fall continually, and indeed you know that I expect to fall more or less, as it may happen, every day I live, so that you certainly will not expect from me anything so impracticable and fanatical as unblemished virtue! You know we have none of us any idea of being perfect in the present life—we don't believe in any such thing!"

Now let me ask you to look at this woman and hear what she has to say. Can you hear her talk so, without having your soul filled with horror? What! is this woman a *wife*, and does she think and talk in this way about conjugal fidelity?

And yet this is not to be compared in shocking guilt and treason with the case of the Christian who says, "I expect to sin every day I live," and who says this with unmoved carelessness. You expect to be a traitor to Jesus each day of your life; to crucify Him afresh each day; to put Him each day to open shame; each day to dishonor His name, and grieve His heart, and to bring sorrow and shame upon all who love Christ's cause; and yet you talk about having a good hope through grace! But tell me, does not every true Christian say, "Do not let me live at all if I cannot live without sin; for how can I bear to go on day by day sinning against Him whom I so much love!"

Those who are really opposed to this idea are either very ignorant of what the Gospel is or they are impenitent and of course do not care to be delivered from their sins; or at best, they are guilty of great unbelief. Into which of these classes the opposers of the doctrine may fall is a question for themselves to settle, as between their own consciences and their God.

There are two distinct views of salvation entertained among professed Christians; and correspondingly, two distinct classes of professors—often embraced within the same church. The one class regard the Gospel as a salvation from sin. They think more of this and value it more than the hope of heaven or of earth. The great thing with them is to realize the idea of deliverance from sin. This constitutes the charm and glory of the Gospel. They seek this more than to be saved from hell. They care more, by far, to be saved from sin itself than from its penal consequences. Of the latter they think and pray but little. It is their glory and their joy that Christ is sent to deliver them from their bondage in iniquity—to lift them up from their wretched state and give them the liberty of love. This they labor to realize; this is to them the good news of Gospel salvation.

The other class are mostly anxious to be saved from hell. The punishment due for sin is the thing they chiefly fear. In fact, fear has been mainly the spring of their religious efforts. The gospel is not thought of as a means of deliverance from sin, but as a great system of *indulgences*—a vast accommodation to take off the fear and danger of damnation, while yet it leaves them in their sin. Now, here I do not by any means imply that they will call their system of gospel faith a scheme of indulgences; the name doubtless will be an offense to them. They may not have distinctly considered this point, and they may have failed to notice that in fact it is such and nothing better.

They seem not to notice that a scheme of salvation that removes the fear of damnation for sin, and which yet leaves them in their sins to live for themselves, to please themselves, and which holds that Christ will at last bring them to heaven notwithstanding their having lived in sin all their days, must be *a vast scheme of indulgences.* Indeed, it is a *compromise* on a most magnificent scale. By virtue of it, the whole Church is expected to wallow on in sin through life, and be none the less sure of heaven at last.

These opposite views are so prevalent and so palpable you will see them everywhere as you go round among the churches. You will find many in the Church who are altogether worldly and selfish; who live conformed to the world in various neglects of duty, and who expect to indulge themselves in sin more or less all the way through life. You may ask them; "Do you think that is right?" They answer, "No." "Why, then, do you do it?" "Oh, we are all imperfect, and we can't expect to be any better than imperfect while here in the flesh." Yet they expect to be saved at last from hell, and to have all their sins forgiven; but how? Not on condition of sincerely turning away from all their sins, but on the assumption that the gospel is a vast system of indulgences—more vast by far than Pope Leo X. ever wielded and worked to comfort sinning professors in his day. For here are not merely those that sin *occasionally* as *there,* but those who live in sin and know they do, and expect they shall as long as they live, yet expect to be saved without fail at last.

The other class of professed Christians have no expectation of being saved except they have a pure heart and live above the world. Talk to them about living in sin; they hate and dread the very thought. To them the poison of asps is in it. Sin is bitter to their souls. They dread it as they dread death itself.

No one can go round within this church or any other without finding these two classes as distinct in their apprehension of the gospel as I have described them to be. The one class are in agony if they find themselves even slipping, and they are especially cautious so as not to expose themselves to temptation.

Not so with the other class. There were two ministers of the gospel together; one urged the other strongly to engage in a certain service. The other declined. "Why not go?" asked the first. "Because I do not think myself justified in exposing myself to such and so much temptation," said the other.

"But why stop for that? We expect to sin more or less always; and all we have to do is repent of it afterwards," replied the first.

Horror-smitten, the other could only say, "I hold to a different gospel from that altogether."

Suppose a wife should say to her husband, "I am determined I will go to the theatre." "But, my dear," says he, "you know bad people congregate there, and you may be tempted." But she replies, "Never mind; if I sin I will repent of it afterwards."

The real Christian may be known by this, that the very thought of being drawn into sin drives him to agony. He cannot bear the idea of living in sin, no, not for one moment.

The young people here who are truly Christians will be careful about this ensuing vacation. You will be on your guard, for you are afraid you may be ensnared into sin. I do not mean that you need fear to go where God calls you, but it is a terrible thing to be ensnared into sin, and you cannot but feel it to be so. If you know what it is to be wounded by the arrows of sin in your soul, you will go abroad into apparent danger, walking softly, and with caution, and much prayer. You will surely be much on your guard. But if you say, "Oh, if I sin I will repent," what shall I say of you? You will repent, will you? And this will make it all right again so easily? Suppose you foresaw that in going abroad for vacation you would get drunk a few times, and would commit one or two murders, would you say, "Oh, I may be a good Christian notwithstanding. I will be careful to repent of it after it is all over." *Horrible!* And yet you can think yourself a good Christian! Let me tell you, a Christian man who repents of sin, repents of it *as* sin. He makes no such discriminations as between a little secret sin and a great sin; for example, a murder. He knows no distinction between sins that allow him to commit the one class without scruple and to shrink from the other. With him anything that grieves God is a horrible thing. Anything that displeases God makes him cry out, "God will see it; it will grieve His heart!" How it will affect God—this is all in all with him. One who knows what it is to appear guilty of sin before God, and then who knows also what it is to be delivered from this condition, will understand how the Christian ought to feel in circumstances of temptation, where he feels himself in danger of sinning. His hair all stands on end! How awful to sin against God! Hence, anything that seems likely to bring him into danger will rouse up all his soul within him and put him on his guard.

The unbelief of the Church regarding what they may receive from Christ is the great stumbling-block, hindering themselves and others from experiencing deliverance. Not only is this a great curse to professed Christians, but it is also a great grief to Jesus Christ and a sore trial.

Many seem to have hardened their hearts against all expectation of this deliverance from sin. They have heard the doctrine preached. They have seen some profess to be in this state of salvation from sin, but they have also seen some of this class fall again, and now they deliberately reject the whole doctrine. But is this consistent with really embracing the gospel? What is Christ to the believer? What was His errand into the world? What is He doing and what is He trying to do?

He has come to break the power of sin in the heart, and to be the life of the believer, working in him a perpetual salvation from sin, aiming to bring him thus, and only thus, to heaven at last. What is faith? What but the actual giving of yourself up to Christ that He may do this work for you and in you? What are you to believe of Christ if not this, that He is to save His people from their sins? Can you tell of anything else? Does the Bible tell you to expect something different and less than this? The fact is that it has been the great stumbling-block to the Church that this thing has not been well understood. The common experience of nominal Christians has misrepresented and belied the truth. The masses forming their views much more from this experience than from the Bible, or at best applying this experience to interpret the Bible, have adopted exceedingly defective, if not to say false, opinions as to the nature and design of the gospel. They seem to forget altogether that Paul, writing to Christians at Rome, assures them that if they are under grace, sin shall not have dominion over them.

When Christians do not expect this blessing from Christ, they will not get it. Since they expect so little, no wonder they get so little. According to their faith, and not ever very much beyond it, need they expect to receive.

It is often the case that sanctification is held as a theory, while the mind does not yet by any means embrace the truth in love. The case is analogous to that of impenitent sinners who hold in theory that they must have a new heart. They profess to believe thus, but do they really understand it? No. Suppose it were revealed to their minds so that they should really see it as it is, would they not see a new thing? Would they not be startled to see how utterly far they are, while impenitent, from being acceptable to God, and how great the change they must experience before they can enter the kingdom? So of sanctification. Although this class of persons profess to hold it in theory, yet the passages of Scripture which describe it do not enter into their experience. They do not see the whole truth. If they were to see the whole truth, and should then reject it, I believe it would be in them the unpardonable sin. When the Spirit of God discloses to them the real meaning of the gospel, then if they deliberately reject it, how can the sin be less than what the Scriptures represent as the unpardonable sin? Having once been enlightened, and having received the knowledge of the truth that they might be saved, then if they turn back, is it not thenceforth impossible that they should be renewed again to repentance? One thing, at least, must be said; there is a peril which many of the professed Christians of our day seem not to realize. Since they have so much light before their minds regarding the provisions made in the gospel for present sanctification, if they reject this light practically and live still in sin as if the gospel made no provision to save the Christian from his sins, then they are in great peril. Into this awful peril how many rush blindly and to their own destruction!

6

THE WAGES OF SIN*
Romans 6:23

"The wages of sin is death."

The death here spoken of is that which is due as the penal sanction of God's law.

In presenting the subject of our text, I must:

I. *Illustrate the nature of sin.*
II. *Specify some of the attributes of the penal sanctions of God's law.*
III. *Show what this penalty must be.*

I. *An illustration will give us the best practical view of the nature of sin.* You have only to suppose a government established to secure the highest well-being of the governed, and of the ruling authorities also. Suppose the head of this government to embark all his attributes in the enterprise—all his wealth, all his time, all his energies—to compass the high end of the highest general good. For this purpose he enacts the best possible laws—laws which, if obeyed, will secure the highest good of both subject and Prince. He then takes care to affix adequate penalties; else all his care and wisdom must come to naught. He devotes to the interests of his government all he is and all he has, without reserve or abatement.

But some of his subjects refuse to sympathize with this movement. They say, "Charity begins at home," and they are for taking care of themselves in the first place; in short, they are thoroughly selfish.

It is easy to see what this would mean in a human government. The

Sermons on Gospel Themes, pp. 37-56.

man who does this becomes the common enemy of the government and of all its subjects. *This is sin.* This illustrates precisely the case of the sinner. Sin is selfishness. It sets up a selfish end; and to gain it, uses selfish means; so that in respect to both its end and its means, it is precisely opposed to God and to all the ends of general happiness which He seeks to secure. It denies God's rights; discards God's interests. Each sinner maintains that his own will shall be the law. The interest he sets himself to secure is entirely opposed to that proposed by God in His government.

All law must have sanctions. Without sanctions it would be only advice. It is therefore essential to the distinctive and inherent nature of law that it have sanctions.

These are either remuneratory or vindicatory. They promise reward for obedience, and they also threaten penalty for disobedience. They are vindicatory, inasmuch as they vindicate the honor of the violated law.

Again, sanctions may be either natural or governmental. Often both forms exist in other governments than the divine.

Natural penalties are those evil consequences which naturally result without any direct interference by the government to punish. In the divine government, compunctions of conscience and remorse fall into this class, and indeed many other things which naturally result to obedience on the one hand and to disobedience on the other.

There should also be governmental sanctions. Every governor should manifest his displeasure against the violation of his laws. To leave the whole question of obedience to mere natural consequences is obviously unjust to society. Inasmuch as governments are established to sustain law and secure obedience, they are bound to put forth their utmost energies in this work.

Another incidental agency of government, under some circumstances, is that which we call discipline. One object of discipline goes before the infliction of penalty, and forces open unwilling eyes to see that law has a government to back it up and that the sinner has a fearful penalty to fear. Coming upon men during their probation, while as yet they have not seen or felt the fearfulness of penalty, it is designed to admonish them—to make them think and consider. Thus its special object is the good of the subject on whom it falls and of those who may witness its administration. It does not propose to sustain the dignity of law by exemplary inflictions. This belongs exclusively to the province of penalty. Discipline, therefore, is not penal in the sense of visiting crime with deserved punishment, but aims to dissuade the subject of law from violating its precepts.

Disciplinary agency could scarcely exist under a government of pure law, for the reason that such a government cannot defer the infliction of penalty. Discipline presupposes a state of suspended penalty. Hence penal inflictions must be broadly distinguished from disciplinary.

We are sinners, and therefore have little occasion to dwell on the remuneratory features of God's government. We can have no claim to remuneration under law; this is precluded utterly by our sin. But with the penal features we have everything to do. I therefore proceed to enquire.

II. *What are the attributes of the penal sanctions of God's law?*

God has given us reason. This affirms intuitively and irresistibly all the great truths of moral government. There are certain attributes which we know must belong to the moral law; e.g. one is, *intrinsic justice.* Penalty should threaten no more and no less than is just. Justice must be an attribute of God's law; else the whole universe must inevitably condemn it.

Intrinsic justice means and implies that the penalty is equal to the obligation violated. The guilt of sin consists in its being a violation of obligation. Hence the guilt must be in proportion to the magnitude of the obligation violated, and consequently the penalty must be measured by this obligation.

Governmental justice is another attribute. This feature of law seeks to afford security against transgression. Law is not governmentally just unless its penalty be so graduated as to afford the highest security against sin which the nature of the case admits. Suppose under any government the sanctions of law are trifling, not at all proportioned to the end to be secured. Such a government is unjust to itself, and to the interests it is committed to maintain. Hence a good government must be governmentally just, affording in the severity of its penalties and the certainty of their just infliction the highest security that its law shall be obeyed.

Again, penal sanctions should be worthy of the end aimed at by the law and by its author. Government is only a means to an end; this proposed end being universal obedience and its consequent happiness. If law is indispensable for obtaining this end, its penalty should be graduated accordingly.

Hence the penalty should be graduated by the importance of the precept. If the precept be of fundamental importance—of such importance that disobedience to it saps the very existence of all government—then it should be guarded by the greatest and most solemn sanctions. The penalties attached to its violation should be of the highest order.

Penalty should make an adequate expression of the lawgiver's views of the value of the end he proposes to secure by law; also of his views of the sacredness of his law; also of the intrinsic guilt of disobedience. Penalty aims to bring forth the *heart* of the lawgiver—to show the earnestness of his desire to maintain the right, and to secure that order and well-being which depend on obedience. In the greatness of the penalty the lawgiver brings forth his heart and pours the whole influence of his character upon his subjects.

The object of executing penalty is precisely the same; not to gratify revenge, as some seem to suppose, but to act on the subjects of government with influences toward obedience. It has the same general object as the law itself has.

Penal sanctions should be an adequate expression of the lawgiver's regard for the public good and of his interest in it. In the precept he gave some expression; in the penalty, he gives yet more. In the precept we see the object in view and have a manifestation of regard for the public interest; in the penalty, we have a *measure* of this regard, showing us how *great* it is. For example, suppose a human law were to punish murder with only a trifling penalty. Under the pretence of being very tender-hearted, the lawgiver amerces this crime of murder with a fine of fifty cents! Would this show that he greatly loved his subjects and highly valued their life and interest? Far from it. You cannot feel that a legislator has done his duty unless he shows how much he values human life, and unless he attaches a penalty commensurate in some good degree with the end to be secured.

One word as to the infliction of capital punishment in human governments. There is a difference of opinion as to which is most effective; solitary punishment for life, or death. Leaving this question without remark, I have it to say that no man ever doubted that *the murderer deserves to die.* If some other punishment than death is to be preferred, it is not by any means because the murderer does not deserve death. No man can doubt this for a moment. It is one of the unalterable principles of righteousness, that if a man sacrifices the interest of another, he sacrifices his own; an eye for an eye; life for life.

We cannot but affirm that no government lays sufficient stress on the protection of human life unless it guards this trust with its highest penalties. Where life and all its vital interests are at stake, there the penalty should be as great and as solemn as is possible.

Moral agents have two sides to their sensibility: hope and fear; to which you may address the prospect of good or the dread of evil. I am now speaking of penalty. This is addressed only to fear.

I have said in substance that the penalty should adequately assert and vindicate the rightful authority of the lawgiver; should afford if possible an adequate rebuke of sin, and should be based on a just appreciation of its nature. God's moral government embraces the whole intelligent universe, and stretches with its vast results onward through eternity. Hence the sweep and breadth of its interests are absolutely unlimited; and consequently, the penalties of its law, being set to vindicate the authority of this government and to sustain these immeasurable interests, should be beyond measure dreadful. If anything beyond and more dreadful than the threatened penalty could be conceived, all minds would say, "This is not enough." With any just views of the relations and the guilt of sin, they could not be satisfied unless the penalty is the greatest that is conceivable. Sin is so vile, so mischievous, so terribly destructive and so far-sweeping in its ruin, that moral agents could not feel that enough is done so long as more can be.

III. *What is the penalty of God's moral law?*

Our text answers, "*death.*" This certainly is not *animal death*, for saints die and animals also, neither of whom can be receiving the wages of sin. Besides, this would be no penalty if, after its infliction, men went at once to heaven. Such a penalty, considered as the wages of sin would only be an insult to God's government.

Again, it cannot be *spiritual death*, for this is nothing else than a state of entire disobedience to the law. You cannot well conceive anything more absurd than to punish a man for disobedience by subjecting him to perpetual disobedience—an effort to sustain the law by dooming such offenders to its perpetual violation—and nothing more.

But this death *is* endless misery, corresponding to the death-penalty in human governments. Everybody knows what this is. It separates the criminal from society forever; debars him at once and utterly from all the privileges of the government, and consigns him over to hopeless ruin. Nothing more dreadful can be inflicted. It is the extreme penalty, fearful beyond any other, that is possible for man to inflict.

There can be no doubt that death as spoken of in our text is intended to correspond to the death-penalty in human governments.

You will also observe that in our text the "gift of God" which is "eternal life through Jesus Christ our Lord," is directly contrasted with death, the wages of sin. This fact may throw light on the question respecting the nature of this death. We must look for the antithesis of *"eternal life."*

Now this eternal life is not merely an eternal existence. Eternal life never means merely an eternal existence, in any case where it is used in Scripture; but it does mean a state of eternal blessedness, implying eternal holiness as its foundation. The use of the term "life" in Scripture in the sense of *real life*—a life worth living—*i.e.*, real and rich enjoyment, is so common as to supersede the necessity of special proof.

The penalty of death is therefore the opposite of this—viz., eternal misery.

I must here say a few words upon the *objections* raised against this doctrine of eternal punishment.

All the objections I have ever heard amount only to this, *that it is unjust.* They may be expressed in somewhat various phraseology, but this is the only idea which they involve, of any moment at all.

1. It is claimed to be unjust because "life is so short."

How strangely men talk! Life so short that men have not time to sin enough to deserve eternal death! Do men forget that *one sin* incurs the penalty due for sinning? How many sins ought it to take to make one transgression of the law of God? Men often talk as if they supposed it must require a great many. As if a man must commit a great many murders before he has made up the crime of murder enough to fall under the sentence of the court! What? Shall a man come before the court and plead that although he has broken the law to be sure, yet he has not lived long enough, and has not broken the law times enough, to incur its penalty? What court on earth ever recognized such a plea as proving any other than the folly and guilt of him who made it?

2. It is also urged that "man is so small, so very insignificant a being that he cannot possibly commit an infinite sin." What does this objection mean? Does it mean that sin is an act of creation, and to be mea-

sured therefore by the magnitude of that *something* which it creates? This would be an exceedingly wild idea of the nature of sin. Does the objection mean that man cannot violate an obligation of infinite strength? Then his meaning is simply *false*, as everybody must know. Does he imply that the guilt of sin is not to be measured by the obligation violated? Then he knows not what he says, or wickedly denies known truth. What? Man so little that he cannot commit much sin! Is this the way we reason in analogous cases? Suppose your child disobeys you. He is very much smaller than you are! But do you therefore exonerate him from blame? Is this a reason which nullifies his guilt? Can no sin be committed by inferiors against their superior? Have sensible men always been mistaken in supposing that the younger and smaller are sometimes under obligations to obey the older and the greater? Suppose you smite down the magistrate; suppose you insult, or attempt to assassinate the king; is this a very small crime, almost too excusable to be deemed a crime at all, because forsooth, you are in a lower position and he in a higher? You say, "I am so little, so very insignificant! How can I deserve so great a punishment?" Do you reason so in any other case except your own sins against God? Never.

3. Again, some men say, "Sin is not an infinite evil." This language is ambiguous. Does it mean that sin would not work infinite mischief if suffered to run on indefinitely? This is false, for if only one soul were ruined by it, the mischief accruing from it would be infinite. Does it mean that sin is not an infinite evil, as seen in its present results and relations? Suppose we admit this; it proves nothing to our purpose, for it may be true that the sum total of evil resulting from each single sin will not all be brought out in any duration less than eternity. How then can you measure the evil of sin by what you see today?

But there are still other considerations to show that the penalty of the law must be infinite. Sin is an infinite *natural* evil. It is so in this sense, that there are no bounds to the natural evil it would introduce if not governmentally restrained.

If sin were to ruin but one soul, there could be no limit set to the evil it would thus occasion.

Again, sin involves infinite guilt, for it is a violation of infinite obligation. Here it is important to notice a common mistake growing out of confusion about the ground of obligation. From this, results mistakes in regard to what constitutes the guilt of sin. Here I might show that when you misapprehend the ground of obligation, you will almost of necessity misconceive the nature and extent of sin and guilt. Let us return to our former illustration. Here is a government wisely framed to secure the highest good of the governed and of all concerned. Whence arises the obligation to obey? Certainly from the intrinsic value of the end sought to be secured. But how broad is this obligation to obey; or, in other words, what is its true measure? I answer, it exactly equals the value of the end which the government seeks to secure, and which obedience will secure, but which sin will destroy. By this measure of God the penalty must be graduated. By this the lawgiver must determine how much sanction, remuneratory and vindicatory, he must attach to his law in order to meet the demands of justice and benevolence.

Now God's law aims to secure the highest universal good. Its chief and ultimate end is not, strictly speaking, to secure supreme homage to God, but rather to secure the highest good of all intelligent moral beings—God and all His creatures. So viewed, you will see that the intrinsic value of the end to be sought is the real ground of obligation to obey the precept. The value of this end being estimated, you have the value and strength of the obligation.

This is plainly infinite in the sense of being unlimited. In this sense we affirm obligation to be without limit. The very reason why we affirm any obligation at all is that the law is good and is the necessary means of the highest good of the universe. Hence, since we affirm any penalty at all, we are compelled to affirm the justice and the necessity of an infinite penalty. We see that intrinsic justice must demand an infinite penalty for the same reason that it demands any penalty whatever. If *any* penalty be just, it is just because law secures a certain good. If this good aimed at by the law be unlimited in extent, so must be the penalty. Governmental justice thus requires endless punishment; else it provides no sufficient guaranty for the public good.

Again, the law not only *designs* but *tends to secure* infinite good. Its tendencies are direct to this end. Hence, its penalty should be infinite. The law is not just to the interests it both aims and tends to secure unless it arms itself with infinite sanctions.

Nothing less than infinite penalty can be an adequate expression of God's view of the value of the great end on which His heart is set. When men talk about eternal death being too great a penalty for sin, what do they think of God's efforts to restrain sin all over the moral universe? What do they think of the death of His well-beloved Son? Do they suppose it possible that God could give an adequate or a corresponding expression to His hatred of sin by any penalty less than endless?

Nothing less could give an adequate expression to His regard for the authority of law. Oh, how fearful the results and how shocking the very idea, if God should fail to make an adequate expression of His regard for the sacredness of that law which underlies the entire weal of all His vast kingdom?

You would insist that He shall regard the violation of His law as Universalists do. How surely He would bring down an avalanche of ruin on all His intelligent creatures if He were to yield to your demands! Were He to affix anything less than endless penalty to His law, what holy being could trust the administration of His government!

His regard to the public good forbids His attaching a light or finite penalty to His law. He loves His subjects too well. Some people have strange notions of the way in which a ruler should express his regard for his subjects. They would have him so tender-hearted toward the guilty that they should absorb his entire sympathy and regard. They would allow him perhaps to fix a penalty of sixpence fine for the crime of murder, but not much if anything more. The poor murderer's wife and children are so precious you must not take away much of his money, and as to touching his liberty or his life—neither of these is to be thought of. What! Do you not know that human nature is very frail and temptable, and therefore you ought to deal very sparingly with penalties for murder? Perhaps they would say, you may punish the murderer by keeping him awake one night—just one, no more; and God may let a guilty man's conscience disturb him about to this extent for the crime of murder! The Universalists do tell us that they will allow the most High God to give a man conscience that shall trouble him a little if he commits murder—a little, say for the first and perhaps the second offense; but they are not wont to notice the fact that under this penalty of a troubling conscience, the more a man sins, the less he has to suffer. Under the operation of this descending scale, it will soon come to this that a murderer would not get so much penalty as the loss of one night's sleep. But such are the notions that men reach when they swing clear of the affirmations of an upright reason and of God's revealing Word.

Speaking now to those who have a moral sense to affirm the right as well as eyes to see the operation of law, I know you cannot deny the logical necessity of the death penalty for the moral law of God. There is a logical clinch to every one of these propositions which you cannot escape.

No penalty less than infinite and endless can be an adequate expression of God's displeasure against sin and of His determination to resist and punish it. The penalty should run on as long as there are subjects to be affected by it—as long as there is need of any demonstration of God's feelings and governmental course toward sin.

Nothing less is the greatest God can inflict, for He certainly can inflict an endless and infinite punishment. If therefore the exigency demands the greatest penalty He can inflict, this must be the penalty—*banishment from God and endless death.*

But I must pass to remark that the gospel everywhere assumes the same. It holds that by the deeds of the law no flesh can be justified before God. Indeed, it not only affirms this, but builds its entire system of atonement and grace upon this foundation. It constantly assumes that there is no such thing as paying the debt and cancelling obligation; and therefore, that the sinner's only relief is forgiveness through redeeming blood.

Yet again, if the penalty be not endless death, *what is it*? Is it temporary suffering? Then how long does it last? When does it end? Has any sinner ever got through; served out his time and been taken to heaven? We have no testimony to prove such a case, not the first one; but we have the solemn testimony of Jesus Christ to prove that there never can be such a case. He tells us there can be no passing from hell to heaven or from heaven to hell. A great gulf is fixed between, over which none shall ever pass. You may pass from earth to heaven, or from earth to hell; but these two states of the future world are wide extremes, and no man or angel shall pass the gulf that divides them.

But you answer my question, "What is the penalty?" by the reply, "It is only the natural consequences of sin as developed in a troubled conscience." Then it follows that the more a man sins the less he is punished, until it amounts to an infinitesimal quantity of punishment, for which the sinner cares just nothing at all. Who can believe this? Under this system, if a man fears punishment, he has only to pitch into sinning with the more will and energy; he will have the comfort of feeling that he can very soon get over all his compunctions, and get beyond any penalty whatever! And do you believe this is God's only punishment for sin? You cannot believe it.

Universalists always confound discipline with penal sanctions. They overlook this fundamental distinction and regard all that men suffer here in this world as only penal. Whereas it is scarcely penal at all, but is chiefly disciplinary. They ask, "What good will it do a sinner to send him to an endless hell? Is not God perfectly benevolent; and if so, how can He have any other object than to do the sinner all the good He can?"

I reply, "Punishment is not designed to do good to that sinner who is punished. It looks to other, remoter, and far greater good. Discipline, while he was on earth, sought mainly *his* personal good; penalty looks to other results. If you ask, 'Does not God aim to do good to the universal public by penalty?' I answer, 'Even so; that is precisely what He aims to do.' "

Under human governments, the penalty may aim in part to reclaim. So far, it is discipline. But the death penalty, after all suspension is past and the fatal blow comes, aims not to reclaim, and is not discipline, but is only penalty. The guilty man is laid on the great public altar and made a sacrifice for the public good. The object is to make a fearful, terrible impression on the public mind of the evil of transgression and the fearfulness of its consequences. Discipline looks not so much to the support of law as to the recovery of the offender. But the day of judgment has nothing to do with reclaiming the lost sinner. That and all its issues are purely penal. It is strange that these obvious facts should be overlooked.

There is yet another consideration often disregarded, viz., that, underlying any safe dispensation of discipline, there must be a moral law, sustained by ample and fearful sanctions, to preserve the lawgiver's authority and sustain the majesty and honor of his government. It would not be safe to trust a system of discipline, and indeed it could not be expected to take hold of the ruined with much force, if it were not sustained by a system of law and penalty. This penal visitation on the unreclaimed sinner must stand forever, an appalling fact, to show that justice is realized, law vindicated, God honored; and to make an enduring and awful impression of the evil of sin and of God's eternal hostility against it.

Remarks

We hear a great many cavils against future punishment. At these we should not so much wonder, but for the fact that the gospel assumes this truth, and then proposes a remedy. One would naturally suppose the mind would shrink from those fearful conclusions to which it is pressed when the relations of mere law are contemplated; but when the gospel interposes to save, then it becomes passing strange that men should admit the reality of the gospel, and yet reject the law and its penalties. They talk of *grace*; but what do they mean by grace? When men deny the fact of sin, there is no room and no occasion for grace in the gospel. Admitting nominally the fact of sin, but virtually denying its guilt, grace is only a name. Repudiating the sanctions of the law of God and laboring to disprove their reality, what right have men to claim that they respect the gospel? They make it only a farce—or at least a system of *amends* for unreasonably severe legislation under the legal economy. Let not men who so traduce the law assume that they honor God by applauding His gospel!

The representations of the Bible with regard to the final doom of the wicked are exceedingly striking. Spiritual truths are revealed by natural objects: e.g., the gates and walls of the New Jerusalem, to present the splendors and glories of the heavenly state. A spiritual telescope is put into our hands; we are permitted to point it towards the glorious city "whose Builder and Maker is God"; we may survey its inner sanctuary, where the worshipping hosts praise God without ceasing. We see their flowing robes of white, the palms of victory in their hands, the beaming joy of their faces, the manifestations of ineffable bliss in their souls. This is heaven portrayed in symbol. Who supposes that this is intended as hyperbole? Who arraigns these representations as extravagant in speech, as if designed to overrate the case, or raise unwarrantable expectations? No man believes this. No man ever brings this charge against what the Bible says of heaven. What is the object in adopting this figurative mode of representation? Beyond question, the object is to give the best possible conception of the facts.

Then we have the other side. The veil is lifted and you come to the very verge of hell to see what is there. Whereas on the one hand all was glorious, on the other all is fearful and full of horrors.

There is a bottomless pit. A deathless soul is cast therein; it sinks and sinks and sinks, going down that awful pit which knows no bottom, weeping and wailing as it descends, and you hear its groans as they echo and re-echo from the sides of that dread cavern of woe!

Here is another image. You have a "lake of fire and brimstone," and you see lost sinners thrown into its waves of rolling fire; and they lash its burning shore and gnaw their tongues for pain. There the worm dieth not, and their fire is not quenched, and "not one drop of water" can reach them to "cool their tongues," "tormented in that flame."

What think you? Has God said these things to frighten our poor souls? Did He mean to play on our fears for His own amusement? Can you think so? Nay, does it not rather grieve His heart that He must build such a hell, and *must* plunge therein the sinners who will not honor His law, who will not embrace salvation from sinning through His grace? Ah, the waves of death roll darkly under the eye of the Holy and compassionate One! He has no pleasure in the death of the sinner! But He must sustain His throne and save His loyal subjects if He can.

Turn to another scene. Here is a deathbed. Did you ever see a sinner die? Can you describe the scene? Was it a friend, a relative, dear, very dear to your heart? How long was he dying? Did it seem to you the death-agony would never end? When my last child died, the struggle was long; Oh, it was fearfully protracted and agonizing! Twenty-four hours in the agonies of dissolving nature! It made me sick; I could not see it! But suppose it had continued till this time I should long since have died myself under the anguish and nervous exhaustion of witnessing such a scene. So would all our friends. Who could survive to the final termination of such an awful death? Who would not cry out, "My God, cut it short, cut it short in mercy!" When my wife died, her death struggles were long and heart-rending. If you had been there, you would have cried mightily to God, "Cut it short! Oh, cut it short and relieve this dreadful agony!" But suppose it had continued, on and on, by day and by night, day after day, through its slow moving hours, and night after night, *long* nights, as if there could be no morning. The figure of our text supposes an eternal dying. Let us conceive such a case. Suppose it should actually occur in some dear circle of sympathizing friends. A poor man cannot die! He lingers in the death-agony a month, a year, five years, ten years, till all his friends are broken down, and fall into their graves under the insupportable horror of the scene: but still the poor man cannot die! He outlives one generation, then another and another; one hundred years he is dying in mortal agony and yet he comes no nearer to the end! What would you think of such a scene? It would be an illustration—that is all—a feeble illustration of the awful "*second death*"!

God would have us understand what an awful thing sin is and what fearful punishment it deserves. He would fain show us by such figures how terrible must be the doom of the determined sinner. Did you ever see a sinner die? And did you not cry out, "Surely the curse of God has fallen heavily on this world!" Ah, this is only a faint emblem of that heavier curse that comes in the "*second death*"!

The text affirms that death is the "wages of sin." It is just what sin deserves. Labor earns wages and creates a rightful claim to such remuneration. So men are conceived as earning wages when they sin. They become entitled to their pay. God deems himself obligated to give them their well-deserved wages.

As I have often said, I would not say one word in this direction to distress your souls, if there were no hope and no mercy possible. Would I torment you before the time? God forbid! Would I hold out the awful penalty before you and tell you there is no hope? No. I say these things to make you feel the need of escaping for your life.

Think of this: "the wages of sin is death!" God is aiming to erect a monument that shall proclaim to all the universe—*Stand in awe and sin not!* So that whenever they shall look on this awful expression, they shall say, "What an awful thing sin is!" People are wont to exclaim, "Oh, how horrible the *penalty!*" They are but too apt to overlook the horrible *guilt* and *ill-desert* of sin! When God lays a sinner on his death-bed before our eyes, He invites us to look at the *penalty of sin.* There he lies, agonizing, groaning, quivering, racked with pain, yet he lives, and lives on. Suppose he lives on in this dying state a day, a week, a month, a year, a score of years, a century, a thousand years, a thousand ages, and still he lives on, "dying perpetually, yet never dead"; finally, the universe passes away; the heavens are rolled together as a scroll, and what then? There lies that sufferer yet! He looks up and cries, out, "*How long*, Oh, how long?" Like the knell of eternal death, the answer comes down to him, "*Eternally*, eternally." Another cycle of eternal ages rolls on, and again he dares to ask, *how long*? and again the answer rolls back, "*Eternally*, eternally!" O how this fearful answer comes down thundering through all the realms of agony and despair!

We are informed that in the final consummation of earthly scenes that "the judgment shall sit and the books shall be opened." We shall be there, and what is more, *there* to close up our account with our Lord and receive our allotment. Which will you have on that final settlement day? The wages of sin? Do you say, "Give me my wages—give me my wages; I will not be indebted to Christ"? Sinner, you shall have them. God will pay you without fail or stint. He has made all the necessary arrangements, and has your wages ready. But take care what you do! Look again before you take your final leap. Soon the curtain will fall, probation close, and all hope will have perished. Where then shall I be? And you, *where*? On the right hand or on the left?

The Bible locates hell in the sight of heaven. The smoke of their torment as it rises up forever and ever is in full view from the heights of the Heavenly City. There, you adore and worship; but as you cast your eye afar off toward where the rich man lay, you see what it costs to sin. There, not one drop of water can go to cool their burning tongues. Thence the smoke of their torment rises and rises for evermore! Take care what you do today!

Suppose you are looking into a vast crater, where the surges of molten lava boil and roll up, and roll and swell, and ever and anon belch forth huge masses to deluge the plains below. Once in my life, I stood in sight of Etna, and dropped my eye down into its awful mouth. I could not forbear to cry out "*tremendous*, tremendous!" There, said I, is an image of hell! Oh, sinner, think of *hell*, and of yourself thrust into it. It pours forth its volumes of smoke and flame forever, never ceasing, never exhausted. Upon that spectacle the universe can look and read, "The wages of sin is death! Oh, sin not, since such is the doom of the unpardoned sinner!" Think what a demonstration this is in the government of God! What an exhibition of His holy justice, of His inflexible purpose to sustain the interests of holiness and happiness in all His vast dominions! Is not this worthy of God, and of the sacredness of His great scheme of moral government?

Sinner, you may now escape this fearful doom. This is the reason why God has revealed hell in His faithful Word. And now shall this revelation, to you, be in vain and worse than in vain?

What would you think if this whole congregation were pressed by some resistless force close up to the very brink of hell; but just as it seemed that we are all to be pushed over the awful brink, an angel rushes in, shouting as with seraphic trump, "*Salvation is possible—Glory to God*, glory to God, GLORY TO GOD!"

You cry aloud, "Is it possible?" "Yes, yes," he cries, "let me take you up in my broad, loving arms and bear you to the feet of Jesus, for He is mighty and willing to save!"

Is all this mere talk? Oh, if I could wet my lips with the dews of heaven, and bathe my tongue in its founts of eloquence, even then I could not describe the realities.

Christian people, are you figuring round and round to get a little property, yet neglecting souls? Beware, lest you ruin souls that can never live again! Do you say, "I thought they knew it all"? They reply to you, "I did not suppose you believed a word of it yourselves. You did not act as if you did. Are you going to heaven? Well, I am going down to hell! There is no help for me now. You will sometimes think of me then, as you shall see the smoke of my woe rising up darkly athwart the glorious heavens. After I have been there a long, long time, you will sometimes think that I, who once lived by your side, am there. Oh, remember, you cannot pray for me then; but you will remember that once you might have warned and might have saved me."

Oh, methinks, if there can be bitterness in heaven, it must enter through such an avenue and spoil your happiness there!

7

LEGAL EXPERIENCE*
Romans 7

The seventh chapter of the Epistle to the Romans.

I have more than once had occasion to refer to this chapter, and have read some portions of it and made remarks. But I have not been able to go into a consideration of it as fully as I wished, and therefore thought I would make it the subject of a separate lecture. In giving my views, I shall pursue the following order:

I. *Mention the different opinions that have prevailed in the church concerning this passage.*

II. *Show the importance of understanding this portion of scripture correctly, or of knowing which of these prevailing opinions is the true one.*

III. *Lay down several facts and principles which have a bearing on the exposition of this passage.*

IV. *Refer to some rules of interpretation which ought always to be observed in interpreting either the Scriptures or any other writing or testimony.*

V. *Give my own view of the real meaning of the passage and my reasons for them.*

I shall confine myself chiefly to the latter part of the chapter, since that has been chiefly the subject of dispute. You see from the manner in which I have laid out my work that I design to simplify the subject as much as possible, so as to bring it within the compass of a single lecture. Otherwise I might make a volume, so much having been written to show the meaning of this chapter.

Lectures to Professing Christians (1880), pp. 320-338.

I. *I am to show what are the principal opinions that have prevailed concerning the application of this chapter.*

1. One opinion that has extensively prevailed, and still prevails, is that the latter part of the chapter is an epitome of Christian experience.

It has been supposed that it describes the situation and exercises of a Christian, and that it was designed to exhibit the Christian warfare with indwelling sin. However, that is, comparatively, a modern opinion. No writer is known to have held this view of the chapter for centuries after it was written. According to Professor Stuart, who has examined the subject more thoroughly than any other man in America, Augustine was the first writer that exhibited this interpretation, and he resorted to it in his controversy with Pelagius.

2. The only other interpretation given is that which prevailed in the first centuries, and which is still generally adopted on the continent of Europe, as well as by a considerable number of writers in England and in America, that this passage describes the experience of a sinner under conviction, who was acting under the motives of the law, and not yet brought to the experience of the gospel. In this country, the most prevalent opinion is that the seventh chapter of Romans delineates the experience of a Christian.

II. *I am to show the importance of a right understanding of this passage.*

A right understanding of this passage is fundamental. If this passage in fact describes a sinner under conviction, or a purely legal experience, and if a person supposing that it is a Christian experience finds his own experience corresponds with it, then his mistake is a fatal one. It must be a fatal error to believe that his experience is that of a real Christian because it corresponds with the seventh of Romans, if Paul in fact is giving only the experience of a sinner under legal motives and considerations.

III. *I will lay down some principles and facts that have a bearing on the elucidation of this subject.*

1. It is true that mankind acts in all cases, and from the nature of mind must always act, as on the whole they feel to be preferable.

Or, in other words, the will governs the conduct. Men never act against their will. The will governs the motion of the limbs. Voluntary beings cannot act contrary to their will.

2. Men often desire what, on the whole, they do not choose.

The desires and the will are often opposed to each other. The conduct is governed by the choice not by the desires. The desires may be inconsistent with the choice. You may desire to go to some other place tonight, and yet on the whole choose to remain here. Perhaps you desire very strongly to be somewhere else, and yet choose to remain in meeting. A man wishes to go on a journey to some place. Perhaps he desires it strongly. It may be very important to his business or his ambition. But his family is sick, or some other object requires him to be at home, and on the whole he chooses to remain. In all cases, the conduct follows the actual choice.

3. Regeneration, or conversion, is a change in the choice.

It is a change in the supreme controlling choice of the mind. The regenerated or converted person prefers God's glory to everything else. He chooses it as the supreme object of affection. This is a change of heart. Before, he chose his own interest or happiness as his supreme end. Now, he chooses God's service in preference to his own interest. When a person is truly born again, his choice is habitually right, and of course his conduct is in the main right.

The force of temptation may produce an occasional wrong choice, or even a succession of wrong choices, but his habitual course of action is right. The will, or choice, of a converted person is habitually right, and of course his conduct is so. If this is not true, I ask, in what does the converted differ from the unconverted person? If it is not the character of the converted person that he habitually does the commandments of God, what is his character? But I presume this position will not be disputed by anyone who believes in the doctrine of regeneration.

4. Moral agents are so constituted that they naturally and necessarily approve of what is right.

A moral agent is one who possesses understanding, will, and conscience. Conscience is the power of discerning the difference among moral objects. It will not be disputed that a moral agent can be led to see the difference between right and wrong, so that his moral nature shall approve of what is right. Otherwise, a sinner never can be brought under conviction. If he has not a moral nature, that can see and highly approve the law of God, and justify the penalty, then he cannot be convicted. For this is conviction, to see the goodness of the law that he has broken and the justice of the penalty he has incurred. But in fact, there is not a moral agent in heaven, earth, or hell, that cannot be made to see that the law of God is right, and whose conscience does not approve the law.

5. Men may not only approve the law as right, but they may often, when it is viewed abstractly and without reference to its bearing on themselves, take real pleasure in contemplating it.

This is one great source of self-deception. Men view the law of God in the abstract, and love it. When no selfish reason is present for opposing it, they take pleasure in viewing it. They approve of what is right, and condemn wickedness in the abstract. All men do this, when no selfish reason is pressing on them. Who ever found a man so wicked that he approved of evil in the abstract? Where was a moral being ever found that approved the character of the devil, or that approved of other wicked men unconnected with himself? How often do you hear wicked men express the greatest abhorrence and detestation of enormous wickedness in others. If their passions are in no way enlisted in favor of error or of wrong, men always stand up for what is right. And this merely constitutional approbation of what is right may amount even to delight, when they do not see the relations of right interfering in any manner with their own selfishness.

6. In this constitutional approbation of truth and the law of God,

and the delight which naturally arises from it, there is no virtue.

It is only what belongs to man's moral nature. It arises naturally from the constitution of the mind. Mind is constitutionally capable of seeing the beauty of virtue. And so far from there being any virtue in it, it is in fact only a clearer proof of the strength of their depravity; that when they know the right, and see its excellence, they do not obey it. It is not, then, that impenitent sinners have within themselves something that is holy. But their wickedness is herein seen to be so much the greater. For the wickedness of sin is in proportion to the light that is enjoyed. And when we find that men may not only see the excellence of the law of God, but even strongly approve of it and take delight in it, and yet not obey it, then it shows how desperately wicked they are, and makes sin appear exceedingly sinful.

7. It is a common use of language for persons to say, "I would do so and so, but cannot," when they only mean to be understood as desiring it, but not as actually choosing to do it. And so they say, "I could not do so," when they only mean that they would not do it; and, they could if they would.

Not long ago I asked a minister to preach for me the next Sabbath. He answered, "I can't." I found out afterwards that he could if he would. I asked a merchant to take a certain price for a piece of goods. He said, "I can't do it." What did he mean? That he had not the power to accept such a price? Not at all. He could, if he would, but he did not choose to do it. You will see the bearing of these remarks, when I come to read the chapter. I proceed now.

IV. *To give several rules of interpretation, that are applicable to the interpretation not only of the Bible, but to all written instruments, and to all evidence whatever.*

There are certain rules of evidence which all men are bound to apply in ascertaining the meaning of instruments and the testimony of witnesses and of all writings.

1. We are always to put that construction on language which is required by the nature of the subject.

We are bound always to understand a person's language as it is applicable to the subject of discourse. Much of the language of common life may be tortured into anything, if you lose sight of the subject, and take the liberty to interpret it without reference to what they are speaking of. How much injury has been done, by interpreting separate passages and single expressions in the Scriptures, in violation of this principle. It is chiefly by overlooking this simple rule that the Scriptures have been tortured into the support of errors and contradictions innumerable and absurd beyond all calculation. This rule is applicable to all statements. Courts of justice never would allow such perversions as those which have been committed upon the Bible.

2. If a person's language will allow it, we are bound always to construe it so as to make him consistent with himself.

Unless you observe this rule, you can scarcely converse five minutes with any individual on any subject and not make him contradict himself. If you do not hold to this rule, how can one man ever communicate his ideas so that another man will understand them? How can a witness ever make known the facts to the jury, if his language is to be tortured at pleasure without the restraints of this rule?

3. In interpreting a person's language, we are always to keep in view the point to which he is speaking.

We are to understand the scope of his argument, the object he has in view, and the point to which he is speaking. Otherwise, we shall of course not understand his language. Suppose I were to take up a book, any book, and not keep my eye on the object the writer had in view in making it, and the point at which he was aiming, I never could understand that book. It is easy to see how numerous errors have grown out of a practice of interpreting the Scriptures while disregarding the first principles of interpretation.

4. When you understand the point to which a person is speaking, you are to understand him as speaking to that point; and not put a construction on his language unconnected with his object or inconsistent with it.

· By losing sight of this rule, you may make nonsense of everything. You are bound always to interpret language in the light of the subject to which it is applied or about which it is spoken.

V. *Having laid down these rules and principles, I proceed, in the light of them, to give my own view of the meaning of the passage, and my reasons for them.* But first I will make a remark or two.

1st Remark. Whether the apostle was speaking of himself in this passage, or whether he is supposing a case, is not material to the right interpretation of the language.

It is supposed by many that because he speaks in the first person he is to be understood as referring to himself. But it is a common practice, when we are discussing general principles, or arguing a point, to suppose a case by way of illustration or to establish a point. And it is very natural to state it in the first person, without at all intending to be understood (and in fact without ever being understood) as declaring an actual occurrence or an experience of our own. The apostle Paul was pursuing a close train of argument, and he introduces this simply by way of illustration. And it is no way material whether it is his own actual experience or a case supposed.

If he is speaking of himself, or if he is speaking of another person, or if he is supposing a case, he does it with a design to show a general principle of conduct, and that all persons under like circumstances would do the same. Whether he is speaking of a Christian, or of an impenitent sinner, he lays down a general principle.

The apostle James, in the 3rd chapter of James, speaks in the first person, even in administering reproof: "My brethren, be not many masters, knowing that we shall receive the greater condemnation. For in many things we offend all. Therewith bless we God, even the Father; and therewith curse we men, which are made after the similitude of God."

The apostle Paul often says, "I," and uses the first person when discussing and illustrating general principles: "All things are lawful unto me, but all things are not expedient: all things are lawful for me, but I will not be brought under the power of any." And again, "Conscience, I say, not thine own, but of the other: for why is my liberty judged of another man's conscience? For if I by grace be a partaker, why am I evil spoken of for that for which I give thanks? For now we see through a glass, darkly; but then face to face: now I know in part; but then shall I know even as also I am known. And now abideth faith, hope, charity, these three; but the greatest of these is charity." So also, "For if I build again the things which I destroyed, I make myself a transgressor." In 1 Cor. 4:6., he explains exactly how he uses illustrations, "And these things, brethren, I have in a figure transferred to myself, and to Apollos, for your sakes: that ye might learn in us not to think of men above that which is written, that no one of you be puffed up for one against another."

2nd Remark. Much of the language which the apostle uses here is applicable to the case of a backslider, who has lost all but the form of religion. He has left his first love, and has in fact fallen under the influence of the legal motives of hope and fear, just like an impenitent sinner. If there be such a character as a real backslider, who has been a real convert, he is then actuated by the same motives as the sinner, and the same language may be equally applicable to both. And, therefore, the fact that some of the language before us is applicable to a Christian who has become a backslider does not prove at all that the experience here described is Christian experience, but only that a backslider and a sinner are in many respects alike. I do not hesitate to say this much; at least, that no one, who was conscious that he was actuated by love to God, could ever have thought of applying this chapter to himself. If anyone is not in the exercise of love to God, this describes his character; and whether he is backslider or sinner, it is all the same thing.

3rd Remark. Some of the expressions used in this chapter are supposed to describe the case of a believer, who is not an habitual backslider, but who is overcome by temptation and passion for a time and who speaks of himself as if he were all wrong. A man is tempted, we are told, when he is drawn away by his own lusts and enticed. And in that state, no doubt, he might find expressions here that would describe his own experience while under such influence. But that proves nothing regarding the design of the passage, for while he is in this state he is under a certain influence, but the impenitent sinner is all the time under just such influence. The same language, therefore, may be applicable to both without inconsistency.

Although some expressions may bear this plausible construction, yet a view of the whole passage makes it evident that it cannot be a delineation of Christian experience. *My own opinion, therefore, is that the apostle designed here to represent the experience of a sinner, not careless, but strongly convicted, and yet not converted.* The reasons are these:

1. The apostle is here manifestly describing the habitual character of someone, and this one is wholly under the dominion of the flesh. It is not on the whole a description of one who, under the power of present temptation, is acting inconsistently with his general character, but his general character is so. It is one who uniformly and habitually falls into sin, notwithstanding his approval of the law.

2. It would have been entirely irrelevant to his purpose to state the experience of a Christian as an illustration of his argument. That was not what was needed. He was laboring to vindicate the law of God in its influence on a carnal mind. In a previous chapter, he had stated the fact that justification was only by faith and not by works of law. In this seventh chapter, he maintains not only that *justification* is by faith, but also that *sanctification* is only by faith. "Know ye not brethren, (for I speak to them that know the law) how that the law hath dominion over a man as long as he liveth? So then, if while her husband liveth, she be married to another man, she shall be called an adulteress; but if her husband be dead, she is free from that law; so that she is no adulteress, though she be married to another man." What is the use of all this? Why, this, "Wherefore, my brethren, ye also are become dead to the law by the body of Christ; that ye should be married to another, even to him who is raised from the dead, that we should bring forth fruit unto God." While you were under the law, you were bound to obey the law and hold to the terms of the law for justification. But now being made free from the law as a rule of judgment, you are no longer influenced by the legal considerations of hope and fear, for Christ to whom you are married has set aside the penalty that by faith you might be justified before God.

"For when we were in the flesh"; that is, in an unconverted state, "the motions of sins, which were by the law, did work in our members to bring forth fruit unto death. But now we are delivered from the law, that being dead wherein we were held; that we should serve in newness of spirit, and not in the oldness of the letter." Here he is stating the real condition of a Christian; he serves in newness of spirit and not in the oldness of the letter. He found that the fruit of the law was only death, and by the gospel he was brought into true subjection to Christ. What is the objection to this? "What shall we say then? Is the law sin? God forbid. Nay, I had not known sin, but by the law: for I had not known lust, except the law had said, Thou shalt not covet. And the commandment which was ordained to life, I found to be unto death." The law was enacted that people might live by it, if they would perfectly obey it; but when we were in the flesh, we found it unto death. "For sin, taking occasion by the commandment, deceived me, and by it slew me. Wherefore the law is holy, and the commandment holy, and just, and good." Now he brings up the objection again. How can anything that is good be made death unto you? "Was, then, that which is good made death unto me? God forbid. But sin, that it might appear sin, working death in me by that which is good; that sin by the commandment might be exceeding sinful." And he vindicates the law by showing that it is not the fault of the law but the fault of sin, and that this very result shows at once the excellence of the law and the exceeding sinfulness of sin. Sin must be a horrible thing if it can work such a perversion as to take the good law of God and make it the means of death.

"For we know that the law is spiritual; but I am carnal, sold under sin." Here is the hinge on which the whole question turns. Now mark; the apostle is here vindicating the law against the objection that if the law is a means of death to sinners it cannot be good. Against this objection, he goes to show that all its action on the mind of the sinner proves it to be good. Keeping his eye on this point, he argues that the law is good and that the evil comes from the motions of sin in our members. Now he comes to that part which is supposed to delineate a Christian experience and which is the subject of controversy. He begins by saying, "the law is spiritual but I am carnal." This word "carnal" he used once, and only once, in reference to Christians, and then it was in reference to persons who were in a low state of religion. "For ye are yet carnal; for whereas there is among you envying, and strife, and divisions, are ye not carnal, and walk as men." These Christians had backslidden and they acted as if they were not converted persons but were carnal. The term itself is generally used to signify the worst of sinners. Paul here defines it so; "carnal, sold under sin." Could that be said of Paul himself at the time he wrote this epistle? Was that his own experience? Was he sold under sin? Was that true of the great apostle? No, but he was vindicating the law, and he used an illustration by supposing a case. He goes on, "For that which I do, I allow not; for what I would, that I do not; but what I hate, that do I."

Here you see the application of the principles I have laid down. In the interpretation of this word "would," we are not to understand it of the choice or will, but only a desire. Otherwise the apostle contradicts a plain matter of fact, which everybody knows to be true, that the will governs the conduct. Professor Stuart has very properly rendered the word desire; "what I desire, I do not, but what I disapprove, that I do." Then comes the conclusion, "If, then, I do that which I would not, I consent unto the law, that it is good. If I do that which I disapprove, if I disapprove of my own conduct, if I condemn myself, I thereby bear testimony that the law is good." Now, keep your eye on the object the apostle has in view and read the next verse, "Now then it is no more I that do it, but sin that dwelleth in me." Here, as it were, he divides himself against himself, or speaks of himself as possessing two natures, or, as some of the heathen philosophers taught, as having two souls, one which approves the good and another which loves and chooses evil. "For I know that in me (that is, in my flesh) dwelleth no good thing: for to will is present with me; but how to perform that which is good I find not." Here "to will" means to approve, for if men really *will* to do a thing, they do it. This everybody knows. Where the language will admit, we are bound to interpret it so as to make it consistent with known facts. If you understand "to will" literally, you involve the apostle in the absurdity of saying that he willed what he did not do, and so acted contrary to his own will, which contradicts a notorious fact. The meaning must be desire. Then it coincides with the experience of every convicted sinner; *he knows what he ought to do, and he strongly approves it, but he is not ready to do it.* Suppose I were to call on you to do some act. Suppose, for instance, I were to call on those of you who are impenitent to come forward and take that seat so we might see who you are, and pray for you, and should show you your sins and that it is your duty to submit to God; some of you would exclaim, "I know it is my duty, and I greatly desire to do it, but I cannot." What do you mean by it? Why, simply, that on the whole, the balance of your will is on the other side.

In the 20th verse he repeats what he had said before, "Now if I do that I would not, it is no more I that do it, but sin that dwelleth in me." Is that the habitual character and experience of a Christian? I admit that a Christian may fall so low that this language may apply to him; but if this is his general character, how does it differ from that of an impenitent sinner? If this is the habitual character of a Christian, there is not a word of truth in the scripture representations that the saints are those who really obey God; for here is one called a Christian, of whom it is said expressly that he never does obey.

"I find then a law, that when I would do good, evil is present with me." Here he speaks of the actions of the carnal propensities being so constant and so prevalent that he calls it a "law." "For I delight in the law of God after the inward man." Here is the great stumbling block. Can it be said of an impenitent sinner that he "delights" in the law of God? I answer, Yes. I know the expression is strong, but the apostle was using strong language all along on both sides. It is no stronger language than the prophet Isaiah uses in chapter 58. He was describing as wicked and rebellious a generation as ever lived. He says, "Cry aloud, spare not; lift up thy voice like a trumpet, and show my people their transgression, and the house of Jacob their sins." Yet he goes on to say of this very people, "Yet they seek me daily, and delight to know my ways, as a nation that did righteousness, and forsook not the ordinance of their God; they ask of me the ordinances of justice; they *take delight* in approaching to God." Here is one instance of impenitent sinners manifestly delighting in approaching to God. So in Ezekiel 33:32. "And lo thou art unto them as a very lovely song of one that hath a pleasant voice, and can play well on an instrument: for they hear thy words, but do them not." The prophet had been telling how wicked they were. "And they come unto thee as the people cometh, and they sit before thee as my people, and they hear thy words, but they will not do them: for with their mouth they show much love, but their heart goeth after their covetousness." Here were impenitent sinners, plainly enough, yet they love to hear the eloquent prophet. How often do ungodly sinners delight in eloquent preaching or powerful reasoning by some able minister! It is to them an intellectual feast. And sometimes they are so pleased with it as really to think they love the Word of God. This is consistent with entire depravity of heart and enmity against the true character of God. Nay, it sets their depravity in a stronger light, because they know and approve the right, and yet do the wrong.

So, notwithstanding this delight in the law, he says, "But I see another law in my members, warring against the law of my mind, and bringing me into captivity to the law of sin which is in my members. O wretched man that I am! Who shall deliver me from the body of this death?" Here the words, "I thank God, through Jesus Christ our Lord," are plainly a parenthesis, and a break in upon the train of thought. Then he sums up the whole matter, "So then, with the mind I myself serve the law of God, but with the flesh the law of sin."

It is as if he had said, "My better self, my unbiased judgment, my conscience, approves the law of God; but the law in my members, my passions, have such a control over me, that I still disobey." Remember, the apostle was describing the habitual character of one who was wholly under the dominion of sin. It was irrelevant to his purpose to adduce the experience of a Christian. He was vindicating the law; therefore, it was necessary for him to take the case of one who was under the law. If he was describing Christian experience, he was reasoning against himself; for if it was Christian experience, this would prove, not only that the law was inefficacious for the subduing of passion and the sanctification of men, but that the gospel also was inefficacious. Christians are under grace and it is irrelevant, in vindicating the law, to adduce the experience of those who are not under the law but under grace.

Another conclusive reason is that he actually states the case of a believer as entirely different in verses four and six. He speaks of those who are not under law and not in the flesh; that is, not carnal, but delivered from the law and actually serving or obeying God in spirit.

Then, in the beginning of the eighth chapter, he goes on to say, "There is therefore now no condemnation to them which are in Christ Jesus, who walk not after the flesh, but after the Spirit. For the law of the Spirit of life in Christ Jesus, hath made me free from the law of sin and death." He had alluded to this in the parenthesis above, "I thank God," etc. "For what the law could not do, in that it was weak through the flesh, God sending his own Son in the flesh, and for sin, condemned sin in the flesh: that the righteousness of the law might be fulfilled in us who walk not after the flesh but after the Spirit." Who is this of whom he is now speaking? If the person in the last chapter was one who had a Christian experience—whose experience is this? Here is something entirely different. The other was wholly under the power of sin, and under the law, and while he knew his duty, never did it. Here we find one for whom what the law could not do, through the power of passion, the gospel has done, so that the righteousness of the law is fulfilled, or what the law requires is obeyed. "For they that are after the flesh, do mind the things of the flesh; but they that are after the Spirit, the things of the Spirit. For to be carnally minded is death; but to be spiritually minded is life and peace: because the carnal mind is enmity to God: for it is not subject to the law of God, neither indeed can be. So then they that are in the flesh cannot please God." There it is. Those whom he had described in the seventh chapter, as being carnal, cannot please God. "But ye are not in the flesh, but in the Spirit, if so be that the Spirit of God dwell in you. Now, if any man have not the Spirit of Christ, he is none of his. And if Christ be in you, the body is dead because of sin; but the Spirit is life because of righteousness." But here is an individual whose body is dead. Before the body had the control, and it dragged him away from duty and from salvation; but now the power of passion is subdued.

Now I will give you the sum of the whole matter:

(1.) The strength of the apostle's language cannot decide this question, for he uses strong language on both sides. If it be objected that the individual he is describing is said to "delight in the law," he is also said to be "carnal, sold under sin." When a writer uses strong language, it must be so understood so not to make it irrelevant or inconsistent.

(2.) Whether he spoke of himself, or of some other person, or merely supposed a case by way of illustration, is wholly immaterial to the question.

(3.) It is plain that the point he wished to illustrate was the vindication of the law of God regarding its influence on a carnal mind.

(4.) The point required by way of illustration; the case of a convicted sinner, who saw the excellence of the law, but in whom the passions had the ascendancy.

(5.) If this is spoken of Christian experience, it is not only irrelevant, but proves the reverse of what he intended. He intended to show that the law though good, could not break the power of passion. But if this is Christian experience, then it proves that the gospel, instead of the law, cannot subdue passion and sanctify men.

(6.) The contrast between the state described in the seventh chapter and that described in the eighth chapter proves that the experience of the former was not that of a Christian.

Remarks

1. Those who find their own experience written in the seventh chapter of Romans are not converted persons. *If that is their habitual character, they are not regenerated; they are under conviction, but not Christians.*

2. You see the great importance of using the law in dealing with sinners; to make them prize the gospel, to lead them to justify God, and to condemn themselves. Sinners are never made truly to repent, unless they are convicted by the law.

3. At the same time, you see the entire insufficiency of the law to convert men. The case of the devil illustrates the highest efficacy of the law in this respect.

4. You see the danger of mistaking mere desires for piety. Desire that does not result in right choice has nothing good in it. The devil may

have such desires. The wickedest men on earth may desire religion, and no doubt often do desire it, when they see that it is necessary to their salvation or to control their passions.

5. Christ and the gospel present the only motives that can sanctify the mind. The law only convicts and condemns.

6. Those who are truly converted and brought into the liberty of the gospel do find deliverance from the bondage of their own corruptions.

They do find the power of the body over the mind broken. *They may have conflicts and trials, many and severe; but as an habitual thing, they are delivered from the thraldom of passion, and get the victory over sin, and find it easy to serve God.* His commandments are not grievous to them. His yoke is easy, and His burden light.

7. *The true convert finds peace with God.* He feels that he has it. He enjoys it. *He has a sense of pardoned sin, and of victory over corruption.*

8. You see, from this subject, the true position of a vast many church members. They are all the time struggling under the law. They approve of the law, both in its precept and its penalty, they feel condemned, and desire relief. But still they are unhappy. They have no spirit of prayer, no communion with God, no evidence of adoption. They only refer to the 7th of Romans as their evidence. Such a one will say, "There is my experience exactly." Let me tell you, that if this is your experience, you are yet in the gall of bitterness and the bonds of iniquity. You feel that you are in the bonds of guilt, and you are overcome by iniquity, and surely you know that it is as bitter as gall. Now, don't cheat your soul by supposing that with such an experience as this you can go and sit down by the side of the apostle Paul. You are yet carnal, sold under sin, and unless you embrace the gospel you will be damned.*

---

*Two recent studies discuss the view advocated in this sermon. See Wenham's and Gundry's articles on Romans 7:7-25 in *Pauline Studies* edited by Hagner and Harris, Paternoster Press or Eerdmans, 1980. The editor was not able to acquire these contributions in honor of F. F. Bruce in time for this book, and is indebted to the book review in *The Expository Times*: Vol. 92, No. 8, May 1981, p. 245.

8

CHRIST THE HUSBAND OF THE CHURCH*
Romans 7:4

"Wherefore, my brethren, ye also are become dead to the law by the body of Christ; that ye should be married to another, even to him who is raised from the dead, that we should bring forth fruit unto God."

In the discussion of this subject, the following is the order in which I shall direct your thoughts:

I. *Show that the marriage state is abundantly set forth in the Bible, as describing the relation between Christ and the church.*
II. *Show what is implied in this relation.*
III. *The reason for the existence of this relation.*
IV. *Show the great guilt of the church in behaving towards Christ as she does.*
V. *The forbearance of Christ towards the church.*

I. *I am to show that the marriage state is abundantly set forth in the Bible, as describing the relation between Christ and the church.*

Christ is often spoken of as the husband of the church. "Thy Maker is thy husband, the Lord of Hosts is his name." "Turn, O backsliding children, saith the Lord, for I am married unto you." The church is spoken of as the bride, the Lamb's wife. "The Spirit and the Bride say, Come." That is, Christ and the church say, "Come." In 2 Cor. 11:2, the apostle Paul says, "For I am jealous over you with godly jealously: for I have espoused you to one husband, that I may present you as a chaste virgin to Christ." I can merely refer to these passages. You that are acquainted with your Bibles will not need for me to take up time to show that this relation is often adverted to in the Bible, in a great variety of forms.

Lectures to Professing Christians (1880), pp. 453-468.

II. *I am to show what is implied in this relation.*

1. The wife gives up her own name and assumes that of her husband. This is universally true in the marriage state. And the church assumes the name of Christ, and when united with Him is baptized into His name.

2. The wife's separate interest is merged in that of her husband.

A married woman has no separate interest and no right to have any. So the church has no right to have a separate interest from the Lord Jesus Christ. If a wife has property, it goes to her husband. If it is real estate, the life interest passes to him; and if it is personal estate, the whole merges in him.

The reputation of the wife is wholly united to that of her husband, so that his reputation is hers, and her reputation is his. What affects her character, affects his; and what affects his character, affects hers. Their reputation is one; their interests are one. So with the church, whatever concerns the church is just as much the interest of Christ, as if it were personally His own matter. As the husband of the church, He is just as much pledged to do everything that is needful to promote the interest of the church, as the husband is pledged to promote the welfare of his wife. As a faithful husband gives up his time, his labor, his talents, to promote the interest and happiness of his wife; so Jesus Christ gives himself up to promote the welfare of His church. He is as jealous of the reputation of His church, as ever a husband was of the reputation of his wife. Never was a human being so pledged, so devoted to the interest of his wife, or felt so keenly an injury as Jesus Christ feels when His church has her reputation or her feelings injured. He declares that it were better a man had a mill-stone hanged about his neck, and he were cast into the depths of the sea, than that he should offend one of these little ones that believe in Him.

3. The relation between husband and wife is such, that if any thing is the matter with one, the other is full of sympathy.

So Christ feels for all the sufferings of the church, and the church feels for all the sufferings of Christ. When a believer comprehends the sufferings of Christ, there is nothing in the universe that so affects and dissolves his mind with sorrow. Never has a wife felt such distress, such brokenhearted grief, when she has witnessed the suffering or death of her husband, as the Christian feels when he views his sins as the reason for the death of Jesus Christ. Let me ask some of these married women present: "How would you feel, if your husband to redeem you from *merited ignominy* and death, had volunteered the greatest suffering and pain, and even death for you? When you were reminded of it by any circumstance, would it melt you down in brokenhearted grief? Now have you never understood that your sins caused the death of Christ, and that He died for you just as absolutely, as if you had been the only sinner in all God's world?" He suffered pain and contempt and death for you. He loves His church and gave himself for it. It is called the church of God, which He purchased with His own blood.

4. The wife pledges herself to yield her will to the will of her husband, and to yield obedience to his will.

She has no separate interest, and ought to have no separate will. The Bible enjoins this and makes it a Christian duty for the wife to conform in all things to the will of her husband. The will of her husband becomes, to the faithful wife, the mainspring of her activity. Her entire life is only carrying out the will of her husband. The relation of the church to Christ is precisely the same. The church is governed by Christ's will. When believers exercise faith, the will of Christ becomes the moving cause of all their conduct.

5. The wife recognizes her husband as her head.

The Bible declares that he is so. In like manner, as from the head proceed those influences that govern the body, so from Christ proceed those influences that govern the church.

6. The wife looks to her husband as her support, her protector, and her guide.

Every believer places himself as absolutely under the protection of Christ, as a married woman is under the protection of her husband. The woman naturally looks to her husband to preserve her from injury, from insult, and from want. She hangs her happiness on him, and expects he will protect her; and he is bound to do it.

So Christ is pledged to protect His church from every foe. How often have the powers of hell tried to put down the church, but her husband has never abandoned her. No weapon formed against the church has ever been allowed to prosper, and never shall. Never will the Lord Jesus Christ so far forget His relation to the church, as to leave His bride unprotected. No. Let all earth and hell conspire against the church, and just as certain as Christ has power to protect the church His church is safe. And each individual believer is just as safe as if he were the only believer on earth, and has Christ as truly pledged for his preservation. The devil can no more put down a single believer, to final destruction, than he can put down God Almighty. He may murder them, but that is no injury. Overcoming a believer by taking his life affords Satan no triumph. He put Christ to death, but what did he gain by it? The grave had no power over Him, to retain Him. So with a believer; neither the grave nor hell has any more power to injure one of Christ's little ones, that believe in Him, than they have to injure Christ himself. He says, "Because I live, ye shall live also." And, "He that believeth in me, though he were dead, yet shall he live; and whosoever liveth and believeth in me, shall never die." There is no power in the universe that can prevail against a single believer, to destroy him. Jesus Christ is the Head of the church, and Head over all things to the church, and the church is safe.

7. The legal existence of the wife is so merged in that of her husband that she is not known in law as a separate person.

If any actions or civil liabilities come against the wife, the husband is responsible. If the wife has committed a trespass, the husband is answerable. It is his business to guide and govern her, and her business to obey; and if he does not restrain her from breaking the laws, he is responsible. And if the wife does not obey her husband, she has it in her power to bring him into great trouble, disgrace and expense. In like manner, Jesus Christ is Lord over His church; and if He does not actually restrain His church from sin, He has it to answer for; and He is brought into great trouble and reproach by the misconduct of His people. By human laws, the husband is not liable for capital crimes committed by the wife, because the law in these cases recognizes her separate existence so as to punish her. But Christ has assumed the responsibility for His church, for *all* her conduct. He took the place of His people, when they were convicted of capital crimes and sentenced to eternal damnation. This is answering in good earnest. And now it is His business to take care of the church, control her, keep her from sin, and care for every sin of every member. Jesus Christ is responsible, and must answer for our sins. And He does answer for them. He has made an atonement to cover all this, and ever liveth to make intercession for His people. He holds himself responsible before God for all the conduct of His church. Every believer is so a part of Jesus Christ, and so perfectly united to Him, that whatever any of them may be guilty of, Jesus Christ takes upon himself to answer for it. This is abundantly taught in the Bible.

What an amazing relation! Christ has here assumed the responsibility, not only for the civil conduct of His church, but even for the capital crime of rebellion against God. There is a sense, therefore, in which the church is lost in Christ and has no separate existence known in law. God has so given up the church to Christ, by the covenant of grace, that, strictly speaking, the church is not known in law. I do not mean that crimes committed by believers against the moral law are not sin, but that the law cannot get hold of them for condemnation. There is now no condemnation to them that are in Christ Jesus. The penalty of the law is forever remitted. The crimes of the believer are not taken into account so as to bring him under condemnation; no, in no case whatever. Whatever is to be done falls upon Christ. He has assumed the responsibility for bringing them from under the power of sin, as well as from under the law, and stands pledged to give them all the assistance they need to gain *a complete victory.*

III. *I am to explain the reason why this relation is constituted between Christ and His church.*

1. The first reason is assigned in the text, "that we should bring forth fruit unto God." A principal design of the institution of marriage is the propagation of the species. So it is in regard to the church. Through the instrumentality of the church, children are to be born to Christ; He is to see His seed, and to see the travail of His soul and be satisfied by the converts multiplied as the drops of morning dew. It is not only through the travail of the Redeemer's soul, but through the travail of the church, that believers are born unto Jesus Christ. As soon as Zion tra-

vailed, she brought forth children.

2. Another object of the marriage institution is the protection and support of those who are naturally helpless and dependent. If the law of power prevailed in society, everybody knows that females, being the weaker sex, would be universally enslaved. The design of the institution of marriage is to secure protection and support to those who are so much more frail, so that by the law of force they would not be continually enslaved. So Jesus Christ upholds His church and affords her all the protection against her enemies, and all the powers of hell, that she needs.

3. The mutual happiness of the parties is another end of the marriage institution.

The same is true of the relation between Christ and His church. Perhaps you will think it strange if I tell you that the happiness of Christ is increased by the love of the church. But what does the Bible say? "Who, for the joy set before him, endured the cross, despising the shame." What was the joy set before Him if the love of the church was not a part of it? It would be very strange to hear of a husband contributing to the happiness of his wife and not enjoying it himself. Jesus Christ enjoys the happiness of His church, but much more, since He loves His church better than any husbands love their wives.

4. The alleviation of mutual sufferings and sorrows is one end of marriage.

Sharing each other's sorrow is a great alleviation. Who does not know this? In like manner Christ and His church share each other's sorrows. The apostle Paul says he was always bearing about in his body the dying of the Lord Jesus; "For as the sufferings of Christ abound in us, so our consolation also aboundeth by Christ." And he declared that one end of his toils and self-denial was that he might know "the fellowship of Christ's sufferings." And he rejoiced in all his sufferings that he might fill up that which was behind of the afflictions of Christ. The church feels keenly every reproach cast upon Christ, and Christ feels keenly every injury inflicted on the church.

5. The principal reason for this union of Christ with His church is so He may sanctify the church.

Read what is said in Ephesians 5:22-27. "Wives, submit yourselves unto your own husbands, as unto the Lord. For the husband is the head of the wife, even as Christ is the head of the church; and he is the Saviour of the body. Therefore as the church is subject unto Christ, so let the wives be to their own husbands in every thing. Husbands, love your wives, even as Christ also loved the church, and gave himself for it; that he might sanctify and cleanse it with the washing of water by the word. That he might present it to himself a glorious church, not having spot or wrinkle, or any such thing; but that it should be holy and without blemish."

Here, then, is set forth the great design of Christ in marrying the church. It is that He might sanctify it, and cleanse it, or that it should be perfectly holy and without blemish. John, in the Revelation, informs us that he saw those who had "washed their robes and made them white in the blood of the Lamb," See how beautifully the bride, the Lamb's wife, is described in the 21st chapter, coming down from God out of heaven, prepared as a bride adorned for her husband.

IV. *I will make a few remarks on the wickedness of the church in behaving towards Christ as she does.*

1. Vast multitudes of those who profess to be a part of the church, the bride of Christ, really set up a separate interest.

They have pretended to merge their self-interest in the interest of Christ, but manifestly keep up a separate interest. And if you attempt to make them act on the principle that they have no separate interest, they will plainly show that they have no such design. What would you think of a wife keeping up a separate interest from her husband? You would say it was plain that she did not love her husband as she ought.

2. The church is not satisfied with Christ's love.

Everybody knows what an abominable thing it is for a wife not to be satisfied with the love of her husband, but to be continually seeking other lovers, and always associating with other men. Yet, how plain it is that the church is not satisfied with the love of Christ, but it is always seeking after other lovers. What are we to think of those members of the church who are not satisfied with the love of Christ for happiness, but must have the riches and pleasures and honors of the world to make them happy?

Still more horrible would be the conduct of a wife, who should select her lovers from the enemies of her husband, and should bring them home with her, and make them her chosen friends. Yet how many who profess to belong to Christ go away, and give their affections to Christ's enemies. Some will even marry those whom they know to be haters of God and religion. Horrible! Is that the way a bride should do?

3. Everyone knows that it is a disgraceful thing for the wife to play the harlot.

Yet God often speaks of His church as going astray and committing spiritual whoredom. And it is true. He does not make this charge, as a man makes it against his wife, when he is determined to leave her and cast her off. But He makes it with grief and tenderness, and accompanies it with moving expostulations, and the most melting entreaties that she would return.

4. What would you think of a married woman who should expect, at the very time of her marriage, that she would get tired of her husband, and leave him and play the harlot?

Yet, how many there are, professors of religion, who when they made a profession had no more expectation of living without sin, than they expected to have wings and fly. They have come into His house, and pledged themselves to live entirely for Him, and married Him in this public manner, covenanting to forsake all sin, and to live alone for Christ, and be satisfied with His love, and have no other lovers; and yet all the while they are doing it, they expect in their minds that they shall scatter their ways to strangers upon every high hill, and commit sin and dishonor Christ.

5. What are we to think of a woman, who, at the very time of her marriage, expected to continue in her course of adultery as long as she lived in spite of all the commands and expostulations of her husband?

Then what are we to think of professors of religion, who deliberately expect to commit spiritual adultery and continue in it as long as they live?

6. But the most abominable part of such a wife's wickedness is when she turns round and charges the blame of her conduct upon her faithful husband.

Now the church does this. Christ has done all that He could do, short of using absolute force, to keep His church from sinning, yet the church charges her sin upon Him, as if He had laid her under an absolute necessity of sinning by not making any adequate provision for preserving His people against temptation. And they are horrified now at the very name of Christian Perfection, as if it were really dishonoring Christ to believe that He is able to keep His people from committing sin and falling into the snare of the devil. And so it has been, for hundreds of years, that with the greater part of the church it has not been orthodox to teach that Jesus Christ really has made such provision that His people may live free from sin. And it is really considered a wonder that anybody should teach that the bride of the Lord Jesus Christ is expected to do as she pretends to do. Has He married a bride and made no provision adequate to protect her against the arts and seductions of the devil? Well done! That must be the ridicule of hell.

7. Suppose a wife should refuse to obey her husband and then make him responsible for her conduct.

Yet the church refuses to obey Jesus Christ, and then makes Him answer for her sins. This is the great difficulty with the church; she is continually blaming her Head for her delinquencies.

8. The church is continually dishonoring Christ.

The reputation of husband and wife is one. Whatever dishonors one, dishonors the other. Now, the church, instead of avoiding every appearance of evil is continually causing the enemies of God to blaspheme by her conduct.

V. *I will say a few words on the forbearance of Christ towards the church.*

What other husband, in such circumstances, would suffer the connection to remain and bear what Christ bears? Yet He still offers to be reconciled, and lays himself out to regain the affections of His bride. Sometimes a husband really loses his affection towards his wife, and treats her so like a brute that, although she once loved him, she loves him no more. But where can anything be found in the character and conduct of Christ to justify the treatment He receives? He has laid himself out to the utmost to engross the affections of the church. What could He have done more? Where can any fault or any deficiency be found in

Him. And even after all that the church has done against Him. What is He doing now? Suppose a husband should for years follow his wandering guilty wife, from city to city, beseeching and entreating her with tears to return to his house and be reconciled; and after all, she should persist in going after her lovers, and yet he continues to cry after her and beg her to come back and live with him, and he will forgive and love her still. Is there any such forbearance and condescension known among men?

Remarks

1. Christians ought to understand the bearing of their sins.

Your sins dishonor Christ, and grieve Christ, and injure Christ, and then you make Christ responsible for them. You sustain a relation to Him so you ought to know what is the effect of your sin. How does a wife feel when she had disgraced her husband? How blushes cover her face and tears fill her eyes! When her justly-offended husband comes into her presence, how she falls down at his feet with a full heart and confesses her fault, and pours her penitential tears into his bosom. She is grieved and humbled, and though she loves him, his very presence is a grief until she breaks down before him and feels that he has forgiven her.

Now how can a Christian fail to recognize this; and when he is betrayed into sin and has injured Christ, how can he sleep? How can you help realizing that your sins take hold of Jesus Christ and injure Him in all these tender relations?

2. One great difficulty of Christians is when they expect to live in sin, because this expectation insures their continuance in sin.

If an individual expects to live in sin, he in fact means to live in sin and of course he will live in sin. It is very much to be feared that many professors of religion never really meant to live without sin. The apostle insists that believers should reckon themselves dead to sin; that they should henceforth have no more to do with it than if they were dead, and they should no more expect to sin than a dead man should expect to walk. They should throw themselves upon Christ, and receive Him in all His relations, and expect to be preserved and sanctified and saved by Him. If they would do this, do you not suppose they would be kept from sin? Just as certainly as they believe in Christ for it. To believe that Christ will keep them insures the result that He will. The reason why they do not receive preserving grace at all times, as they need and all they need, is that they do not expect it; and they do not trust in Christ to preserve them in perfect love. The man tries to preserve himself. Instead of throwing himself upon Christ, he throws himself upon his own resources; then in his weakness he expects to sin, and of course he does sin. If he knew his own entire emptiness, and if he would throw himself upon Christ as absolutely, and rest upon Christ as confidently, for sanctification as for justification, then the one is just as certain as the other.

No one who has trusted in God for anything He has promised ever failed to receive according to his faith the very thing for which he trusted. If you trust in God for what He has not promised, that is tempting God. If Peter had not been called by Christ to come to Him on the water, it would have been tempting God for him to get down out of the ship into the water, and he would have lost his life for his presumption and folly. But as soon as Christ told him to come, it was merely an act of sound and rational faith for him to do it. It was a pledge on the part of Christ that he should be sustained; and so, he was sustained as long as he had faith. Now, if the Bible has promised that those who receive Christ as their sanctification shall be sanctified, then you who believe in Him for this end have just as much reason to expect it as Peter had to expect he should walk on the waves. It is true; we do not expect a miracle to be wrought to sustain the believer as it was to sustain Peter. But it is promised that he shall be sustained, and if miracles were necessary, no doubt they would be performed, for God would move the universe, and turn the course of nature upside down, sooner than one of His promises should fail to them that put their trust in Him. If God is pledged to anything, a person that ventures on that pledge will find it redeemed, just as certainly as God possesses almighty power. Has God promised sanctification to them that trust Him for it? If He has not, then to go to Him in faith for preservation from temptation and sin is tempting God. It is fanaticism. If God has left us to the dire necessity of getting along with our own watchfulness and our own firmness and strength, then we must submit to it and do the best we can. But if He has made any promises, then He will redeem them to the uttermost, though all earth and all hell should oppose. And so it is regarding the mistakes and the errors which Christians fall into. If there were no promise that they shall be guided as far as they need, and be led into the truth and in the way of duty and of peace; then for a Christian to look to God for knowledge, wisdom, guidance, and direction, without any promises, is tempting God. But if there are promises on this subject, depend on it, they will be fulfilled to the very last mite to the believer who trusts in them; and exercising confidence in such promises is only a sober and rational faith in the Word of God.

I believe that the great difficulty of the church on the subject of Christian Perfection lies here; she has not fully understood how the Lord Jesus Christ is wholly pledged in all these relations, and that she has just as much reason and is just as much bound to trust in Him for sanctification as for justification. What saith the scripture? "Who of God is made unto us wisdom and righteousness, and sanctification, and redemption." When did the idea spring up in the church that Jesus Christ is our redemption, and that He has made himself responsible for the meanest individual who would throw himself on Him for justification? This has been universally admitted in the church in all ages. But why is it no more plainly or more abundantly taught, than it is, that Jesus Christ is promised and pledged for wisdom and for sanctification to all that receive Him in these relations? Has He not promised that if any man lack wisdom, he may ask of God, and if he asks in faith, God will give it to him? What then? Is there then no such thing as being preserved by Christ from falling into this and that delusion and error? God has made this broad promise; that Christ is as much pledged for our wisdom and our sanctification, if we only trust on Him, as He is for our justification. If the church would only renounce any expectation from herself and die as absolutely to her own wisdom and strength as she does to her own righteousness, or the expectation of being saved by her own works, then Jesus Christ is as much pledged for the one as for the other. The only reason why the church does not realize these results is that Christ is trusted for justification, and as for wisdom and sanctification He is not trusted.

The truth is that a great body of believers having begun in the Spirit are now trying to be made perfect by the flesh. We have thrown ourselves on Christ for justification, and then have been attempting to sanctify ourselves. If it is true, as the apostle affirms, that Christ is to the church both wisdom and sanctification, what excuse have Christians for not being sanctified?

3. If individuals do not as much expect to live without sin against Christ, as they expect to live without open sins against men, such as murder or adultery, then it must be for one of three reasons:

(1) Either we love our fellowmen better than we do Christ, and so are less willing to do them an injury.

(2) Or we are restrained by a regard to our own reputation; and this proves that we love reputation more than Christ.

(3) Or we think we can preserve ourselves better from these disgraceful crimes than we can from less heinous sins.

Suppose I were to ask any of you if you expect to commit murder, or adultery? "Horrible!" you say. But why not? Are you so virtuous that you can resist any temptation which the devil can offer? If you say so, you do not know yourself. If you have any real power to keep yourself, so as to abstain from openly disgraceful sins in your own strength, you have power to abstain from all sins. But if your only reliance is on Jesus Christ to keep you from committing murder and adultery, how is it that you should get the idea that He is not equally able to keep you from all sin? Oh, if believers would only throw themselves wholly on Christ, and make Him responsible by placing themselves entirely at His control, then they would know His power to save, and they would live without sin.

4. What a horrible reproach is the church to Jesus Christ.

5. You see why it is that converts are what they are.

Degenerate plants of a strange vine sure enough! The church is in such a state that it is no wonder those who are brought in, with few exceptions, prove a disgrace to religion. How can it be otherwise? How can the church, living in such a manner, bring forth offspring that shall do honor to Christ? The church does not, and individual believers do not in general, receive Christ in all His offices as He is offered in the Bible. If they did, it would be impossible for them to live like such loathsome harlots.

9

TOTAL DEPRAVITY*
Romans 8:7

"The carnal mind is enmity against God, for it is not subject to the law of God, neither indeed can be."

The law spoken of is the moral law; or that law which requires men to love God with all their heart and their neighbour as themselves. The facts affirmed by the apostle are that the carnal mind is enmity against God; and for that reason, it is not subject to the law of God; that is, it does not obey the law of God; neither, of course, can it obey this law while it continues to be enmity against God. The apostle does not affirm that a sinner cannot love God, but that a carnal mind cannot love God; for, to affirm that a carnal mind can love God is the same as to affirm that enmity itself can be love. In speaking from these words, I design to show:

    I. *What is not meant by the carnal mind.*
    II. *What the carnal mind, as used in the text, does mean.*
    III. *That all men, who have not been born by the Spirit of God, have a carnal mind.*
    IV. *That this carnal mind is enmity against God.*

    I. *I am to show what is not meant by the carnal mind, as used in the text.*
    1. It is *not* meant that any part of the substance of the soul or the body is enmity against God.
    2. It is *not* meant that there is anything in the constitution, or substance of body or mind, that is opposed to God. The mind is not saturated or soaked with enmity.

Sermons on Important Subjects, pp. 115-143.

3. *Nor* is it meant that the mind or body is so constructed that, from the *constitution of our nature*, we are opposed to God.

4. It is *not* meant that there are appetites or propensities that are constitutional which are enmity against God.

5. *Nor* is it meant that all unconverted men *feel sensible emotions* of enmity or hatred to God. Enmity may exist in the mind either as a volition or an emotion. When existing in the form of a *volition*, it is a settled *aversion* to His character and government, and is of such a nature that while it may have an abiding influence over our conduct, it may not have a *felt* existence in the mind.

When existing in the form of an *emotion*, it then constitutes what we call *feeling*; and its existence is a matter of consciousness. I said that enmity may exist in the form of a volition, or a settled aversion to God, and have an abiding influence over our conduct. Enmity can lead us to treat God as an enemy, without rising into the form of an emotion that may be sensibly felt and be the object of consciousness. Emotions exist in the mind only when those objects are before it which are calculated to produce them; and a principal reason why sinners do not more frequently exercise such emotions of hatred to God, as to be sensible of their enmity against Him, is, that they seldom think of God. God is not in all their thoughts. And when they do think of Him, they do not think justly, or think of Him as He really is. They deceive themselves with vain imaginations, and hide from their own view His real character, and thus cover up their enmity.

II. *I am to show what is meant by the carnal mind, as used in the text.* The proper translation of this text is, "*the minding of the flesh is enmity against God.*" It is a voluntary state of mind. It is that state of supreme selfishness in which all men are, previous to their conversion to God.

It is a state of mind; in which, probably, they are not born, but into which they appear to fall very early after their birth. The gratification of their appetites is made by them the supreme object of desire and pursuit, and becomes the law of their lives; or that law in their members that wars against the law of their minds, of which the apostle speaks.

They conform their lives and all their actions to this rule of action, which they have established for themselves, which is nothing more nor less than voluntary selfishness; or a controlling and abiding preference of self-gratification above the commandments, authority, and glory of God.

It should be well understood, and always remembered, that the carnal mind, as used by the apostle, is not the *mind itself*, but is a voluntary action of the mind. In other words, it is not any part of the mind, or body, but a *choice* or preference of the mind. It is a *minding of the flesh*. It is preferring self-gratification before obedience to God.

The constitutional appetites, both of body and mind, are in themselves innocent; but, making their gratification the supreme object of pursuit is enmity against God. It is the direct opposite of the character and the requirements of God. God requires us to subordinate all our appetites of body and mind to His glory, and to aim supremely at honouring and glorifying Him. To love Him with all our hearts is to bring all our powers of body and mind under obedience to the law of love; and whatever we do, whether we eat or drink, we should do all to the glory of God. Now the carnal mind, or the minding of the flesh, is the direct opposite of this. It is pursuing as a supreme end that which is the direct opposite of the requirements and character of God. It is a choice, a preference, an abiding temper, or disposition of the mind which consists in a determination to gratify self, and to make this the high and supreme object of pursuit.

III. *I am to show that, previous to conversion, all men are in this state of enmity against God.* The Bible speaks of men as possessing by nature one common heart or disposition. This text does *not* say that the carnal minds of some men are enmity against God, but that the carnal *mind* is enmity against God. In another place, God says, "Every imagination of the thoughts of their *heart* [not hearts] is only evil continually." Another passage says, "The *heart* of the sons of men is full of evil, and madness is in their *heart* while they live." Indeed, unconverted men throughout the Bible are spoken of as having a common heart, and what the Bible asserts is seen to be a matter of fact. Go throughout all the ranks of the human family from the sensitive female, who faints at the sight of blood, to the horrid pirate, whose eyes flash fire and whose lips burn with blasphemy; and present to them all, the claims of God and the gospel of His Son, then require them to repent and give their hearts to God. With one assent, they will plead their *inability*. Go to the refined and unrefined; the learned and unlearned; the high and low; rich and poor; old and young; male and female; bond and free, of every country and of every clime; and not one of them can be persuaded to embrace the gospel without the interposition of the Holy Ghost. Now, how is it possible to account for this notorious fact but upon the principle that however the external deportment of different individuals may be modified by circumstances, however much the natural temper may be made to differ (by education, by animal temperament, by the state of the nervous system, and a variety of other considerations), still with regard to God, they possess the same disposition, and will, all with one assent, begin to make excuses for not loving and obeying him.

IV. *I am to show that this carnal mind, or minding of the flesh, is enmity against God.*

In my former discourse on the subject of depravity, I endeavoured to demonstrate, by an appeal to facts, that unconverted men *do not love God.**

The first point to be established, under the fourth head of this dis-

---

*Editor's Note: Sermon IV, "Total Depravity," John 5:42, pp. 91-114 of *Sermons on Important Subjects*. If the carnal mind hates God, as Finney will demonstrate, surely we can deduce that unconverted men do not love God.

course, is that impenitent sinners *hate* God.

I shall pursue the same method, appeal to the same sources for proof, and go into the same field and gather facts, to establish the truth of this position that I did in proof of the position that men do not love God. My appeal is to the well-known laws of mind, as they are seen to develop themselves in the transactions of every day.

1. *We are naturally pleased with those things that are displeasing to our enemies.* Hatred is ill-will. Therefore, whatever displeases or disobliges our enemy, gratifies our ill-will. It is a contradiction to say that we hate an individual with a malevolent hatred, and yet have no satisfaction in what displeases him. It is the same as to say that the gratification of our desires is not pleasing to us. We witness the developments of this law of mind, not only in our own case, but in the manifested feelings of those around us. See that man, if something has happened greatly to disoblige his enemy, he cannot conceal the pleasure he takes in this event. If the same event has in some measure injured himself, and he is in some degree partaker in the common calamity; yet, if it has much more deeply injured or completely ruined his bitter enemy, then he feels upon the whole gratified with the event, and considers the ruin of his enemy as more than a compensation for his own loss and does not mind bearing the portion that has fallen to him inasmuch as it has overwhelmed the man that he so deeply hates. Now, whatever he may say (under whatever hypocritical pretence he may conceal the satisfaction that he feels in this event), it remains certain that his hatred is gratified; that he really at heart takes pleasure in an event which has gratified his malignant opposition to his enemy.

We see this same law of mind developing itself toward God. Sinners manifest the greatest pleasure in sin. It is the element in which they live and move. They roll it as a sweet morsel under their tongue. They drink in iniquity like water. They even weary themselves to commit iniquity. They not only do these things themselves, but have pleasure in them that do them. The very things that are the most displeasing to God are most pleasing to them. And the things that are the most pleasing to God are most displeasing to them. They love what God hates, and hate what God loves. This demonstrates that they are in a state of mind which is the direct opposite of the character and will of God. The whole bent, current, and inclination of their minds are the direct opposite of God's requirements, and are enmity against Him. This is matter of fact.

Again, *We are naturally gratified to see the friends of our enemy forsake and dishonour him.* If a man hate another, and the children or friends of this enemy of his do anything to grieve, or dishonour, or injure him in any way, then he may speak of it as if he regretted it; but, if he pretends to regret it, he is a hypocrite. It is just as certain upon the whole that he rejoices in it as it is that he hates him. He rejoices in it, because it gratifies his hatred. You see this law of mind manifesting itself with equal uniformity and strength toward the blessed God. When the professed friends of God forsake His cause, and do anything to dishonour

Him, you may perceive that impenitent sinners are gratified. They will speak of it with exultation; and while Christians converse about it with sorrow, weep over it, and betake themselves to prayer that God will wipe away the reproach, it will become the song of the drunkard and the wicked in bar-rooms and in the corners of the streets they will laugh at it and rejoice over it.

Again, *We are apt to see and magnify the faults of the friends of our enemies.* With what scrutiny will politicians search after the faults of the friends and supporters of an opposing candidate. How eagle-eyed is that man in searching out all the failings of those that favour his enemy. How politicians, and others, will not only see their *real* faults, but will greatly magnify them and dwell upon them until they fill their whole field of vision. They give their attention so exclusively to their faults so as to forget that they have any virtues. So enormous do their faults appear that where they have the appearance of virtue it is ascribed to duplicity and hypocrisy.

Now, you see this same spirit often manifesting itself toward God. With what a searching and malignant gaze are the eyes of unconverted men fastened upon the professed friends of God. How eagerly they note their faults. How enormously they magnify them, and how apt are they to ascribe every appearance of virtue in them to bigotry and hypocrisy.

Again, *We are apt to misinterpret the motives and put the worst construction upon the conduct of the enemies of our friends.* If they are favouring the interests, and endeavouring to promote the happiness, of one whom we greatly hate, then we behold all their conduct through a jaundiced eye. The best things in them are often ascribed by us to the worst of motives; and those things in them which deserve the most praise are often, by us, the most severely reprobated. Your acquaintance with your own hearts, and with the developments of the human character around you, will instantly supply abundant proofs of this remark. This feature of the human character often most odiously develops itself toward God. How frequently we do hear impenitent sinners ascribing the most praiseworthy deeds of God's professed friends to the most unworthy motives. How often their acts of greatest self-denial, those things in which they most humbly serve and most nearly resemble God, are misrepresented, ascribed to the basest of motives, and made the very reasons upon which they ground their pertinacious opposition to them. It is impossible to account for this upon any other principle than that of their enmity against God; for the *persons* against whom this enmity is vented are often entire strangers to them; individuals against whom they can have no personal hostility. It is manifestly not enmity against *them*, any further than they resemble God, which calls forth these expressions of hatred; but enmity against the cause in which they are engaged, against the master whom they serve.

Again, *We naturally shun the friends of our enemies.* We naturally avoid the society of one who we know to be particularly friendly to our enemy; his company and conversation is irksome to us. We see this same spirit manifested by impenitent sinners toward the friends of God. They avoid them and feel uneasy in their company. Their presence seems to impose restraints upon sinners, and they cannot abuse God with quite as much freedom when Christians are present. They are therefore glad to dispense with their company. How often do you observe impenitent sinners, in making up a party for a stagecoach or railroad car, so arrange matters as to exclude a minister or any engaged Christian from their company? They feel uneasy at his presence and manifest the same temper that we should witness, if some distinguished friend of their greatest enemy were present with them. How can this be accounted for, on any other principle, than that of enmity against God? With these ministers or professors of religion, they have, perhaps, very little personal acquaintance; they have never had any misunderstanding with them, nor has any personal controversy existed between them. It must be on account of the cause in which they are engaged, and the master whom they serve; they wish to avoid them.

Again, *We naturally admire—magnify the virtues—and overlook the vices of the enemies of those we hate.* How enthusiastic are politicians in their admiration of the talents, wisdom, and virtues of those who take sides with them and are opposed to the election of their political enemy. If any man has an enemy, he regards it as an evidence of wisdom in anyone else to be opposed to the same man. He is inclined greatly to over-rate the number, the talents, and the influence of those who are opposed to his enemy. If he hears of a few that are opposed to him, and among them any men of more than ordinary talents, he is apt to imagine that almost everybody is opposed to him, and especially all the talented and virtuous part of the community, and to think that nobody favours him but the weak, the servile, and the interested.

It is just so on the subject of religion. How often do you hear impenitent sinners boasting of the talents, the numbers, and the virtues of infidels and of those that make no pretension to religion? Boasting of the excellent characters, high standing, and great influence of the leaders among the irreligious; while, at the same time, they depreciate both the numbers and the talents of those that are the friends of God. They often consider them as a sickly, a bigoted, and a priest-ridden people; and this too, without any definite knowledge of their numbers, their characters, or their influence. What is this but the outbreakings of enmity against God and the cause which they hate?

Again, *We naturally hate to think of our enemies.* The human mind is so constituted that malevolent emotions distress it and are the source of misery. Whenever our thoughts are intensely occupied in thinking of an individual whom we hate, those malevolent emotions will naturally arise which are condemned by the conscience, and which of themselves constitute misery. For this reason, unless it be for the purpose of studying revenge, or in some way to gratify our hatred, we naturally turn our thoughts away from an object which we hate. And while, as I have shown in a former discourse, we naturally dwell upon a beloved object; we just as naturally abstract our thoughts from a hated one. Behold the developments of this law of mind in its action toward God. Sinners banish God from their thoughts. They are "unwilling to retain God in their knowledge"; and if at any time the thought of God is intruded upon them, then they manifest uneasiness and immediately divert their attention. If they are really convinced that they are sinners and are in danger of His wrath, then their selfish regard to their own happiness may lead them to reflection and induce them to think of God, for the purpose of devising some means of escaping His just indignation.

Again, *We dislike to converse about those that we hate;* and unless it be for the purpose of calumniating them, and pouring forth our malignant hostility against them, we choose to remain silent and say nothing about them. You often hear a man say of his enemy, "I desire not to talk about him." As I have shown, in the former discourse, we love to converse about our friends, because such conversation at once enkindles and expresses our love for them. Such conversation gratifies us. But we hate to converse about our enemies. For although there is a kind of gratification in giving vent to our enmity, it is at the same time the source and essence of pain. Who has not witnessed the manifestations of this law of mind on the subject of religion? Who does not know that sinners are averse to talking about God? That they converse about Him seldom, reservedly, and in a manner that shows they have no pleasure in it; but, on the contrary, that such conversation gives them pain?

Again, *We are naturally pained to hear our enemy praised.* For example, a party of ladies and gentlemen are assembled, and all of them but one are particularly friendly to a distinguished and absent individual. This one is his bitter enemy. His enmity, however, is unknown to the company, and they, of course, bring up their favourite as the subject of their conversation. They indulge themselves in enthusiastic commendations of their absent friend, and are delighted with the common bond of sympathy that exists among them upon this subject. But mark the embarrassment and distress of this enemy. While they, without heeding his agony, indulge themselves in the most lavish pouring forth of applause, this enemy is filled with the most irrepressible distress and indignation. He looks at his watch; takes out his snuffbox; walks to the window; tries to read a newspaper; turns up and down the room; tries to divert the attention of the company, and introduce some other topic of conversation. Now, suppose that one of the *ladies* turns to him and demands his opinion, remarking, that he seems to be absent-minded and does not enjoy the conversation. If he is a gentleman, he may wish to be very civil to the lady and endeavour to waive an answer to her question. But suppose she presses him and wonders at his hesitancy until his conduct attracts the attention of the other members of the party, and then they all, with one consent, agree with the lady and insist upon an expression of his opinion. Now, an hundred to one, if, in spite of his good breeding, he does not manifest the enmity of his heart and clearly exhibit to the company the deep malignity of his feelings.

Under similar circumstances, you may often witness the outbreakings of enmity against God. Let a company of Christians, in a steamboat or stage-coach, engage in conversation upon their favourite topic. Let them converse of Jesus Christ; and after a warm conversation, let them appeal to impenitent sinners in the midst of them for an expression of their opinion. Or if, when in a proper place, they propose to conclude the interview with prayer, how often they are offended. Go and visit a family, some of whose members are Christians and others not; sit down and converse warmly with the pious wife on the subject of religion in the presence of her husband and unconverted family: what looks you will instantly perceive about the house. Perhaps one will go out at this door, and another at that door; if any of the impenitent remain, then turn and direct your conversation to one of them. If it be the husband, perhaps he will almost forget that he is a gentleman and abuse you to your face. Perhaps he will say that his religion is a matter between him and God. That he does not thank you for your impertinence. That it is none of your business and that he does not thank you for coming there to disturb him and his family upon the subject of religion. Now, why does he consider this a disturbance? Why does he look upon it as an impertinence? Why is he so displeased? Certainly he has no reason to fear that you will injure him or his family. If he loved the subject and loved God, is it not certain that he would thank you for your visit and be pleased with the interview? And is it not proof to demonstration that he hates God and religion, when he considers the kind introduction of the subject as an intrusion and a vexation?

Again, *We are naturally pained and incredulous on hearing of the prosperity of our enemy.* If we hear that our enemy is gaining friends or popularity or property or influence, it distresses us. We are inclined to disbelieve it. And, if there be any room for doubt, we are sure to hang a doubt on every point that admits debate. See that man with his hypocritical face; he has heard of the prosperity of his enemy, and he professes to rejoice in it. But if he believes it, he only mentions it on occasions where he cannot avoid it; and then, the spirit and manner of his conversation, if he pretend to rejoice in it, will, to a discerning mind, reveal the deep hypocrisy of his heart. But if there be a possibility of calling the truth of it in question, you will find that he disbelieves it altogether. You will find him dwelling upon and greatly magnifying any little circumstance that will render it improbable; while he depreciates, and casts into the shade, the weighty considerations that demonstrate its truth. Who has not witnessed the exhibitions of this principle on the subject of religion? Let a report of the prosperity of religion and of great revivals be circulated through the community, and see how Universalists, and other impenitent sinners, will manifest uneasiness and try to disprove it all; they will question the evidence, and try to pour contempt upon the report and upon those that believe it. They do not believe that so many have been converted; "you will see," say they, "that the professed converts will all go back again and be worse than ever." "The reports," say they, "are greatly exaggerated; and if there are any Christians in these revivals, then there are probably ten hypocrites to one Christian." Such facts as these speak for themselves.They manifest a state of mind that cannot be mistaken. It is the boiling over of enmity against God.

Again, *We naturally hate efforts to promote the interests of our enemies.* We are very apt to cavil at the measures which they use, to call their motives into question, and to find a great deal of fault with the spirit and manner of their efforts; when we are opposed to the *end* which they have in view. If it be to promote the interests of our enemy, we are naturally watching for objections and are captious and ill-natured with regard to their movements. We are apt to ridicule and oppose such efforts; and anything like zeal, in such a case, is looked upon by us as enthusiasm and madness. Witness the conduct of impenitent sinners on the subject of religion. If any efforts are made to promote the interests of the kingdom of God, to honour and glorify Him, they are offended. They get up an opposition. They not infrequently ridicule their meetings; speak evil of those that are engaged in them; denounce their zeal as enthusiasm and madness and something for which they deserve the execration of all their neighbours. People may get together and dance all night, and impenitent sinners do not think it objectionable. The theatre may be opened every night, at great expense, and the actors and multitudes of others may be engaged all day in preparing for the entertainment of the evening; and thus, the *devil* may get up a protracted meeting, and continue it for years, and they see no harm in it: no enthusiasm in all this. *Ladies* may go, and stay till midnight every evening. Poor people may go, and spend their time and money and waste their health and lives and ruin their souls; and there is no harm in all this. But let Christians do anything like this, and exercise one-tenth part of this zeal in promoting the honour of God and the salvation of souls; why, it would be talked of from Dan to Beersheba. Sinners may go to a ball or party, and stay nearly all night; but excessively indecorous it is for ladies to go out to *evening* prayer meetings. For Christians to have protracted meetings and to pray till 10 o'clock at night is considered abominable! Why, such things are spoken against in the newspapers. They are the subjects of remark and reprobation, in steamboats, stagecoaches, barrooms, and wherever impenitent sinners are assembled. Politicians may manifest the greatest zeal on the subject of politics; may hold their caucuses; post up their handbills; blaze away in the public journals; appoint their ward committees; ransack every nook and corner; parade through the streets with their music; fire their guns; show their flags; transport their frigates through the streets on wheels; send their coaches up and down the streets, with handbills posted on their sides to bring men to the polls; spend hundreds of thousands of dollars to carry an election; and all this is well enough! But, Oh, let Christians but begin to serve God with such zeal, and make such efforts to build up His kingdom, and save the souls of men; and ten to one, if the wicked did not absolutely mob them, and cry out that such efforts would ruin the nation, they would brand such proceedings as the most arrant enthusiasm and downright madness. But is it because politics are of so much more importance than the salvation of souls? Is it because no effort is necessary to arouse a slumbering world, and bring sinners to act and think and feel as they ought to on the subject of salvation? No, there is reason enough for the highest possible degree of Christian effort, and sinners know it very well; but their enmity against God is so great that such efforts cannot be made without arousing all the hell there is within them.

Again, *We easily believe an ill report of one whom we hate.* If a man hears any evil of an enemy, he believes it on the slightest testimony. He does not care to inquire whether the report may be relied upon, but he eagerly listens to every breath of slander, and yields the most unqualified credence to almost any and every falsehood that serves to blacken the reputation of his enemy. The reason for this is that his ill-will is gratified with such reports. He hopes that they are true, and therefore easily believes them. How frequently do we see this feature of the human heart developing itself on the subject of religion. With what eagerness do sinners listen to every false and slanderous report that may be circulated about the friends of God. It is surprising to see what absurd and ridiculous things they will believe. They manifest the most unequivocal desire to believe evil of those who profess friendship to God. It is amazing to see the enmity of their hearts manifesting itself to such a degree; that often, there is nothing too absurd, ridiculous, and contradictory for them to believe, if it only has a tendency to cast contempt and ridicule upon the cause of God.

Again, *We naturally love to give publicity to any evil report about our enemies.* We desire to have others feel toward them as we do. It gratifies our malignant feelings to hear and to circulate those reports that are injurious to the enemy we hate. Hear that man. He meets with a neighbour, and says, "Have you heard such and such a report of such an individual?" "No, I have not." "Ah, I supposed that you knew it, or I should have said nothing about it." Now hear him go into the whole subject, and relate and aggravate every circumstance of which he has heard, and comment upon them as he goes along; at length he closes by saying, "I hope you will not mention this, but it is a matter of fact." And now he goes abroad, and falls in with another neighbour and relates the same to him as a great secret; hopes he will say nothing about, but thinks the fact cannot be disputed.

Everywhere he goes, he takes this course; he hopes the thing will not get abroad to the injury of the poor man. This is a mournful event. He is truly sorry that any such thing has happened. In all this he is a hypocrite and he knows it. He is glad the event has happened and he delights to publish it. He seems to covet the exclusive privilege of being the bearer of the first intelligence to every door. How often do we witness the developments of this principle against God? If something takes place that is disgraceful among the professed friends of God, and injurious to the interests of religion, how ready sinners are to give it universal publicity.

They will talk about it. Publish it on all occasions; blaze it abroad in the public prints, and send it in every direction upon the wings of the wind. If anyone becomes deranged, in connection with a revival of religion, alas, what an ado is made about it. Thirty thousand citizens of the United States may be murdered every year by strong drink. The groceries may fill bedlam with maniacs. Homicide, suicide, and all manner of abominations may be the result of rum selling; and yet, the indignation of sinners is not aroused. But if some nervous individual becomes deranged, in view of his abominable crimes against his Maker and in connection with a revival or a protracted meeting, then the press groans under the burden of the doleful complainings that are poured out upon the public ear.

2. Under this 4th general division of the subject, I observe that *impenitent sinners hate God with a MORTAL HATRED.*

That is, were it in their power, they would destroy His very existence. Probably very few sinners are sensible that they have this degree of enmity, and may feel shocked at the assertion. Nevertheless, it is true. There are several reasons why they may never have known that such was the state of their hearts. It is probable that most of them have never dared to indulge any such feelings. Another reason why they never have desired to destroy God is that they have never thought it possible to destroy Him. There are many things which sinners have never designed or desired to do, because they have never thought it possible. Did any of you ever design to be a king. Did you ever entertain a thought of being a king? Have you ever felt any ambition to be a king? Probably you never did. And for the very reason that you have never thought it possible. Suppose a throne, a crown, and a sceptre were put within your reach; and the robe of royalty was tendered to your acceptance: do you not think that you have pride and ambition enough, under such circumstances, to desire to be a king? And suppose, when you had accepted the crown and swayed the sceptre over one nation that you had the opportunity of extending your empire and making your dominion universal over all nations, do you not believe that you would instantly desire to do it? And now, suppose that when all the governments of this world were subject to your sceptre; suppose an opportunity should come for you to extend your dominion over the entire universe of worlds, and you should conceive it possible to subject God himself to your control: are you too good, under such circumstances, to aim at exercising dominion over all the universe and over God himself? Sinners, who would trust the best among you? You know not your hearts, if you suppose that under such circumstances there would be any limit to your ambition.

But again, *Sinners do not realize the greatness of their enmity against God, because, as yet, God lets them go unpunished, and they do not believe that He will send them to hell for their sins.* If God will let them have their own way (as long as He does not interfere to punish them for their sins or disturb them in their courses of iniquity), then their enmity remains comparatively at rest. But who among them would not rise up and murder Him, were it in their power, if He should attempt to punish them for their sins?

No, they would sooner wish Him in hell than consent that He should deal with them in justice.

But again, *It is evident, that the enmity of sinners against God is MORTAL, from the fact that they are in rebellion against Him, and in league with devils to oppose His government, and undermine His throne.* Sinners do not obey Him. The whole weight of their influence and example is opposed to His government. They do everything that the nature of the case admits to annihilate His authority and destroy His government. Rebellion is always aimed at the life of the sovereign, and it is impossible for sinners to be more absolutely in rebellion against God than they are.

But again, *The question has been tried:* God has once put himself as much in the power of men as, in the nature of things, was possible. The second person in the Godhead took to himself human nature, and put His human nature within the power of men. And what was the result? They rested not till they had murdered Him. Do you say that those were the Jews? That you are of a different spirit? This has always been the favourite plea of sinners.

The ancient Jews persecuted and murdered the prophets. The Jews of Christ's day professed to honour the prophets, built their sepulchres, and insisted that if they had lived in the days of the prophets, then they would not have persecuted them. But they persecuted and murdered Christ; and Christ himself informs them that by persecuting Him, they showed that they approved the deeds of their fathers. Now sinner, suppose you lived under a government that was a monarchy. Suppose your fathers had rebelled against the rightful king, and placed an usurper upon the throne; and that you, their children, although you did not participate in the original rebellion, yet now, you maintain the same ground which they took, support the usurper, and refuse obedience to your rightful sovereign. Now, is not this, in law and in equity, is it not to all intents and purposes justifying the conduct of your fathers; becoming a partaker in their crimes? Suppose you did not originally murder Christ; still, is it not a fact that you now refuse to obey Him as your rightful sovereign? That you support the authority of Satan, who has usurped the government of this world by refusing to repent, by withholding your service and your heart from Jesus Christ. Do you not to all intents and purposes, become a partaker in the crime of those who murdered Him? He claimed their obedience, and they arose and imbrued their hands in His blood. He claims your obedience, and you utterly refuse it; and thus show that you approve the deeds of the Jews. And that, were He in your power, sooner than submit to His authority, you would murder Him again. This conduct makes you, in the eye of common law, a partaker in their crime. In the eye of conscience, of reason, and of common sense; in the eye of God, and in the judgment of heaven, earth and hell, you are guilty of the blood of Christ, and prove to a demonstration, that were it in your power you would dethrone and murder the Almighty.

3. Sinners hate God *supremely*. That is, they hate Him more than they do anything and everything, anybody and everybody else in the universe. Do not startle at this; as if it were a rash and extravagant assertion. It is a sober but an awful truth. Look at this! All other enmity can be overcome by kindness. The greatest enemy you have on earth may subdue your enmity by kindness, and win you over to become his friend. But how is it that all the kindness of God (infinitely greater kindness than any human being has had it in his power to show you) has not overcome your enmity and you still remain in rebellion against Him?

Again, *A mere change of circumstances in any other case of enmity will change your heart.* Here are two political opponents between whom an hereditary enmity exists. They have both believed and spoken all evil of each other. Now let a change of politics bring them both upon the same side of a political question, and they instantly become friends. Let them have an opportunity to play into each other's hands; let both their hearts be set upon the election of the same candidate, and see how cordially they will co-operate. How warmly they will take each other by the hand! They will walk and sit and dine together; attend political meetings, defend each other's reputation, magnify each other's virtues, and throw the kind mantle of charity over each other's vices. And all this they will do heartily. Their real feelings toward each other are changed. Their hearts are really changed toward each other, and they can truly say, "Whereas we formerly hated, now we love each other." All this has been effected merely by a change of circumstances without any interference by the Holy Ghost. Let the President of the United States appoint his greatest political opponent to the first office in his gift, and he makes him his friend. Suppose the greatest anti-Jackson man in this city, who has said and done the most of any man in the United States to prevent his election, should be reduced to poverty, and have no means to support himself and family. Now suppose that that news of his extremity should reach the president, and he should appoint him to a post of high honour and emolument, would not this change his heart? Would he complain that he *could not* become the president's friend until the Holy Ghost had changed his heart? No. Such kindness would be like pouring coals of fire upon his head and would melt him down in an instant; would change the whole current of his soul. How then, does it happen, that after all the offers of heaven, and all the threatening of hell, and all the boundless love and compassion manifested in giving His only-begotten and well-beloved Son to die for you; when mercy stoops from heaven with bleeding hands and offers to save, and hell roars from beneath and threatens to devour; when God approaches you with a word of moving, melting motives, gathered from earth and heaven and hell, and rolls their mountainous weight upon you that you say these considerations will never change your heart unless made effectual by the Holy Ghost?

Again, *If men did not hate God supremely they would INSTANTLY*

REPENT. Suppose that when you go home tonight, at the deep hour of midnight, when you are all asleep in an upper apartment of your house that you are awakened by the cry of fire and you look up and find your dwelling wrapt in flames around you. You leap from your bed and find the floor under your feet just ready to give way. The roof over your head is beginning to give way and ready to fall in upon you with a crash. Your little ones awake and are shrieking and clinging to your night-clothes. You see no way of escape. At this moment of unutterable anguish and despair, someone comes dashing through the flames with his hair and clothes on fire; he seizes you in your distraction with one hand, and gathers his other long and strong arm around your little ones, and again rushes through the flames at the hazard of his life. You absolutely swoon with terror. In a few moments, you open your eyes in the street and find yourself supported in the arms of your deliverer. He is rubbing your temples with camphor, and fanning you to restore your fainting life. You look up and see in the scorched and smoky features of him who rescued you, the man whom you have supremely hated. He smiles in your face, and says, "Fear not, your children are all alive; they are all standing around you." Now would you, could you, look coldly at him and say, "Oh, I wish I could repent that I have hated you so much. I wish I could be sorry for my sin against you"? Could you say this? No. You would instantly roll over upon your face, and wash his feet with your tears, and wipe them with the hairs of your head. This scene would change your heart in a moment, and ever after the name of that man would be music in your ears. If you heard him slandered, or saw him abused, it would enkindle your grief and indignation. And now, sinner, how is it that you complain that you cannot repent of your sins against God? Behold His loving kindness and His tender mercy! How can you look up? How can you refrain from repentance? How can you help being dissolved in broken-hearted penitence at His blessed feet? Behold His bleeding hands! See His wounded side! Hark! Hear His deep death-groan when He cries, "It is finished," and gives up the ghost for your sins. Sinner, are you marble or adamant! Has your heart been case-hardened in the fires of hell so that you don't repent? Surely nothing but enmity deep as perdition can be proof against the infinitely moving inducements to repentance.

But perhaps you will say that you do not like to hear about hell and damnation, that you love mercy, and that if ministers would present the love and mercy of God, and present God as a God of mercy, then sinners would love Him. But this is all a mistake. Sinners are as much opposed to the mercy of God as they are to any of His attributes. This is matter of fact and the experience of every day. Hark, what is that din and outcry? Whence are those cries of *"crucify him! crucify him!"* that load down the winds, and break upon our ears from the distance of more than 1800 years? Why, God has revealed His mercy, and all the world are in arms against it: Jesus Christ has come upon the kind errand of salvation, and the world is filled with uproar to murder Him! Mercy is the very attribute of God, against which mankind are arrayed. For thousands of years, the sword of vindictive justice has slept in its scabbard and God has been unfolding and holding out the attribute of mercy. All the opposition in the world to God, and to religion, is aimed particularly at His mercy. What is Christianity? What is the Bible? What are revivals of religion? What are all those things that have called forth so much of the opposition of earth and hell, but so many exhibitions of the mercy of the blessed God. When justice ascends the throne, then the cavilling mouths of sinners will be stopped. Justice will soon hush the tumult, and the loud opposition of sinners against their Maker. Then every mouth shall be stopped, and all the world shall be found guilty before God. But now is the dispensation of His mercy, and all the earth is up in arms against it! And why are you such a hypocrite, as to pretend to love the mercy of God? If you love it, why do you not accept it? If you love a God of mercy, why have not all the moving manifestations of it that have passed before you melted you down and subdued your heart? Oh, sinner, sinner, speak no more proudly. Boast not yourself that you love any attribute of God; for if, while you remain impenitent, you say you love Him, you are a liar, and the truth is not in you.

Remarks

I will conclude this discourse with several remarks.

1. You see why Universalists and other sinners are so disturbed with revivals of religion. It is because God comes so manifestly forth in the exercise of His mercy. They cannot bear such an exhibition of God. It disturbs all the sediment and lurking enmity of their hearts. These professed friends of God and men, as soon as God displays himself and men become the recipients of His mercy, are greatly offended by it.

2. You see the importance of preaching clearly and frequently about the enmity of sinners' hearts against God. There is, and has been for ages in most instances, a striking defect in exhibiting this most important subject. Ministers seem to have been afraid to charge men with being the enemies of God. I never heard this doctrine declared in my life, in such a way that I understood it, previous to my own conversion. Many ministers seem to have regarded total depravity as consisting in nothing more than the absence of love to God.

The church does not seem to have realized, or believed, that the carnal mind is absolute enmity against God. Although there is no other truth more abundantly taught in the Word of God, or more unanswerably evident from matter of fact; yet, how few sinners have been made to see and believe it. I have, in hundreds of instances, conversed with persons who have sat under the preaching of the gospel all their days, and who never have been made to see this fundamental truth of the gospel.

It is a truth upon which is founded the necessity of the new birth and the Spirit's influences. And without understanding and believing it, how are we to expect the world to be converted to God?

3. From this subject, it is manifest that if sinners should take their

oath that they hate God, it would not make it at all more evident. If all the men in the universe should take their oath that the sun shines at noonday, it would not add a particle to the evidence that the sun shines, or render it any more certain, in itself, or evident to others. It is a simple matter of fact of which we can have no higher testimony than our own senses. So it is a matter of fact that sinners are the enemies of God. They act it out before all men. It is as evident as that they have an existence, and how it ever came to be questioned, or ever forgotten, or overlooked, is, to me, most mysterious.

4. There are many professors of religion who could not make it more evident that they are the enemies of God if they should take their oath of it. They speak against revivals and those engaged in promoting them. They give publicity to the faults, real or supposed, of those who are the friends of God. They retail slander and manifest their opposition to God in so many ways that their hypocrisy and enmity against God are perfectly manifest.

5. Those persons who have not known by their own experience that they have been enemies of God, have not been converted, nor so much as truly convicted. What have they repented of? Have they repented merely of their outward sins? This is impossible; unless they have understood and condemned the fountain of iniquity from which these abominations have proceeded. The head and front of their offending is that they have been the enemies of God. Nay their minding of the flesh has been of itself enmity against God. And now, do they talk of having repented when they have never so much as known that in which their chief guilt consists. Impossible!

6. Those sinners who deny that they are the enemies of God are never likely to be converted until they confess their enmity. "He that covereth his sins, shall not prosper, but whoso confesseth and forsaketh them, shall have mercy." There are many persons who will confess themselves sinners but will deny that they are the enemies of God. Thus they cover up the great amount of their sins; acknowledge their outward acts of wickedness, but deny the enmity from which they flow. While they do this, God will never forgive them.

7. These discourses exhibit a very different view of total depravity from that which regards depravity as physical, or constitutional, or as belonging to the substance of the body or mind. They exhibit all depravity as *voluntary,* as consisting in voluntary transgression. As the sinner's own act. Something of his own creation. That over which he has a perfect control, and for which he is entirely responsible. Oh, the darkness, and confusion, and utter nonsense, of that view of depravity which exhibits it as something lying back, and the cause of, all actual transgression. Something created in the sinner and born with him. Some physical pollution transmitted from Adam, through the agency of God or the devil, which is in itself sinful and deserving the wrath of God previous to the exercise of voluntary agency on the part of the sinner. This is absurd and impossible.

It is not only absurd and impossible, but is virtually charging all the sin in the world upon God, and if it is firmly believed, renders repentance in every such case a natural impossibility. While the sinner supposes himself to be condemned, not only for his conduct, but for his nature; and while he believes that his conduct is the natural and necessary result of a depraved constitution; and that his nature must be changed before he can obey his Maker, it is manifestly impossible for him to blame himself for his sins. He must cease not only to be a reasonable being but to have common sense before he can justify God, and condemn himself, upon these principles. No wonder that men who maintain such a view of depravity as this should also maintain that sinners are *unable* to repent. It is true that upon these principles of depravity, and with these views, sinners cannot repent of themselves, nor can God make them repent. *The only way in which God can bring a sinner to repentance is by correcting his views, by showing him what sin is, and by causing him to see that it is for his conduct, and not for his nature, that he is to repent; and that his conduct and not his nature needs to be changed.* To teach physical, or constitutional, depravity is not only to teach heresy and nonsense, but it leads the sinner inevitably to justify himself and condemn God; and renders repentance, while the sinner believes it, impossible.

8. You see why sinners find it so difficult to be religious. The total difficulty consists in their unwillingness to yield up their selfishness.

9. It cannot be pretended, with any show of reason, that these discourses amount to any denial of *moral* depravity. I have purposely denied physical depravity, but certainly these discourses maintain *moral* depravity: that for which the sinner is to blame; that of which he must repent in all its length and breadth. It would seem that in the estimation of some a denial that the nature is in itself depraved is a virtual denial of all depravity. In other words, they seem to think it a virtual denial of the *guilty source* of all actual transgression. I have endeavoured to show that the cause of the outbreaking of sin is *not* to be found in a sinful constitution, or nature, but in a wrong original choice, in which the sinner prefers self-gratification to the will of his Maker; and that choice has become the settled preference of his soul, and constitutes the deep fountain from which flow the putrid waters of spiritual and eternal death. I am unable to see by what figure of speech *that* is called *moral* depravity which either consists in a depraved constitution or is the *natural* result of it. Why should it be called *moral* depravity? Certainly it can have no such relation to moral law as to deserve punishment. It is indeed awesome that in the 19th century it should be thought heresy to call sin a transgression of the law, and insist that it must be the *act* of a voluntary agent. Has it come to this that those who virtually deny all *moral* depravity and virtually charge all the sins of the world upon God are gravely to complain of heresy in those who maintain *moral* depravity in all its length and breadth, but who deny physical or constitutional depravity? What next? If it be heresy to say that sin is a transgression of the law certainly the apostle was not orthodox.

10. From this subject it is plain either that sinners must be annihilated, or converted, or forever lost. With a mind that is enmity against God, it is impossible that they should be happy. Infidels have no cause to sneer at the doctrine of the new birth. If there were no Bible in the world, the doctrine of total depravity as exhibited in these discourses would be abundantly manifest as a matter of fact. And it cannot be denied that except men pass through just that change of mind which is in the Bible called the new birth, or a change of heart, they must self-evidently be annihilated or damned to all eternity.

11. Sinners are not almost Christians. We sometimes hear persons say, of such an impenitent sinner, that he is almost a Christian. The truth is that the most moral impenitent sinner in the world is much nearer a devil than a Christian. Look at that sensitive young lady. Is she an impenitent sinner? Then she only needs to die to be as very a devil as there is in hell. Any slight occurrence that should destroy her life would make her a devil. Nay, she needs no positive influence to be exerted upon her to make a fiend of her; only remove all restraints and the very enmity of hell boils over in her heart at once. Let God take from under her His supporting hand. Let Him cease but for a moment to fan her heaving lungs, and she would open her eyes in eternity; and if she dared, would curse Him to His face.

12. How impossible it would be for sinners to enjoy heaven, if permitted to go there in their present state of mind. Only break down the body; let the mind burst forth into the presence of God; let it look abroad and behold His glories, and see holiness to the Lord inscribed on everything around them; let them listen to the song of praise; let them perch upon the loftiest battlement of heaven; let them hear the song "Holy, Holy, holy, Lord God Almighty," and so great would be their enmity, if unconverted, that, if permitted, they would dive into the darkest cavern of hell to escape from the presence of the infinitely holy Lord God.

13. While sinners remain in impenitence, they yield to God no sort of obedience any more than the devil does. Their carnal mind is not subject to the law of God, neither indeed can it be. In this state of mind, until the supreme preference of their mind is changed, until they have given up minding the flesh and decide to obey God, it is in vain to talk of obedience. The first act of obedience that you ever will or can perform is to cease minding the flesh and give your heart to God.

14. You see the wickedness and folly of those parents who think their unconverted children friendly to religion. You cannot teach them a greater heresy than that they are friendly to religion or to God. I have often heard professing parents say that their children were not enemies to religion. No wonder that such children were not converted under such teaching as this. It is just the doctrine that the devil desires you to teach them. You only give your children the impression that they are friendly to religion already, and they will never know why they need a new heart. While in this state of mind, and labouring under this delusion, they can-

not so much as be convicted, much less converted.

15. You see from this subject, the folly and the falsehood of saying of an impenitent sinner, he is a good-hearted man; when the fact is, that his heart is enmity against God.

Lastly, You see how necessary it is that there should be a hell. What shall be done with these enemies of God, if they die in their sins? Heaven is no place for you. It would doubtless be worse to you than hell, if you were allowed to go there. A hell is deserved by sinners, and is evidently needed for those who die in enmity against God. And now, sinner, you see your state; you must be convinced of the truth of what I have said. Remember that your enmity is voluntary. It is of your own creation—that which you have long cherished and exercised. Will you give it up? What has God done that you should continue to hate Him? What is there in sin that you should prefer it to God? Why, Oh, why will you indulge for a moment longer this spirit of horrible rebellion and enmity against the blessed God? Go but a little further; cleave to your enmity but a little longer; and the knell of eternal death shall toll over your damned soul, and all the corners of despair will echo with your groans.

10

ALL THINGS FOR GOOD TO THOSE
THAT LOVE GOD*
Romans 8:28

"And we know that all things work together for good to them that love God."

You will observe that the apostle speaks with all confidence. He does not say, "We expect, or we believe, or we conjecture, that all will be well for God's friends," but he says, "*We know.*" There is no doubt about it. Let us then:

   I. *Inquire what his language means.*
   II. *Show how the result of good to all that love God is secured.*
   III. *Notice some particulars as illustrations of the general truth.*
   IV. *Show how we know it to be true.*

I. *What is the apostle's meaning?*
Here the great question is, "Shall his language be interpreted as strictly universal?"

In words, he announces a universal proposition. "*All things,*" he declares, "work together for good to those that love God." But does he mean to affirm a proposition strictly universal?

Not all universal language should be taken in a strictly universal sense. In the Scriptures, we frequently find it necessary to modify universal language. There may be things in the text or context which forbid the universal sense, or there may be declarations in other parts of the Bible which preclude it; or the nature of the case may render the universal sense either violently improbable, or perhaps absurd, and hence may demand some modification. It should be remembered that the language

---

Sermons on the Way of Salvation, pp. 217-233.

of the Bible is the language of common life, and everybody knows that in the language of common life, we often affirm things in the form of a universal proposition when we really mean something much short of this. For example, it is common to say of a well-known fact, "Everybody says so"; but our "everybody" is by no means intended to embrace all mankind.

But the language of our text I do understand to be used in the strictly universal sense, meaning that absolutely *all* things, present and future—all things, above and beneath, in heaven, earth, and hell—do and will conspire to the ultimate blessedness of the saints. The Bible obviously teaches this doctrine, and I know of no facts in the universe that militate against its universal application.

II. *How does this come about? How is this result secured?*

In order to see this matter in its true light, we need to consider that the happiness of moral agents is conditioned on their holiness, and results from it. Holy persons will of course be happy, and have real enjoyment in proportion to the degree in which they are holy. Still further, let it be considered that the holiness of moral agents is conditioned upon their knowledge. Every moral agent is more or less holy according to what he knows more or less, and he is more or less conformed in heart and life to what he knows. I speak now particularly of the knowledge of God, whether obtained through His Word or through His works.

Now all events are matters of knowledge. All events that occur under God's government, and God himself is an object of knowledge. According to the Bible, all events will ultimately be known to the saints, for the judgment-day will bring them all to light. Hence, we learn that ultimately the entire history of all God's doing will be known to all His creatures. All He has ever done or shall ever do, whether in this world or in other worlds, will be open subjects of knowledge to His creatures, and will be known as fast and as far as their limited capacities will admit.

Now it is very plain that if all things, embracing all events and all the works of God, are matters of knowledge; and if, moreover, knowledge is a condition of real holiness, then all the knowledge which the saints attain will be at once available to their happiness. It will go to enhance their real blessedness. Especially will this be true of their knowledge of God and of His countless works and various ways. All things, the saints will then see, are parts of one great plan; both those which God himself performs by His direct agency, and those which are done through His permissive agency by His creatures. It will then be seen that all things are arranged and planned for the good of His obedient children; and when this great all-controlling principle in God's administraton comes to be seen in all its bearings, the knowledge of this truth cannot fail to be a source of ineffable blessedness to all the holy. God's infinite grace as the great and good Father of all His loving children will be so revealed so as to show that He makes all things work together for their good.

III. *Let us now turn our attention to some particulars as illustrations of the general truth.*

It is generally supposed that what we call mercies and blessings and what we recognize by name as God's good gifts to men are really good things to those that love God. We can see that they are, and men universally recognize them as good.

The same is equally true of what we call judgments and chastisements—the rebukes of God; for all these, too, are means of grace, and are blessed of God for the spiritual good of His children. Their only design as they come from our Father's hand is that they may work out good to His saints. He does not afflict willingly, nor grieve the children of men from caprice, or from any pleasure in their pain, but only and wholly for their profit, that they may the more deeply "partake of his holiness." Under this broad principle, we know that all the losses and crosses which befall the saints, all their burdens of care and responsibility, and all their infirmities, shall be overruled for their good. All these things will conspire to teach the saints more of God and more of themselves. By the aid of such revelations they will be able the better to appreciate God's character and plans of discipline, and their own infinite obligation to His manifold grace.

Nor from the "all things" of our text can we except the sins of God's people. They are indeed altogether blameworthy for all their sins, and none the less so for the good which God educes from them by His overruling agency. The sin of Peter was overruled of God for his good. He was a more humble and a better man as long as he lived. He better knew his own weakness, and better appreciated Christ's tender compassion. He felt the force of the admonition, "When thou art converted, strengthen thy brethren," and there was none among all the original twelve to whom Christ said more emphatically, "Feed my sheep"—"Feed my lambs."

This sin of Peter brought him into great peril. "Satan desired to have him that he might sift him as wheat"—and if Christ had left him to himself, he would doubtless have fallen fatally into the snare of the devil. But Christ did not leave him in this hour of his need. "I have prayed for thee," said He, "that thy faith fail not." Christ kept His hand and eye on him, and soon plucked him from the destroyer's grasp. In this scene Peter learned more of the length and depth of his Saviour's grace than he had ever known before.

This is only a single case, yet it was by no means a peculiar case; and therefore, it serves to illustrate the general law of God's administration over His people.

Similar was the case of David. No thanks to him, but all thanks to God, that his sin was overruled, so that in the outcome he was a more meek, humble, penitent, and holy man.

Not only are the sins of the saints overruled to their good, but so are the sins of others, of sinners, and even of the most wicked. All the mistakes of our associates, their infirmities, the thousand nameless things that try us and perhaps perplex us greatly—all these come in among the "all things" which God makes subservient to the good of His people.

There is a woman whose husband is a bad man. His temper is uncomfortable; his ways are adapted to make his intimate associates unhappy; and hence, he causes his wife many sore trials. Yet, if she loves God, and makes Him the Refuge of her soul, all these little trials shall certainly work out to her good both in this world and in the next.

Not less so of the husband who has a bad wife. Not less so of those unhappy families in which the husband and the wife are great trials to each other. So of parents and children. Parents may be a source of trial to their children, and it often happens that children are a source of the greatest trial to their parents. But howsoever the trials occur, the great principle of our text applies to them all. To those that love God, they shall all work together for good.

The principle also reaches and applies to all the temptations of the devil. Let him poison his darts with demoniac skill and hurl them with hellish malice, they shall not ultimately harm those that sincerely love God. "The name of the Lord is a strong tower into which the righteous run and are safe." The Christian has a panoply complete, wherewith he may be able to withstand all the fiery darts of the devil. And what is more to our present purpose; though wounded by these darts, he shall not be slain; though cast down, he shall not be destroyed; for there is a healing, overruling hand under whose agency even the wounds that Satan inflicts shall be wrought into better health and more spiritual vitality than the saints enjoyed before. God knows how to foil Satan with his own weapons, and make even his apparent temporary success react in terrible defeat and disgrace upon his own head. God knows how not only to rescue His saints, but to do much more than simply to rescue them: He imbues them with new vigor, and sanctifies to them their most bitter and humiliating experience.

Yet further, all events are designed to illustrate God's true character. The whole creation is only a revelation of God, and all events that occur in it only serve to reveal more and more of God to intelligent beings. "The heavens declare the glory of God; the firmament showeth his handiwork." How many lectures on God are read to us by the silent stars! How many lessons are repeated to us, day by day, by His rising suns and nightly dews and timely showers! Where in all the works of God, whether in nature or providence, is there a thing that does not speak His praise, and bear some testimony which He can bless to the souls of His saints?

IV. *We know that all things work together for good to the saints.* So says Paul. *How* did he and his brethren know this to be true? Perhaps they knew it by revelations already made in God's Word; or it may be that his mind rested this truth upon the general knowledge of God enjoyed. *It is a matter of revelation.* The Bible amply affirms this truth. *And it is also a plain dictate of reason.* When we come to understand what God's attributes are, as affirmed by the reason, we shall see that such a God can allow nothing to occur which shall not in some way result in good to His friends. This must be so; if it be true that God loves His friends, studies to promote their highest good, has all events under His control, had His choice in the depths of a past eternity among all possible events, and could determine to cause and allow to exist such only as should subserve the ends that lay near His heart.

It is often a matter of experience and observation in this world that things which seem freighted with destruction turn out to be full of life and salvation. For a time, all looked dark and desolate, but light and joy came out at last. Look at the case of Job. You can scarcely think of one form of grief and sorrow which did not blend in the throng that rushed upon him, as if to crush him; but he lived to see all these things work together for good to himself both for time and eternity. So, in general, I remark, that observation and experience will often show that this doctrine applies even to the present life, and has its exemplification even here. Yet the apostle did not mean to affirm that God's plans have their full development in the present world. His affirmation contemplated a future world in which results but partially unfolded here can have their full and everlasting development.

Remarks

1. Saints will in eternity blame themselves for what they cannot on the whole regret. Seeing the results which God has educed by His overruling agency, they cannot wish they had never done those wicked things; yet surely they will none the less blame themselves for their own sins. As to the blame of sin, no matter how much good may come from our wrongdoing, it never can affect the question of our guilt, nor its measure. Take the case of Judas. No thanks to him that his infamous treason was one of the agencies which provided a Saviour for a ruined world. The good which accrued from the death of Christ changes not the intrinsic character of his sin—cannot in any measure make it less mean, less sordid, less revengeful. Hence he must blame himself as much as if no good, but only evil, had resulted from his betrayal of Christ. It was God alone, by His own infinite wisdom and power, who overruled this sin to great good. All praise therefore to Him, and none the less blame to Judas the traitor.

2. Our subject shows how the saints can be perfectly happy in heaven to all eternity. For there is in many minds a point of obscurity in this matter which needs explanation. The saints will see all their past sins in heaven's clear light, and they cannot but blame themselves for every sin they ever committed. How, then, can they be perfectly happy?

The answer is that they will see how their sins have been overruled for good, and they will rejoice in this good which God brings out of their iniquities. In this exercise of joy, they will be deeply humble, as indeed they will have all reason to be, and their joy will be purely a joy in God, blended with everlasting adoration and praise that He had both the power and the heart to bring so much good out of their own wrongdoings. Every view taken by a saint in heaven of his past sins will redound in praise to God, but in deeper humiliation to himself. Yet this humiliation will by no means conflict with the saint's happiness—for he enjoys being humble—he enjoys giving *all glory and praise* to God.

3. God blames a multitude of things, but has no regrets. He has often expressed himself as we do when we feel regret, but these forms of expression are shaped in accommodation to our modes of speaking, and when used by God should be interpreted in accordance with His known character and known relations. It cannot be that, *on the whole*, under all the circumstances of the case, He really regrets the occurrence of anything that takes place. He blames the guilty author, He condemns the sin—but it has not taken Him by surprise; it is no new thing to Him, and it has not in any wise frustrated His purposes and plans for the government of the universe. Before this sin was committed, or its author existed, God saw how He could overrule it for good, and for so much good, that, on the whole, He judged it better to let its author come into existence and commit this sin, rather than prevent either the one or the other. Yet He blames every sin as much as if no good could be educed from it. The sinner is none the better for this development of good through God's overruling agency. To God alone belongs all the praise for both the good intention and the good results are His alone. But for His good hand interposing, all the results would have been evil, and the sinner's intention is, of course, all evil, and only evil continually.

Yet while God blames both sinners and saints for all their sins, He freely forgives the believing penitent and accepts him as a son. Then, He so overrules the sin so as not to be agonized by anything that occurs.

We sometimes see results corresponding to this in the earthly discipline which parents exercise over their children. The parent sees that his child has sinned; at first he regrets the thing exceedingly; but having, in the fear and help of God, done his utmost to reclaim and improve his child, he sees his efforts crowned with the divine blessing, and he says, "That sin of my dear child almost killed me, but now I see him so much changed for the better that I can no longer regret the means which have resulted in so much good"*

4. From this it does not follow that sin is the necessary means of the greatest good. For if, under the very circumstances in which they sin, men would obey rather than disobey—do right rather than wrong—then yet greater good might accrue than accrues from God's overruling of their sin. But God prefers His own course to any other which He can take. Under the circumstances He always does the wisest and best thing possible to Him; and hence, He has no occasion for regret. He brings out

*Editor's Note: When this sermon was preached, Finney saw no real conflict between God's knowing all our future actions and our freedom of choice—we are still to blame for our sins. It must also be emphazied that God does regret particular sins and evils in themselves, but He rejoices that He has the wisdom and power to bring good and loving results out of all sin and evil. He has no *ultimate* regret.

the greatest good possible to himself. If His creatures, who do in fact sin, would be persuaded to do right instead of wrong, their agency for good, concurrent with His, would educe a still augmented good.

For illustration: a father commands his son to perform some certain work. But he has good reason to believe that the son will not do it unless he himself stays at home to control the son by his presence. Yet it is so important for him to go away that he decides to go, though at the hazard of his son's disobedience. In case the son disobeys, he trusts he can subject him to such discipline as shall bring out some good, and the good to be secured by his own presence elsewhere is too great to be sacrificed. The greatest good possible can be secured only by the concurrent agency of father and son. The father can secure the greatest good possible to himself by going away, even though his son should disobey in his absence.

5. But if sin were overruled so as to be at last the means of the *greatest* good, no thanks to the sinner. Suppose it were the case that the whole world would have been damned if Judas had not betrayed Christ, so that his sin secured the salvation of the world—no thanks to Judas for such a result, for he meant not so, neither did his heart think so. He intended no good to the world, nor to any being in it except himself. His act of betraying his friend would be none the less mean, sordid, and revengeful, for the good which in the case supposed would ensue. The good wrought out would be wholly attributable to God.

6. It is naturally impossible to sin benevolently. There can be no such thing as a benevolent sin. To sin with a design to do good is an absurdity in terms. To say, therefore, that we do evil that good may come, is absurd and impossible. To do evil for the sake and with the motive of securing real good is a self-contradiction. For doing evil implies a wicked intention, and the having a good end in view implies a good intention. But to have both a good intention and a bad intention at the same instant, each determining the same act, is surely a self-contradiction. If a man intends good by his act, it is not sin. No man ever sinned in order that it might redound to the glory of God. No tyrant ever persecuted the saints of God that it might do them good. Suppose a wicked man were to say, "My wife is a good woman; let me plague her now for her good. It will only make her a better woman, so let me torment her all I can. There is no way in which I can do her so much good." He can't do any such thing! It is naturally impossible that a man should be honest in trying to do good by wickedness. This sinning benevolently is a natural impossibility.

7. Saints should always be in a position to fall back upon God in all their trials in this life. They should stand in such relations to God that they can rationally and naturally trust Him to shape and control all events, even here, so as to make them work out good in the highest degree. If they walk humbly before God, they may know that all things shall be made to conspire for their good. Only let them truly love God and trust Him; then they need not fear the outcome of any events what-

ever that may be. None can occur without God's permission, or independently of His direction. They may therefore be assured that God will shape all their bearings for the good of those that love Him.

But if professed Christians are living in sin, they have no claim on this promise and no right to expect its fulfillment to themselves. But if they are not in sin, they may, like Micah, cry out triumphantly, "Rejoice not against me, O mine enemy; when I fall I shall arise; when I sit in darkness, the Lord shall be a light unto me."

8. This truth affords ground for strong consolation to the saints. Why should they ever be sad? Suppose all things do not apparently work well now. Let them still have faith in God and rest in His promises. Has He not said that all things shall work together for good to His loving friends? No wonder saints are often seen smiling through their tears, for joy lies deep in their souls though sadness may overcloud their face. Joys and sorrows are often strangely blended in their bosom. Calamities, disappointments, bereavements, befall them as they do other men; and these things are not for the present joyous but grievous, but their faith in God assures them that all will yet be well. Many things will befall them in life that burn and agonize their sensibility; but deep within are trust and faith in God, and a sweet leaning upon His promises—for they know that the ground of their consolation is as firm and strong as the pillars of the universe!

9. We may rejoice in whatever befalls any of God's real children, whether ourselves or others. Parents may rejoice in whatever befalls their godly children or friends. Many things may occur which cause tears now; yet, as Christians, our watchword should be, *It will surely be well for them in the latter end.* The things which give the severest shock will do the most good. Those things which seem most afflictive, when God has brought out all their results, may be found to be most blest to His saints. Those fearful events which seemed to come with a crash, as if they would break down all the pillars of your foundation, Oh, how sweet to see even those strange things so strangely overruled for the good of the saints!

10. Very few Christians can live a single week, or even a day, without needing the consolation which this truth affords. Hence they ought to hold it fast—to keep it treasured in their memory—lying near their hearts—ready to be applied for consolation and for strength in every emergency.

This truth may well reconcile the saints to any and to all events of divine providence. They can afford to be submissive while they know that their Father will make all things work together for their good. They can afford to have travail and suffering, for even their most intense sorrows shall all conspire to work out good to their souls. Therefore let not unbelief deprive us of this consolation. Apart from the light of faith, many things will occur that are inexplicably dark, but faith illumines and explains all.

How wonderful are God's marvelous works! Well may it be said of

Him, "He is wonderful in counsel and excellent in working." Results may lie hidden long, but they will come out at last in glorious sunlight showing that God's hand has guided events to their results with unerring wisdom. In the light of eternity, if not in the light of time, they shall see it all and seeing it shall wonder and adore. "God," they will shout aloud, "hath done all things well!" Then, do not allow yourselves now to be deprived of this great consolation.

But do you say, "Ah, if I only knew that I am a child of God, if I only knew that I really love God, then I could receive this consolation legitimately; then I could feel that it belongs to me; then I could say, 'Let come anything that God is pleased to send, for I am anchored in His love and on His promises'?"

Now you may be very guilty for these doubts, for surely you may be free from them altogether; but still, if with all your doubtings you are really God's child, then they shall all be overruled for your good, so that in heaven you will have it to say, "How wonderful are God's ways! That He should bring me out of a region so dark and desolate, and then make all my doubts and darkness subserve some useful ends to my own soul and to His glory—that out of such materials He should bring out any good at last—how wonderful!"

Finally, we can see that the volumes of glory and praise to God must be to all eternity continually accumulating. Fresh revelations each hour of His wonderful wisdom and love must evolve from humble and holy hearts fresh accessions of praise and honor to His blessed name. Is it not delightful to think that such a God shall be thus praised and honored through eternity!

11

RELIGION OF THE LAW AND THE GOSPEL*
Romans 9:30-33

"What shall we say then? That the Gentiles, which followed not after righteousness, have attained to righteousness, even the righteousness which is of faith. But Israel, which followed after the law of righteousness, hath not attained to the law of righteousness. Wherefore? Because they sought it not by faith, but as it were by the works of the law. For they stumbled at that stumblingstone; as it is written, Behold, I lay in Zion a stumblingstone and rock of offense: and whosoever believeth on him shall not be ashamed."

In the Epistle to the Romans, the apostle pursues a systematic course of reasoning to accomplish a particular design. In the beginning of it, he proves that not only the Gentiles, but the Jews also, were in a state of entire depravity; and that the Jews were not, as they vainly imagined, naturally holy. He then introduces the moral law, and by explaining it, shows that by works of law no flesh could be saved. His next topic is Justification by Faith in opposition to Justification by Law. The next subject, with which he begins chapter 6, is to show that sanctification is by faith; or that all true religion, all the acceptable obedience there ever was in the world, is based on faith. In the eighth and ninth chapters, he introduces the subject of divine sovereignty; and in the last part of the ninth chapter, he sums up the whole matter, and asks, "What shall we say then? What shall we say of all this? That the Gentiles, who never thought of the law, have become pious and have obtained the holiness which is by faith; but the Jews attempting it by the law have entirely failed. Wherefore?" Because they made the fatal mistake of attempting to become pious by obeying the law, and have always come short, while the Gentiles have obtained true religion by faith in

---

Lectures to Professing Christians (1880), pp. 270-282.

Jesus Christ. Jesus Christ is here called "that stumblingstone," because the Jews were so opposed to Him. But whosoever believeth in Him shall not be confounded.

My design tonight is to point out as distinctly as I can the true distinction between the religion of law and the religion of faith. I shall proceed in the following order:

I.   *Show in what the distinction does not consist.*
II. *Show in what it does consist.*
III. *Bring forward some specimens of both, to show more plainly in what they differ.*

I. *I am to show in what the distinction between the religion of law and the religion of faith does not consist.*

1. The difference does not lie in the fact that under the law men were justified by works without faith. The method of salvation in both dispensations has been the same. Sinners were always justified by faith. *The Jewish dispensation pointed to a Saviour to come, and if men were saved at all, it was by faith in Christ. And sinners now are saved in the same way.*

2. Not in the fact that the gospel has cancelled or set aside the obligations of the moral law. It is true, it has set aside the claims of the ceremonial law, or law of Moses. The ceremonial law was nothing but a set of types pointing to the Saviour, and was set aside, of course, when the great anti-type appeared. It is now generally admitted by all believers that the gospel has not set aside the moral law. But that doctrine has been maintained in different ages of the church. Many have maintained that the gospel has set aside the moral law so that believers are under no obligation to obey it. Such was the doctrine of the Nicolaitans, so severely reprobated by Christ. The Antinomians, in the days of the apostles and since, believed that they were without any obligation to obey the moral law; and held that Christ's righteousness was so imputed to believers, and that He had so fulfilled the law for them, that they were under no obligation to obey it themselves.

There have been many, in modern times, called Perfectionists, who have held that they were not under obligation to obey the law. They supposed that Christ has delivered them from the law, and given them the Spirit, and that the leadings of the Spirit are now to be their rule of life instead of the law of God. Where the Bible says that sin shall not have dominion over believers, these persons understand by it that the same acts which would be sin if done by an unconverted person are not sin in them. The others, they say, are under the law, and so bound by its rules; but they themselves are sanctified, and are in Christ, and if they break the law it is no sin. But all such notions must be radically wrong. *God has no right to give up the moral law. He cannot discharge us from the duty of love to God and love to man for this is right in itself.* And unless God will alter the whole moral constitution of the universe, so as to make that right which is wrong, He cannot give up the claims of the moral law. Besides, this doctrine represents Jesus Christ and the Holy Ghost as having taken up arms openly against the government of God.

3. The distinction between law religion and gospel religion does not consist in the fact that the gospel is any less strict in its claims, or allows any greater latitude of self-indulgence than the law. Not only does the gospel not cancel the obligations of the moral law, but it does in no degree abate them. Some people talk about gospel liberty as though they had gotten a new rule of life, less strict, and allowing more liberty than the law. I admit that it has provided a new method of justification, but it everywhere insists that the rule of life is the same with the law. The very first sentence of the gospel, the command to repent, is in effect a re-enactment of the law, because it is a command to return to obedience. *The idea that the liberty of the gospel differs from the liberty of the law is erroneous.*

4. Neither does the distinction consist in the fact that those called legalists, or who have a legal religion, do, either by profession or in fact, depend on their own works for justification. It is not often the case, at least in our day, that legalists do profess dependence on their own works, for there are few so ignorant as not to know that this is directly in the face of the gospel. Nor is it necessarily the case that they really depend on their own works. Often they really depend on Christ for salvation. But their dependence is false dependence; such as they have no right to have. They depend on him, but they make it manifest that their faith, or dependence, is not that which actually "worketh by love," or that "purifieth the heart," or that "overcometh the world." It is a simple matter of fact that the faith which they have does not do what the faith does which men must have in order to be saved, and so it is not the faith of the gospel. They have a kind of faith, but not that kind that makes men real Christians, and brings them under the terms of the gospel.

II. *I am to mention some of the particulars in which these two kinds of religion differ.*

There are several different classes of persons who manifestly have a legal religion. There are some who really profess to depend on their own works for salvation. Such were the Pharisees. The Hicksite Quakers formerly took this ground, and maintained that men were to be justified by works; setting aside entirely justification by faith. When I speak of works, I mean works of law. And here I want you to distinguish between works of law and works of faith. *This is the grand distinction to be kept in view. It is between works produced by legal considerations, and those produced by faith.* There are but two principles on which obedience to any government can turn: *One is the principle of hope and fear*, under the influence of conscience. Conscience points out what is right or wrong, and the individual is induced by hope and fear to obey. *The other principle is confidence and love.* You see this illustrated in families, where one child always obeys from hope and fear, and another from affectionate confidence. So in the government of God, the only thing that ever produces even the appearance of obedience is one of these two principles.

There is a multitude of things that address our hopes and fears; such as character, interest, heaven, and hell, etc. These may produce external obedience or conformity to the law. But filial confidence leads men to obey God from love. This is the only obedience that is acceptable to God. God not only requires a certain course of conduct, but requires that this should spring from love. There never was and never can be, in the government of God, any acceptable obedience but the obedience of faith. Some suppose that faith will be done away with in heaven. This is a strange notion. As if there were no occasion to trust God in heaven, or no reason to exercise confidence in Him. Here is the great distinction between the religion of law and gospel religion. *Legal obedience is influenced by hope and fear*, and is hypocritical, selfish, outward, constrained. *Gospel obedience is from love*, and is sincere, free, cheerful, true. There is a class of legalists, who depend on works of law for justification, who have merely deified what they call a principle of right, and have set themselves to do right; it is not out of respect to the law of God, or out of love to God, but just because it is right.

There is another distinction here. *The religion of law is the religion of purposes, or desires, founded on legal considerations*, and *not the religion of preference, or love to God.* The individual intends to put off his sins; he purposes to obey God and be religious; but his purpose does not grow out of love to God, but out of hope and fear. It is easy to see that a purpose founded on such considerations is very different from a purpose growing out of love. The religion of the gospel is not a purpose merely, but an actual preference consisting in love.

Again, there is a class of legalists that depend on Christ, but their dependence is not gospel dependence, because the works which it produces are works of law; that is, from hope and fear, not from love. Gospel dependence may produce, perhaps, the very same outward works, but the motives are radically different. The legalist drags on a painful, irksome, moral, and perhaps, outwardly, religious life. The gospel believer has an affectionate confidence in God which leads him to obey out of love. His obedience is prompted by his own feelings. Instead of being dragged to duty, he goes to it cheerfully, because he loves it, and doing it is a delight to his soul.

There is another point. The legalist expects to be justified by faith, but he has not learned that he must be sanctified by faith. Modern legalists do not expect to be justified by works; they know these are inadequate—they know that the way to be saved is by Christ. But they have no practical belief that justification by faith is true, as sanctification by faith is true, and that men are justified by faith only, as they are first sanctified by faith only. And, therefore, while they expect to be justified by faith, they set themselves to perform works that are works of law.

Again, I wish you to observe that the two classes may agree in these points; the necessity of good works, and, theoretically, in what constitutes good works; that is, obedience springing from love to God. And further, they may agree in aiming to perform good works of this kind.

But the difference lies here—in the different influences to which they look to enable them to perform good works. The considerations by which they expect their minds to be affected are different. They look to different sources for motives. And the true Christian alone succeeds in actually performing good works. The legalist, aiming to perform good works, is influenced by hope and fear and a selfish regard to his own interest. He obeys the voice of conscience because he is afraid to do otherwise, and falls entirely short of loving God with all his heart, and soul, and strength. The motives under which he acts have no tendency to bring him to the obedience of love. The true Christian, on the contrary, so appreciates God, so perceives and understands God's character in Christ, that he has such an affectionate confidence in God that he finds it easy to obey from love. Instead of finding it, as a hymn has strangely represented,

"Hard to obey, and harder still to love,"

he finds it no hardship at all. The commandments are not grievous. The yoke is easy, and the burden light. And he finds the ways of wisdom to be ways of pleasantness, and all her paths to be peace.

Is it so with most professors of religion? Is it so with you? Do you feel, in your religious duties, constrained by love? Are you drawn by such strong cords of love that it would give you more trouble to omit duty than to obey? Do your affections flow out in such a strong current to God that you cannot but obey? How is it with those individuals who find it "hard to obey, and harder still to love"? What is the matter? Ask that wife who loves her husband, if she finds it hard to try to please her husband! Suppose she answers, in a solemn tone, "Oh yes, I find it hard to obey and harder still to love my husband," what would the husband think? What would any one of you who are parents say, if you should hear one of your children complaining, "I find it hard to obey my father, and harder still to love"? The truth is that there is a radical defect in the religion of those people who love such expressions and live as if they were true. If any one of you find religion a painful thing, rely on it, you have the religion of the law. Did you ever find it a painful thing to do what you love to do? No. It is a pleasure to do it. The religion of the gospel is no labor to them that exercise it. It is the feeling of the heart. What would you do in heaven, if religion is such a painful thing here? Suppose you were taken to heaven and obliged to grind out just so much religion every week, and month and year, to eternity. What sort of a heaven would it be to you? Would it be heaven, or would it be hell? If you were required to have ten thousand times as much as you have here, and your whole life were to be filled up with this, and nothing else to do or enjoy but an eternal round of such duties, would not hell itself be a respite to you?

The difference, then, lies here. One class are striving to be religious from hope and fear, and under the influence of conscience which lashes them if they do not do their duty. The other class act from love to God, and the impulses of their own feelings, and know what the text means which says, "I will put my law in their inward parts, and write it on their hearts, I will be their God, and they shall be my people."

III. *I will give some specimens of these two classes by way of illustration.*

The first example I shall give is that of the apostle Paul, as he has recorded it in the 7th of Romans, where he exhibits the struggle to obey the law under the influence of law alone. [Here Mr. Finney proceeded, at a considerable length, to comment on the 7th chapter of Romans, but as he has since concluded to give a separate lecture on that subject, these remarks are omitted here. He showed how Paul had struggled, and labored, under the motives of law, until he absolutely despaired of help from that quarter; and how, when the gospel was brought to view, the chain was broken, and he found it easy to obey. He then proceeded.]*

You may see the same in the experience of almost any convicted sinner, after he has become truly converted. He was convicted, the law was brought home to his mind, he struggled to fulfill the law, he was in agony, and then he was filled with joy and glory. Why? He was agonized under the law; he had no rest and no satisfaction; he tried to please God by keeping the law; he went about in pain all the day; he read the Bible; he tried to pray; but the Spirit of God was upon him showing him his sins, and he had no relief. The more he attempts to help himself the deeper he sinks in despair. All the while his heart is cold and selfish. But now let another principle be introduced, and let him be influenced by love to God. The same Holy Spirit is upon him, showing him the same sins that grieved and distressed him so before. But now he goes on his knees, his tears flow like water as he confesses his guilt, and his heart melts in joyful relentings, such as cannot be described, but easily understood by them that have felt it. Now he engages in performing the same duties that he tried before. But, Oh, how changed! The Spirit of God has broken his chains, and now he loves God and is filled with joy and peace in believing.

The same thing is seen in many professors of religion, who find religion a painful thing. They have much conviction, and perhaps much of what they call religion, but their minds are chiefly filled with doubts and fears, doubts and fears all the time. By and by, perhaps, that same professor will come out, all at once, a different character. His religion now is not all complaints and sighs, but the love of God fills his heart, and he goes cheerfully and happily to his duty; and his soul is so light and happy in God that he floats in an ocean of love and joy, and the peace that fills him is like a river.

Here, then, is the difference between the slavery of law and the liberty of the gospel. The liberty of the gospel does not consist in being freed from doing what the law requires, but in a man's being in such a

---

*Editor's Note: See the sermon "Legal Experience." This marginal note in brackets was inserted by the editor of *Lectures to Professing Christians*.

state of mind that doing it is itself a pleasure instead of a burden. What is the difference between slavery and freedom? The slave serves because he is obliged to do so, the freeman serves from choice. The man who is under the bondage of law does duty because conscience thunders in his ears if he does not obey, and he hopes to go to heaven if he does. The man who is in the liberty of the gospel does the same things because he loves to do them. One is influenced by selfishness, the other by disinterested benevolence.

Remarks

1. You can easily see that if we believe the words and actions of most professors of religion, that they have made a mistake; they have the religion of law, and not gospel religion. They are not constrained by the love of Christ, but moved by hopes and fears, and by the commandments of God. They have gone no farther in religion than to be convicted sinners. Within the last year, I have witnessed the regeneration of so many professors of religion that I am led to fear that great multitudes in the church are yet under the law; and although they profess to depend on Christ for salvation, their faith is not that which works by love.

2. Some persons are all faith without works. These are Antinomians. Others are all works and no faith: these are legalists. In all ages of the church, men have inclined first to one of these extremes, and then over to the other. Sometimes they are settled down on their lees, pretending to be all faith, and waiting God's time; then they get roused up, and dash on in works, without regard to the motive from which they act.

3. You see the true character of those professors of religion who are forever crying out "Legality!" as soon as they are pressed up to holiness. When I first began to preach, I found this spirit in many places; so that the moment Christians were urged up to duty, the cry would rise, "This is legal preaching—do preach the gospel; salvation is by faith, not by duty; you ought to comfort saints, not distress them." All this was nothing but rank Antinomianism.

On the other hand, the same class of churches now complain if you preach faith to them, and show them what is the true nature of gospel faith. They now want to do something, and insist that no preaching is good that does not excite them, and stir them up to good works. They are all for doing, doing, doing, and will be dissatisfied with preaching that discriminates between true and false faith, and urges obedience of the heart out of love to God. The Antinomians wait for God to produce right feelings in them. The Legalists undertake to get right feelings by going to work. It is true that going to work is the way, when the church feels right, to perpetuate and cherish right feelings. But it is not the way to get right feeling in the first place, to dash right into the work without any regard to the motives of the heart.

4. Real Christians are a stumbling block to both parties; to those

who wait God's time and do nothing, and to those who bustle about with no faith. The true Christian acts under love to God and to his fellow-man, and he labors to pull sinners out of the fire with such earnestness that the waiting party cry out, "Oh, he is getting up an excitement: he is going to work in his own strength; he does not believe in the necessity of divine influences; we ought to feel our dependence; let us wait God's time, and not try to get up a revival without God." So they sit down and fold their hands, and sing, "We feel our dependence, we feel our dependence; wait God's time; we do not trust in our own works." On the other hand, the legalists, when once they get roused to bustle about, will think their religion is the same as the real Christian's. They make as strenuous outward efforts, and suppose themselves to be actuated by the same Spirit.

You will rarely see a revival in which this does not show itself. If the body of the church are awakened to duty, and have the spirit of prayer and zeal for the conversion of sinners, there will be some who sit still and complain that the church is depending on its own strength; others will be very busy and noisy, but without any feeling; while the third class are so full of love and compassion to sinners that they can hardly eat or sleep, and yet so humble and tender that you would imagine they felt themselves to be nothing. The legalist, with his dry zeal, makes a great noise, deceives himself, perhaps, and thinks he is acting just like a Christian. But mark! The true Christian is stirring and active in the service of Christ, but moves with the holy fire that burns within his bosom. The legalist depends on some protracted meeting, or some other influence from without, to excite him to do his duty.

5. You see why the religion of some persons is so steady and uniform, and that of others is so fitful and evanescent. You will find some individuals who seem to be always engaged in religion. Talk to them anytime on the subject, and their souls will kindle. Others are awake only now and then. Once in a while you may find them full of zeal. The truth is, when one has the anointing that abides, he has something that is durable. But if his religion is only that of the law, he will only have just as much of it as he has of conviction at the present moment, and his religion will be fitful and evanescent, of course.

6. You see why some are so anxious to get to heaven, while others are so happy here. There are some, who have such a love for souls and such a desire to have Christ's kingdom built upon earth that they are perfectly happy here, and willing to live and labor for God, as long as He chooses to have them. Nay, if they were sent to hell, and permitted to labor there for souls, they would be happy. While others talk as if people were never to expect true enjoyment in this life; but when they get to heaven, they expect to be happy. One class have no enjoyment but in hope. The other has already the reality, the very substance of heaven begun in the soul.

Now, beloved, I have, as particularly as I could in the time, pointed out to you the distinction between the religion of the law and the religion of the gospel. And now, what religion have you? True religion is always the same, and consists in disinterested love to God and man.* Have you that kind of religion? Or have you the kind that consists, not in disinterested love, but in the pursuit of happiness as the great end. Which have you? The fruits of the Spirit are love, joy, peace. There is no condemnation of such religion. But if any man have not the Spirit of Christ, he is none of His. Now, don't make a mistake here, and allow yourselves to go down to hell with a lie in your right hand, because you have the religion of the law. The Jews failed here, while the Gentiles attained true holiness by the gospel. Oh, how many are deceived and are acting under legal considerations, while they know nothing of the real religion of the gospel!

---

*Editor's Note: Again, in Finney's day "disinterested" did not mean the same thing as "uninterested," but it meant "unselfish" or "without self-centered concern."

12

ON BELIEVING WITH THE HEART*
Romans 10:10

"For with the heart man believeth unto righteousness."

The subject brought to view in this passage requires of us, that we should:

I. *Distinguish carefully between intellectual and heart faith.*
II. *Notice some of the conditions of intellectual faith.*
III. *What are not, and what are, conditions of heart faith.*
IV. *That heart faith is unto righteousness—real obedience.*

I. *Distinguish carefully between intellectual and heart faith.*

There are several different states of mind which are currently called *faith*; this term being obviously used in various senses. So, also, is the term *heart* used in various senses; and indeed, there are but few terms which are not used with some variety of signification. Hence, it becomes very important to discriminate.

Thus, in regard to faith, the Scriptures affirm that the "devils also believe and tremble," but it surely cannot be meant that they have heart faith. They do not "believe unto righteousness."

Faith in the intellect is a judgment—an opinion. The mind judges and is convinced that the facts are so. Whatever the nature of the things believed, this is an involuntary state of mind. Those things believed may be truth; they may relate to God and may embrace the great fundamental facts and doctrines of religion; yet this faith may not result in righteousness. It is often true that persons have their judgments convinced, yet this conviction reaches not beyond their intelligence. Or per-

---

*Sermons on the Way of Salvation, pp. 313-331.

haps it may go so much further as to move their feelings and play on their sensibility, and yet may do nothing more. It may produce no change in the *will*. It may result in no new moral purpose; may utterly fail to reach the voluntary attitude of the mind; and hence, will make no change in the life.

But heart faith, on the other hand, is true confidence, and involves an earnest committal of one's self and interests to the demands of the truth believed. It is precisely such a trust as we have in those to whom we cling in confidence—such as children feel in their real friends and true fathers and mothers. We know they are naturally ready to believe what is said to them, and to commit themselves to the care of those they love.

The heart is in this. It is a voluntary state of mind—always substantially and essentially an act of the will. This kind of faith will, of course, always affect the feelings, and will influence the *life*. Naturally, it tends towards righteousness, and may truly be said to be "unto righteousness." It implies love, and seems in its very nature to unify itself with the affections. The inspired writers plainly did not hold faith to be so purely an act of will as to exclude the affections. Obviously, they made it *include* the affections.

II. *I must now proceed to notice some of the conditions of intellectual faith.*

1. Sometimes, but not always, faith of the heart is essential to faith of the intellect. Thus, it may be necessary that we have heart faith in a man before we are duly prepared to investigate the facts that relate to his character. So, in relation to God, if we lack heart faith in Him, we are in no state to deal fairly with the evidence of His works and ways. Here it is well to notice the vast difference between the irresistible assumptions of the mind respecting God, and those things which we arrive at by study and reasoning. Heart faith seems essential to any candid investigation.

2. It is also essential to our *conviction* as to the truth. I am not prepared to judge candidly concerning a friend unless I have some of this heart faith in him. Suppose I hear a rumor about my best friend affirming something which is deeply scandalous. My regard for him forbids my believing this scandalous report unless it comes most fully sustained by testimony. On the other hand, if I had no heart confidence in him, my intelligence might be thrown entirely off and I might do both him and myself the greatest injustice.

Many of you have had this experience with regard to faith. Often, in the common walks of life, you have found that if it had not been for your heart confidence, you would have been greatly deceived. Your heart held on; at length, the evidence shone out; you were in a condition to judge charitably, and thus you arrived at the truth.

3. Heart faith is especially essential where there is mystery. Of course there are points in religious doctrine which are profoundly mysterious. This fact is not peculiar to religious truth, but is common to

every part of God's works—which is equivalent to saying, "It is common to all real science." Any child can ask me questions which I cannot answer. Without heart confidence, it would be impossible for society to exist. Happily for us, we can often wisely confide when we cannot, by any means, understand.

In the nature of the case, there must be mysteries about God, for the simple reason that He is infinite and we are finite. Yet He reveals enough of himself to authorize us to cherish the most unbounded confidence in Him. Therefore, let no one stumble at this, as though it were some strange thing; for, in fact, the same thing obtains to some extent in all our social relations. In these, we are often compelled to confide in our friends where the case seems altogether suspicious. Yet we confide, and, by-and-by, the truth comes to light, and we are thankful that our heart faith held us from doing them injustice.

4. Again, heart faith is especially in place where there is contradictory evidence.

Often it may seem to you that God must be partial. Then the mind needs the support of confidence in God. You go on safely if there is, underlying all, the deep conviction that God is and must be right. See that woman, stripped of everything—husband, children, all—how can she give any account of this? You may remember the case of a woman who travelled West with her husband and family; there buried her husband and all but two little ones, and then made her weary way back with these on foot. Pinching want and weariness drove her into a stranger's dwelling at nightfall; there a churlish man would have turned her into the street, but his wife had a human heart, and insisted on letting them stay, even if she herself sat up all night. Think of the trying case of that lone widow. She does not sleep; her mingled grief and faith find utterance in the words, *"My heart is breaking, but God is good"*!

How could she make it out that God is good? Just as you would in the case of your husband, if one should tell you he had gone forever, and proved faithless to his vows. You can set this insinuation aside, and let your heart rise above it. You do this on the strength of your heart faith.

So the Christian is with regard to many mysterious points in God's character and ways. You cannot see how God can exist without even beginning to exist; or how He can exist in three persons, since no other beings known to you exist in more than one. You cannot see how He can be eternally good, and yet suffer sin and misery to befall His creatures. But, with heart faith, we do not need to have everything explained. The heart says to its Heavenly Father, "I do not need to catechise Thee, nor ask impertinent questions, for I know it is all right." I know God can never do anything wrong. And so the soul finds a precious joy in trusting, without knowing how the mystery is solved. Just as a wife, long parted from her husband and under circumstances that need explanation, rushes to meet him with her loving welcome, without waiting for one word of explanation, when he returns. Suppose she had waited for the explanation before she could speak a kind word. This might savor of the intellect, but certainly it would not do honor to her heart. For her heart confidence, her husband loves her better than ever, and well he may!

You can understand this; and can you not also apply it to your relations to God? God may appear to your view to be capricious, but you know He is not; may appear unjust, but you know He cannot be. Ah, Christian, when you comprehend the fact of God's wider reach of vision, and of His greater love, then you will cry out, with Job, "Though he slay me, yet will I trust in him." When you have trusted so, think you not that your heart will be as dear to Christ as ever?

III. *Let us next consider what are not, and what are, conditions of heart faith.*

1. It is *not* conditioned upon comprehending the facts to be believed. We may know a thing to be a fact, while yet we are entirely unable to explain it. The reasons and the explanations are quite a different thing from the evidence which sustains the fact, and commends it to our belief.

2. Let it also be borne in mind that it is *not* half as necessary to know all the reasons in the case of God's ways as in man's. The ground of the difference is that we know, in general, that God is always right—a knowledge which we cannot have in regard to man. Of God, our deepest and most resistless convictions assure us that all is right. Our corresponding convictions in the case of man are far from being irresistible. Yet, even with regard to men, we often find that a conviction of their rectitude, which is far less than irresistible, leads us to trust. How much more should our stronger convictions regarding God lead us evermore to trust in Him!

3. Again, this heart faith in God does not rest on our ability to prove even that God exists. Many an earnest Christian has never thought of this, any more than of proving his own existence. An irresistible conviction gives him both, without other proof.

But, positively, *God must be revealed to your inner being so that you are conscious of His existence and presence.* There is not, perhaps, in the universe, a thing of which we can be more certain than of God's existence. The mind may be more deeply acquainted with God than with any other being or thing. Hence, this heart confidence may be based on God's revelations to the inner soul of man. Such revelations may reach the very highest measure of certainty. I do not mean to imply here that we are not certain of the facts of observation. But this is a stronger assurance and certainty. The mind becomes personally acquainted with God, and is conscious of this direct and positive knowledge.

4. A further condition is that the soul be inwardly drawn to God. In our relations to each other, we are sometimes conscious of a peculiar sympathy which draws us towards a friend. This fact is a thing of consciousness, of which we may be quite unable to give any explanation. A similar attraction draws us to God, and seems to be a natural condition of the strongest forms of heart faith.

5. It is quite essential to heart faith that we have genuine love to

God. In the absence of goodwill towards God, there never can be this faith of the heart. The wife has no heart faith in her husband, except as she loves him. Her heart must be drawn to him in real love—else this heart faith will draw back and demand more evidence.

In view of this principle, God takes measures to win our love and draw our hearts to himself. As human beings do towards each other, so *He* manifests His deep interest in us—pours out His blessings on us in lavish profusion, and, in every way, strives to assure us that He is truly our friend. These are His methods to win the confidence of our hearts. When it becomes real to us that we owe everything to God—our health, gifts, all our comforts—then we can bear many dark and trying things. Then we know that God loves us, even though He scourge us; just as children know that parents love them, and mean their good, even though they chastise them. Under these broad and general manifestations of love, they confide, even though there be no present manifestations of love. You may remember how Cecil taught his little daughter the meaning of gospel faith. She came to him, one day, with her hands full of little beads, greatly delighted, to show them. He said to her calmly, "You had better throw them all into the fire." She was almost confounded; but, when she saw he was in earnest, she trustfully obeyed, and cast them in. After a few days, he brought home for her a casket of jewels. "There," said he, "my daughter, you had faith in me the other day, and threw your beads into the fire; that was *faith*; now I can give you things much more precious. Are not these far better?" So you should always believe in God. He has jewels for those who will believe and who will cast away their sins.

IV. *Again, I observe, heart faith is unto righteousness—real obedience.* This trustful and affectionate state of heart naturally leads us to obey God. I have often admired the faith manifested by the old theologian philosophers who held fast to their confidence in God, in spite of the greatest of absurdities. Their faith could laugh at the most absurd principles involved in their philosophy of religious truth. It is a remarkable fact that the greater part of the church have been in their philosophy *necessitarians*, holding not the freedom, but the bondage, of the will—their doctrine being that the will is determined *necessarily* by the strongest motive. President Edwards held these philosophical views, but despite them, he believed that God is supremely good; the absurdities of this philosophy did not shake his faith in God. So all the really Old School theologians hold the absurdities of hyper-Calvinism; as, for example, that God absolutely and supremely controls all the moral actions of all His creatures.

Dr. Beecher, in controversy with Dr. Wilson some years ago, held that obligation implied ability to obey. This Dr. Wilson flatly denied. Whereupon Dr. B. remarked that few men could march up and face such a proposition without winking. It is often the case that men have such heart confidence in God that they will trust Him despite the most flagrant absurdities. There is less superstition in this than I used to suppose and more faith. Men forget their dogmas and philosophy, and, in spite of both, love and confide.

Some men have held monstrous doctrines—even that God is the author of sin, and puts forth His divine efficiency to make men sin, as truly as, by His Spirit, to make them holy. This view was held by Dr. Emmons; yet he was eminently a pious man, of childlike, trustful spirit. It is indeed strange how such men could hold these absurdities at all, and, scarcely less so, how they could hold them and yet confide sweetly in God. Their hearts must have been fixed in this faith by some other influence than that of these monstrous notions in philosophy and theology. For these views of God, we absolutely know were contrary to their *reason* though not to their *reasonings*—a very wide and essential distinction which is sometimes overlooked. The intuitive affirmations of their reason were one thing; the points which they reached by their philosophical reasonings were quite another thing. The former could not lie about God, the latter could. The former laid that sure foundation for heart faith; the latter went to make up their intellectual notions—the absurdities of which (we notice with admiration) never seemed to shake their Christian faith. While these reasonings pushed them on into the greatest absurdities, their reason held their faith and piety straight.

The faith of the heart is proof against all forms of infidelity. Without this, nothing is proof. For if men without piety drop the affirmations of their intuitive reason, and then attempt, philosophically, to reason out all the difficulties they meet with, they almost inevitably stumble.

Heart faith carries one over the manifold mysteries and difficulties of God's providence. In this field there must be difficulties, for no human vision can penetrate to the bottom of God's providential plans and purposes.

So, also, does this faith of the heart carry one over the mysteries of the atonement. It is indeed curious to notice how the heart gets over all these. It is generally the case that the atonement is accepted by the heart unto salvation before its philosophy is understood. It was manifestly so with the apostles; so with their hearers; and so, even with those who heard the Lord Jesus Christ himself. The Bible says but very little indeed on the point of the *philosophy* of the atonement.

So, also, of the doctrine of the Trinity; and so of other doctrines generally. They were known and taught as practical truths, and were accepted as such, long before their philosophy was especially investigated. If any difficulties arose in minds especially inquisitive, it was overcome by heart faith, or settled by the intuitive affirmations of the reason, and not by speculative reasoning.

It is in no sense unreasonable that God should require us to have such faith in Him. Properly considered, He does not require us to believe what we do not know to be true. He does not ask us to renounce our common sense, and exercise a groundless credulity. When we trust His general character, and accept certain dark dispensations of providence as doubtless right, what is it that we believe? Not the special reason for this mysterious dispensation, but we believe that despite its dark aspect to us, God's hand in it is both wise and good. We believe this because we have abundant ground to confide in His general character. It is as if you were to tell me that a known and tried friend of mine had told a lie. I should say, "I cannot believe it. I know him too well." But you say, "Here is the evidence. It looks very dark against him." "Very likely," I reply, "but yet I cannot believe it. There will be some explanation of this. I cannot believe it."

Now I consider myself fully authorized to reject at once all surmises and rumors against my known friend. I am bound to do so until the evidence against him becomes absolutely conclusive. This is altogether reasonable. How much more so in the case of dark things in God's doings!

For it should be considered that man may deceive us; God never can. We do not know man's heart always, to the very core; and if we did, it may change; what once was true, becomes false. But not so with God: our intuitive convictions affirm that God is always good, and always wise; and moreover, that there can never be any declension in His love, or any revolution in His character.

Consequently, Christians are often called on to believe God, not only without, but against, present evidence.

Abraham was called out of his home and country to go into a strange land. He obeyed, not knowing whither he went. He might have asked many questions about the reasons; he does not appear to have asked any.

Commanded to offer up Isaac, he might, with apparent propriety, have expostulated earnestly. He might have said, "Lord, that would be murder! It would outrage the natural affection which Thou hast planted in my bosom. It would encourage the heathen around us in their horrid abominations of making their children pass through the fire to Moloch." All this, and more, he might have said; but, so far as appears, he said nothing—save this: "The Lord commands, and I obey. If He pleases He can raise up my Isaac from the dead." So he went on and virtually offered up his son Isaac, and, "in a figure, received him again from the dead." And God fixed the seal of his approbation on this act of faith, and held it out before all ages as a model of faith and obedience, in spite of darkness and objections.

So Christians are often called to believe without present evidence, other than what comes from their knowledge of God's general character. For a season, God lets everything go against them; yet they believe. Said a woman, passing through great trials, with great confidence in God, "O Lord, I know Thou art good, for Thou hast shown me this; but, Lord, others do not understand this; they are stumbled at it. Canst Thou not show them so that they shall understand this?"

Remarks

1. The demand for reasons often embarrasses our faith. This is one of

the tricks of the devil. He would embarrass our faith by telling us we must understand all God's ways before we believe. Yet we ought to see that this is impossible and unreasonable. Abraham could not see the reasons for God's command to offer Isaac a bloody sacrifice; he might have expostulated; but he did not. The simplicity and beauty of his faith appears all along in this very thing—that *he raised no questions.* He had a deeper insight into God's character. He knew too much of God to question His wisdom or His love. For, a man might understand all the reasons of God's ways, yet this knowledge might do him no good; his heart might rebel even then.

In this light, you may see why so much is said about Abraham's faith. It was gloriously trustful and unquestioning! What a model! No wonder God commends it to the admiring imitation of the world!

2. It is indeed true that faith must often go forward in the midst of darkness. Who can read the histories of believing saints, as recorded in Scripture, without seeing that faith often leads the way through trials? It would be but a sorry development of faith, if, at every step, God's people must know everything before they could trust Him, and must understand all His reasons. Most ample grounds for faith lie in His general character, so that we do not need to understand the special reasons for His particular acts.

3. We are mere infants—miserably poor students of God's ways. His dealings on every side of us appear to us mysterious. Hence, it should be expected that we shall fail to comprehend His reasons, and consequently we must confide in Him without this knowledge. Indeed, just here lies the virtue of faith, that it trusts God on the ground of His general character, while the mind can by no means comprehend His reasons for particular acts. Knowing enough of God to assure us that He must be good, our faith trusts Him, although the special evidence of goodness in particular cases may be wanting.

This is a kind of faith which many do not seem to possess or to understand. Plainly they do not confide in God's dealings.

4. It is manifestly needful that God should train Christians to exercise faith here and now; since in heaven we shall be equally unable to comprehend all His dealings. The holy in heaven will no doubt believe in God; but they must do it by simple faith—not on the ground of a perfect knowledge of God's plans. What a trial of faith it must have been to the holy in heaven to see sin enter our world! They could see few, perhaps none, of the reasons, before the final judgment, and must have fallen back upon the intuitive affirmations of their own minds. The utmost they could say was, "We know God must be good and wise; therefore, we must wait to see the results, and humbly *trust.*"

5. It is not best for parents to explain everything to their children; and especially, they should not take the ground of requiring nothing of which they cannot explain all the reasons. Some profess to take this ground. It is, for many reasons, unwise. God does not train His children so.

Faith is really natural to children. Yet some will not believe their children converted until they can be real theologians. This assumes that they must have all the great facts of the gospel system explained so that they can comprehend their philosophy before they believe them. Nothing can be further from the truth.

6. It sometimes happens that those who are converted in childhood become students of theology in more advanced years; and then, getting proud of their philosophy and wisdom, lose their simple faith and relapse into infidelity. Now I do not object to their studying the philosophy of every doctrine up to the limits of human knowledge; but I do object to their casting away their faith in God. For there is no lack of substantial testimony to the great doctrines of the gospel. Their philosophy may stagger the wisest man; but the evidence of their truth ought to satisfy all alike, the child and the philosopher. Last winter I was struck with this fact—which I mention because it seems to present one department of the evidences of Christianity in a clear light. One judge of the court said to another, "I come to you with my assertion that I inwardly know Jesus Christ, and as truly and as well as I know you. Can you reject such testimony? What would the people of this State say to you if you rejected such testimony on any other subject? Do you not every day let men testify to their own experience?" The judge replied, "I cannot answer you."

"Why, then," replied the other, "do you not believe this testimony? I can bring before you thousands who will testify to the same thing."

7. Again I remark, it is of great use to study the truths of the gospel system theologically and philosophically, for thus you may reach a satisfactory explanation of many things which your heart knew, and clave to, and would have held fast till the hour of your death. It is a satisfaction to you, however, to see the beautiful harmony of these truths with each other, and with the known laws of mind and of all just government.

Yet theological students sometimes decline in their piety, and for a reason which it were well for them to understand. One enters upon this study simple hearted and confiding; but, by-and-by, study expands his views; he begins to be charmed with the explanations he is able to give of many things not understood before; becomes opinionated and proud; becomes ashamed of his former simple heart faith, and thus stumbles fearfully, if not fatally. If you will hold on with all your simple heart confidence to the immutable love and wisdom of God, all will be well. But it never can be well to put your intellectual philosophy in the place of the simplicity of gospel faith.

8. Herein is seen one reason why some students do not become pious. They determine that they will understand everything before they become Christians. Of course they are never converted. Quite in point, here is a case I saw a few years ago. Dr. B., an intelligent but not pious man, had a pious wife, who was leading her little daughter to Christ. The Doctor, seeing this, said to her, "Why do you try to lead that child to Christ? I cannot understand these things myself, although I have

been trying to understand them these many years; how, then, can she?" But some days after, as he was riding out alone, he began to reflect on the matter; the truth flashed upon his mind, and he saw that neither of them could understand God unto perfection—not he any more than his child; while yet either of them could know enough to believe unto salvation.

9. Again, gospel faith is voluntary—a will to trust. I recollect a case in my own circle of friends. I could not satisfy my mind about one of them. At length, after long struggling, I said, "I will repel these things from my mind, and rule out these difficulties. My friend is honest and right; I will believe it, and will trust him none the less for these slanders." In this I was right.

Towards God this course is always right. *It is always right to cast away from your mind all those dark suspicions about Him who can never make mistakes, and who is too good to purpose wrong.* I once said to a sister in affliction, "Can you not believe all this is for your good, though you cannot see *how* it is?" She brightened up, saying, "I must believe in God, and I will."

Who of you have this heart faith? Which of you will now commit yourself to Christ? If the thing required were intellectual faith, I could explain to you how it is reached. It must be through searching the evidence in the case. But heart faith must be reached by simple effort—by a voluntary purpose to *trust*. You who say, "I cannot do this," bow your knees before God and commit yourself to His will; say, "Oh my Saviour! I take You at Your word." This is a simple act of will.

13

CONFORMITY TO THE WORLD*
Romans 12:2

"Be not conformed to this world."

It will be recollected by some who are present that some time ago I made use of this text in preaching in this place, but the object of this evening's discourse is so far different that it is not improper to employ the same text again. The following is the order in which I design to discuss the subject:

I. *To show what is NOT meant by the command of the text.*
II. *To show what is meant by the command, "Be not conformed to this world."*
III. *To mention some of the reasons why this requirement is made upon all who will live a godly life.*
IV. *To answer some objections that are made to the principles laid down.*

I. *I am to show what is not meant by the requirement, "Be not conformed to this world."*

I suppose it is not meant that Christians should refuse to benefit by the useful arts, improvements, and discoveries of the world. It is not only the privilege but the duty of the friends of God to avail themselves of these, and to use for God all the really useful arts and improvements that arise among mankind.

II. *I am to show what is meant by the requirement.*

It is meant that Christians are bound not to conform to the world in the three following things. I mention only these three, not because there

---

Lectures to Professing Christians (1880), pp. 128-154.

are not many other things in which conformity to the world is forbidden, but because these three classes are all that I have time to examine to-night; and further, because these three are peculiarly necessary to be discussed at the present time. The three things are three departments of life, in which it is required that you be not conformed to this world. They are

BUSINESS, FASHION, POLITICS.

In all these departments it is required that Christians should not do as the world does. They should neither receive the maxims, nor adopt the principles, nor follow the practices of the world.

III. *I am to mention some reasons for the command, "Be not conformed to this world."*

You are by no means to act on these same principles, nor from the same motives, nor pursue your object in the same manner that the world does, either in the pursuits of business, or of fashion, or of politics. I shall examine these several departments separately.

FIRST—*Of Business.*

1. The first reason why we are not to be conformed to this world in business is that the principle of the world is that of supreme selfishness. This is true universally in the pursuit of business. The whole course of business in the world is governed and regulated by the maxims of supreme and unmixed selfishness. It is regulated without the least regard to the commands of God, or the glory of God, or the welfare of men. The maxims of business generally current among businessmen, and the habits and usages of businessmen, are all based upon supreme selfishness. Who does not know that in making bargains the businessmen of the world consult their own interest, and seek their own benefit, and not the benefit of those they deal with? Who has ever heard of a worldly man of business making bargains, and doing business for the benefit of those he dealt with? No, it is always for their own benefit. And are Christians to do so? They are required to act on the very opposite principle: "Let no man seek his own, but every man another's wealth." They are required to copy the example of Jesus Christ. Did He ever make bargains for His own advantage? And should His followers adopt the principle of the world—a principle that contains in it the seeds of hell! If Christians do this, is it not the most visionary thing on earth to suppose the world is ever going to be converted to the gospel?

2. They are required not to conform to the world, because conformity to the world is totally inconsistent with the love of God or man.

The whole system recognizes only the love of self. Go through all the ranks of businessmen, from the man that sells candy on the sidewalk at the corner of the street to the greatest wholesale merchant or importer in the United States, and you will find that one maxim runs through the whole: to "buy as cheap as you can, and sell as dear as you can, to look out for number one"; and to do always, as far as the rules of honesty will allow, all that will advance your own interests—let what will become of the interest of others. Ungodly men will not deny that these are the maxims on which business is done in the world. The man who pursues this course is universally regarded as doing business on business principles. Now, are these maxims consistent with holiness, with the love of God and the love of man, with the spirit of the gospel or the example of Jesus Christ? Can a man conform to the world in these principles, and yet love God? Impossible! No two things can be more unlike. Then Christians are by no means to conform to the business maxims of the world.

3. These maxims, and the rules by which business is done in the world, are directly opposite to the gospel of Jesus Christ and the spirit He exhibited, and the maxims He inculcated, and the rules which He enjoined that all His followers should obey on pain of hell.

What was the spirit Jesus Christ exemplified on earth? It was the spirit of self-denial, of benevolence, of sacrificing himself to do good to others. He exhibited the same spirit that God does, who enjoys His infinite happiness in going out of himself to gratify His benevolent heart in doing good to others. This is the religion of the gospel, to be like God, not only doing good, but enjoying it, joyfully going out of self to do good. This is the gospel maxim: "It is more blessed to give than to receive." And again, "Look not every man on his own things, but every man also on the things of others." What says the businessman of the world? "Look out for number one." These very maxims were made by men who knew and cared no more for the gospel than the heathen do. Why should Christians conform to such maxims as these?

4. To conform to the world in the pursuits of business is a flat contradiction of the engagements that Christians make when they enter the church.

What is the engagement that you make when you enter the church? Is it not to renounce the world and live for God, and to be actuated by the Spirit of Jesus Christ, and to possess supreme love to God, and to renounce self, and to give yourself to glorify God, and to do good to men? You profess not to love the world, its honors, or its riches. Around the communion table, with your hand on the broken body of your Saviour, you avouch these to be your principles, and pledge yourself to live by these maxims. And then what do you do? Go away and follow maxims and rules gotten up by men, whose avowed object is to get the world? Is this your way? Then, unless you repent, let me tell you, you will be damned. It is no more certain that any infidel, or any profligate wretch, will go to hell, than that all such professing Christians will go there, who conform to the world. They have double guilt. They are sworn before God to a different course; and when they pursue the business principles of the world, they show that they are perjured wretches.

5. Conformity to the world is such a manifest contradiction of the principles of the gospel that sinners, when they see it, do not and cannot understand from it the true nature and object of the gospel itself.

How can they understand that the object of the gospel is to raise men above the love of the world, and above the influence of the world, and place them on higher ground, to live on totally different principles? When they see professing Christians acting on the same principles with other men, how can they understand the true principles of the gospel, or know what it means by heavenly-mindedness, self-denial, benevolence, and so on?

6. It is this spirit of conformity to the world that has already eaten out the love of God from the church.

Show me a young convert, while his heart is warm, and the love of God glows out from his lips. What does he care for the world? Call up his attention to it, point him to its riches, its pleasures, or its honors; and try to engage him in their pursuit, and he loathes the thought. But let him now go into business, and do business on the principles of the world one year, and you no longer find the love of God glowing in his heart, and his religion has become the religion of conscience, dry, meagre, uninfluential—anything but the glowing love of God moving him to acts of benevolence. I appeal to every man in this house, and if my voice was loud enough I would appeal to every professor of religion in this city, if it is not true. And if anyone should say, "No, it is not so," I should regard it as proof that he *never* knew what it was to feel the glow of a convert's first love.

7. This conformity to the world in business is one of the greatest stumbling blocks in the way of the conversion of sinners.

What do wicked men think, when they see professing Christians, with such professions on their lips, and pretending to believe what the Bible teaches, and yet driving after the world, as eager as anybody, making the best bargains, and dealing as hard as the most worldly? What do they think? I can tell you what they say. They say, "I do not see but these Christians do just as the rest of us do, they act on the same principles, look out as sharp for number one, drive as hard bargains, and get as high interest as anybody." And it must be said that these are not things of which the world accuses Christians slanderously. It is a notorious fact that most of the members of the church pursue the world, as far as appears, in the same spirit, by the same maxims, and to the same degree, that the ungodly do who maintain a character for uprightness and humanity. The world says, "Look at the church. I don't see it as being any better than I am; they go to the full length that I do after the world." If professing Christians act on the same principles with worldly men, as the Lord liveth, they shall have the same reward. They are set down in God's book of remembrance as black hypocrites, pretending to be the friends of God while they love the world. For whoso loveth the world is the enemy of God. They profess to be governed by principles directly opposite to the world; and if they do the same things with the world, they are hypocrites.

8. Another reason for the requirement, "Be not conformed to this world," is the immense, salutary and instantaneous influence it would have if everybody would do business on the principles of the gospel.

Just turn the tables over, and let Christians do business one year on gospel principles. It would shake the world. It would ring louder than thunder. Let the ungodly see professing Christians, in every bargain, consulting the good of the person they are trading with—seeking not their own wealth, but every man another's wealth—living above the world—setting no value on the world any farther than it can be a means of glorifying God. What do you think would be the effect? What effect *did* it have in Jerusalem, when the whole body of Christians gave up their business, and turned out in a body to pursue the salvation of the world? They were only a few ignorant fishermen, and a few humble women, but they turned the world upside down. Let the church live so now, and it would cover the world with confusion of face, and overwhelm them with convictions of sin. Only let them see the church living above the world, and doing business on gospel principles (seeking not their own interests but the interests of their fellowmen) and infidelity would hide its head, heresy would be driven from the church, and this charming, blessed spirit of love would go over the world like the waves of the sea.

SECOND—*Of Fashions.*

Why are Christians required not to follow the fashions of the world?

1. Because the fashions are directly at war with the spirit of the gospel, and they mind earthly things.

What is minding earthly things, if it is not to follow the fashions of the world, that like a tide are continually setting to and fro, and fluctuating in their forms, and keeping the world continually changing? There are many men of large business in the world, and men of wealth, who think they care nothing for the fashions. They are occupied with something else, and they trust the fashions altogether with their tailor, taking it for granted that he will make things all right. But mind, if he should make a garment unfashionable, you would see that they do care about the fashions, and they never would employ that tailor again. Still, at present their thoughts are not much on the fashions. They have a higher object in view. And they think it is beneath the dignity of a minister to preach about fashions. They overlook the fact that with the greater part of mankind fashion is everything. The greater part of the community are not rich, and never expect to be, but they look to the world to enable them to make a "respectable" appearance, and to bring up their families in a "respectable" manner; that is, to "follow the fashions." Nine-tenths of the population never look at anything higher than to do as the world does, or to follow the fashions. For this they strain every nerve. And this is what they set their hearts on, and what they live for.

The merchant and the rich man deceives himself, therefore, if he supposes that fashion is a little thing. The great body of the people mind this; their minds are set upon it—the thing which they look for in life is to have their dress, equipage, furniture, and so on, like other people in the fashion, or "respectable" as they call it.

2. To conform to the world is contrary to their profession.

When people join the church, they profess to give up the spirit that gives rise to the fashions. They profess to renounce the pomps and vanities of the world, to repent of their pride, to follow the meek and lowly Saviour, to live for God. And now, what do they do? You often see professors of religion go to extremes in fashion. Nothing will satisfy them that is not in the height of fashion. And a Christian female dressmaker who is conscientiously opposed to the following of fashions cannot get her bread. She cannot get employment even among professing Christian ladies, unless she follows the fashions in all their countless changes. God knows it is so, and they must give up their business if their conscience will not permit them to follow the changes of fashion.

3. This conformity is a broad and complete approval of the spirit of the world.

What is it that lies at the bottom of all this shifting scenery? What is the cause that produces all this gaudy show and dash and display? It is the love of applause. And when Christians follow the changes of fashion, they pronounce all this innocent. All this waste of money and time and thought, all this feeding and cherishing of vanity and the love of applause, the church sets her seal to when she conforms to the world.

4. Nay, further, another reason is that when Christians follow the fashions of the world, they show that they do in fact love the world.

They show it by their conduct, just as the ungodly show it by the same conduct. As they act alike, they give evidence that they are actuated by one principle—the love of fashion.

5. When Christian professors do this, they show most clearly that they love the praise of men.

It is evident that they love admiration and flattery just as sinners do. Is not this inconsistent with Christian principle: to go right into the very things that are set up by the pride and fashion and lust of the ungodly?

6. Conforming to the world in fashion, you show that you do not hold yourself accountable to God for the manner in which you lay out money.

You practically disown your stewardship of the money that is in your possession. By laying out money to gratify your own vanity and lust, you take off the keen edge of that truth which ought to cut that sinner in two who is living to himself. It is practically denying that the earth is the Lord's, with the cattle on a thousand hills, and all is to be employed for His glory.

7. You show that reputation is your idol.

When the cry comes to your ears on every wind, from the ignorant and the lost of all nations, "Come over and help us, come over and help us" (and every week brings some call to send the gospel, to send tracts and Bibles and missionaries to those who are perishing for lack of knowledge); if you choose to expend money in following the fashions, it is a demonstration that reputation is your idol. Suppose now, for the sake of argument, that it is not prohibited in the Word of God to follow the fashions, and that professing Christians, if they will, may *innocently* follow the fashions (I deny that it is innocent, but suppose it were): does not the fact that they do follow them, when there are such calls for money, time, thought, and the labor to save souls, prove conclusively that they do not love God nor the souls of men?

Take the case of a woman whose husband is in slavery, and she is trying to raise money enough for his redemption. There she is toiling and saving, rising up early and sitting up late, and eating the bread of carefulness, because her husband, the father of her children, the friend of her youth, is in slavery. Now go to that woman and tell her that it is innocent for her to follow the fashions, and dress, and display like her neighbors—will she do it? Why not? She does not desire to do it. She will scarcely buy a pair of shoes for her feet; she grudges almost the bread she eats—so intent is she on her great object to buy her husband's freedom.

Now suppose a person loved God, and the souls of men, and the kingdom of Christ, does he need an express prohibition from God to prevent him from spending his money and his life in following the fashion? No, indeed, he will rather need a positive injunction to take what is needful for his own comfort and the support of his own life. Take the case of Timothy. Did he need a prohibition to prevent him from indulging in the use of wine? So far from it, he was so cautious that it required an express injunction from God to make him drink a little as a medicine. Although he was sick, he would not drink it till he had the word of God for it, because he saw the evils of it so clearly. Now, show me a man or woman (I care not what their professions are) that follows the fashions of the world, and I will show you what spirit they are of.

Now, do not ask me why Abraham, David, and Solomon, who were so rich, did not lay out their money in spreading the kingdom of God. Ah, tell me, did they enjoy the light that professors now enjoy? Did they even know so much as this, that the world can be converted, as Christians now see clearly that it can? But suppose it were as allowable in you as it was in Abraham or David to be rich, and to lay out the property you possess in display, pomp, and fashion; suppose it were perfectly innocent, who that loves the Lord Jesus Christ would wish to lay out money in fashion when they could lay it out to gratify the *all-absorbing* passion to do good to the souls of men?

8. By conforming to the world in fashion, you show that you differ not at all from ungodly sinners.

Ungodly sinners say, "I don't see but that these Christian men and women love to follow the fashions as well as I do." Who does not know that this leads many to infidelity.

9. By following the fashions, you are tempting God to give you up to a worldly spirit.

There are many now that have followed the world, and followed the fashions, till God seems to have given them over to the devil for the destruction of the flesh. They have little or no religious feeling, no spirit of prayer, no zeal for the glory of God or the conversion of sinners: the Holy Spirit seems to have withdrawn from them.

10. You tempt the church to follow the fashions.

Where the principal members, the elders and leaders in the church with their wives and families, are fashionable Christians, they drag the whole church along with them into the train of fashion; and everyone apes them as far as they can, even the lowest servant. Only let a rich Christian lady come out to the house of God in full fashion, and the whole church are set agog to follow as far as they can, and it is a chance if they do not run in debt to do it.

You tempt yourself to pride and folly and a worldly spirit, when you seek to follow the fashions.

Suppose a man, who had been intemperate and was reformed, should go and surround himself with wine and brandy and every seductive liquor, keeping the provocatives of appetite always under his eye, and from time to time tasting a little; does he not tempt himself? Now see that woman who has been brought up in the spirit of pride and show, and who has been reformed, and who has professed to abandon them all; let her keep these trappings, and continue to follow the fashions, and pride will drag her backwards as sure as she lives. She tempts herself to sin and folly.

12. You are tempting the world.

You are setting the world into a more fierce and hot pursuit of these things. The very things that the world loves, and that they are sure to have scruples about their being right, professing Christians fall in with and follow, and thus tempt the world to continue in the pursuit of what will destroy their souls in hell.

13. By following the fashions, you are tempting the devil to tempt you.

When you follow the fashions, you open your heart to him. You keep it for him, empty, swept, and garnished. Every woman that allows herself to follow the fashions may rely upon it. She is helping Satan to tempt her to pride and sin.

14. You lay a great stumbling block before the greatest part of mankind.

There are a few persons who are pursuing greater objects than fashion. They are engaged in the scramble for political power, or they are eager for literary distinction, or they are striving for wealth. And they do not know that their hearts are set on fashion at all. They are following selfishness on a larger scale. But the great mass of the community are influenced mostly by these fluctuating fashions. To this class of persons it is a great and sore stumbling block, when they see professing Christians just as prompt and as eager to follow the changing of fashion as themselves. They see, and say, "What does their profession amount to, when they follow the fashions as much as anybody?" or "Certainly it is right to follow the fashions, for see the professing Christians do it as much as we."

15. Another reason why professing Christians are required not to be conformed to the world in fashion is the great influence their disregarding fashion would have on the world.

If professing Christians would show their contempt for these things, and not pretend to follow them, or regard them, how it would shame the world, and convince the world because they were living for another object—for God and for eternity! How irresistible it would be! What an overwhelming testimony in favor of our religion! Even the apparent renunciation of the world, by many orders of monks, has doubtless done more than anything else to put down the opposition to their religion, and give it currency and influence in the world. Now suppose all this was hearty and sincere, and coupled with all that is consistent and lovely in Christian character, and all that is zealous and bold in labors for the conversion of the world from sin to holiness. What an influence it would have! What thunders it would pour into the ears of the world to wake them up to follow after God!

THIRD—*In Politics.*

I will show why professing Christians are required not to be conformed to the world in politics.

1. Because the politics of the world are perfectly dishonest.

Who does not know this? Who does not know that it is the proposed policy of every party to cover up the defects of their own candidate, and the good qualities of the opposing candidate? And is not this dishonest? Every party holds up its candidate as a piece of perfection, and then aims to ride him into office by any means fair or foul. No man can be an honest man who is committed to a party to go with them, let them do what they may. And can a Christian do it, and keep a conscience void of offense?

2. To conform to the world in politics is to tempt God.

By falling in with the world in politics, Christians are guilty of setting up rulers over them by their own vote, who neither fear nor love God, and who set the law of God at defiance, break the Sabbath, and gamble, and commit adultery, and fight duels, and swear profanely, and leave the laws unexecuted at their pleasure, and that care not for the weal or woe of their country, so long as they can keep their office. I say Christians do this. "For it is plain that where parties are divided, as they are in this country, there are Christians enough to turn the scale in any election. Now let Christians take the ground that they will not vote for a dishonest man, or a Sabbath-breaker, or gambler, or whoremonger, or duelist, for any office, and no party could ever nominate such a character with any hope of success." But on the present system, where men will let the laws go unexecuted, and give full swing to mobs, lynch-murders, or robbing the mails, or anything else, so they can run in their own candidate who will give them the offices; any man is a dishonest man who will do it, be he professor or non-professor. And can a Christian do this and be blameless?

3. By engaging with the world in politics, Christians grieve the Spirit of God.

Ask any Christian politician if he ever carried the Spirit of God with him into a political campaign? Never. I would by no means be understood to say that Christians should refuse to vote and to exercise their lawful influence in public affairs. But they ought not to follow a party.

4. By following the present course of politics, you are contributing your aid to undermine all government and order in the land.

Who does not know that this great nation now rocks and reels, because the laws are broken and trampled under foot, and the executive power refuses or dares not act? Either the magistrate does not wish to put down disorder, or he temporizes and lets the devil rule. And so it is in all parts of the country, and with all parties. And can a Christian be consistent with his profession and vote for such men to office?

5. You lay a stumbling block in the way of sinners.

What do sinners think when they see professing Christians acting with them in their political measures which they themselves know to be dishonest and corrupt? They say, "We understand what we are about, we are after office, we are determined to carry our party into power, we are pursuing our own interest; but these Christians profess to live for another and a higher end, and yet here they come and join with us as eager for the loaves and fishes as the rest of us." What greater stumbling block can they have?

6. You prove to the ungodly that professing Christians are actuated by the same spirit as themselves.

Who can wonder that the world is incredulous as to the reality of religion? If they do not look for themselves into the Scriptures, and there learn what religion is; if they are governed by the rules of evidence from what they see in the lives of professing Christians, they ought to be incredulous. They ought to infer, so far as this evidence goes, that professors of religion do not themselves believe in it. It is the fact. I doubt, myself, whether the great mass of professors believe the Bible.

7. They show, so far as their evidence can go, that there is no change of heart.

What is it? Is it going to the communion table once in a month or two, and sometimes to prayer meeting? Is that a change of heart, when they are just as eager in the scramble for office as any others? The world must be fools to believe in a change of heart on such evidence.

8. Christians ought to cease from conformity to the world in politics, from the influence which such a course would have on the world.

Suppose Christians were to act perfectly conscientious and consistent in this matter, and say, "We will not vote for any man to office, unless he fears God, and will rule the people in righteousness." Ungodly men would not set men as candidates, who set the laws at defiance. No. Every candidate would be obliged to show that he was prepared to act from higher motives, and that he would lay himself out to make the country prosperous, and to promote virtue, and to put down vice and oppression and disorder, and to do all he could to make the people happy and *holy*! It would shame the dishonest politicians to show that the love of God and man is the motive that Christians have in view. And a blessed influence would go over the land like a wave.

IV. *I am to answer some objections that are made against the principles here advanced.*

1. In regard to *business*:

Objection. "If we do not transact business on the same principles on which ungodly men do it, we cannot compete with them, and all the business of the world will fall into the hands of the ungodly. If we pursue our business for the good of others, if we buy and sell on the principle of not seeking our own wealth, but the wealth of those we do business with, we cannot sustain a competition with worldly men, and they will get all the business."

Let them have it, then. You can support yourself by your industry in some humbler calling, and let worldly men do all the business.

Objection. "But then, how should we get money to spread the gospel?"

A holy church that would act on the principles of the gospel would spread the gospel faster than all the money that ever was in New York, or that ever will be. Give me a holy church that would live above the world, and the work of salvation would roll on faster than with all the money in Christendom.

Objection. "But we must spend a great deal of money to bring forward an educated ministry."

Ah! if we had a *holy* ministry, it would be far more important than an educated ministry. If the ministry were holy enough, they would do without so much education. God forbid that I should undervalue an educated ministry. Let ministers be educated as well as they can, the more the better, if they are only holy enough. But it is all a farce to suppose that a literary ministry can convert the world. Let the ministry have the spirit of prayer, let the baptism of the Holy Ghost be upon them, and they will spread the gospel. Only let Christians live as they ought, and the church would shake the world. If Christians in New York would do it, the report would soon fill every ship that leaves the port, and waft the news on every wind, till the earth was full of excitement and inquiry, and conversions would multiply like the drops of morning dew.

Suppose you were to give up your business, and devote yourselves entirely to the work of extending the gospel. The church once did so, and you know what followed. When that little band in Jerusalem gave up their business and spent their time in the work of God, salvation spread like a wave. And I believe, if the whole Christian church were to turn right out, and convert the world, it would be done in a very short time.

And further, the fact is that you would not be required to give up your business. If Christians would do business in the spirit of the gospel, they would soon engross the business of the world. Only let the world see that if they go to a Christian to do business, he will not only deal honestly, but benevolently. He would actually consult the interest of the person he deals with as if it were his own interest, and so who would deal with anybody else? What merchant would go to an ungodly man to trade, who he knew would try to get the advantage of him and cheat him, while he knew that there were Christian merchants to deal with that would consult his interests as much as they do their own? Indeed, it is a known fact that there are now Christian merchants in this city, who regulate the prices of the articles they deal in. Merchants come in from the country, and inquire around to see how they can buy goods, and they go to these men to know exactly what articles are worth at a fair price, and govern themselves accordingly.

The advantage, then, is all on one side. The church can make it for the interest of the ungodly to do business on right principles. The church can regulate the business of the world, and woe to them if they do not.

2. In regard to *fashion*:

Objection. "Is it best for Christians to be singular?"

Certainly; Christians are bound to be singular. They are called to be a peculiar people; that is, a singular people, essentially different from the rest of mankind. To maintain that we are not to be singular is the same as to maintain that we are to be conformed to the world.

But the question now regards fashion, in dress, equipage, and so on. And here I will confess that I was formerly myself in error. I believed, and I taught, that the best way for Christians to live was to dress so as not to be noticed, and to follow the fashions and changes so as not to appear singular, and so nobody would be led to think of their being different from others in these particulars. But I have seen my error, and now wonder greatly at my former blindness. It is your duty to dress so plain as to show to the world that you place no sort of reliance in the things of fashion, and set no value at all on them, but despise and neglect them altogether. But unless you are singular, unless you separate yourselves from the fashions of the world, you show that you do value them. There is no way in which you can bear a proper testimony by your lives against the fashions of the world, but by dressing plainly. I do not mean that you should *study singularity*, but that you should consult *convenience and economy*, although it may be singular.

Objection. "But if we dress plain, the attention of people will be taken with it."

The reason of it is this, so few do it that it is a novelty and everybody stares when they see a professing Christian so strict as to disregard the fashions. Let them all do it, and the only thing you show by it is that you are a Christian, and do not wish to be confounded with the ungodly. Would it not tell on the pride of the world, if all the Christians in it were united in bearing a practical testimony against its vain show?

Objection. "But in this way you carry religion too far away from the multitude. It is better not to set up an artificial distinction between the church and the world."

The direct reverse of this is true. The nearer you bring the church to the world the more you annihilate the reasons that ought to stand out in view to the world for their changing sides and coming over to the church. Unless you go right out from them, and show that you are not of them in any respect, and carry the church so far as to have a broad interval between saints and sinners, how can you make the ungodly feel that so great a change is necessary?

Objection. "But this change which is necessary is a change of heart."

True; but will not a change of heart produce a change of life?

Objection. "You will throw obstacles in the way of persons becoming Christians. Many respectable people will become disgusted with religion, and if they cannot be allowed to dress and be Christians, they will take to the world altogether."

This is just about as reasonable as it would be for a temperance man to think he must get drunk now and then to avoid disgusting the intemperate and to retain his influence over them. The truth is that persons ought to know, and ought to see in the lives of professing Christians, that if they embrace religion, they must be weaned from the world, and must give up the love of the world, and its pride, and show, and folly, and live a holy life, in watchfulness, and self-denial, and active benevolence.

Objection. "Is it not better for us to disregard this altogether, and not pay any attention to such little things, and let them take their course; let the milliner and mantua-maker do as they please, and follow the usages of society in which we live, and the circle in which we move?"

Is this the way to show contempt for the fashions of the world? Do people ordinarily take this course of showing their contempt for a thing by practicing it? Why, the way to show your abhorrence of the world is to follow along in the customs and the fashions of the world! Precious reasoning this.

Objection. "No matter how we dress, if our hearts are right?"

Your heart right! Then your heart may be right when your conduct is all wrong? Just as well might the profane swearer say, "No matter what words I speak, if my heart is right." No, your heart is not right unless your conduct is right. What is outward conduct, but the acting out of the heart? If your heart were right, you would not wish to follow the fashions of the world.

Objection. "What is the standard of dress? I do not see the use of all your preaching, and laying down rules about plain dress unless you give us a standard."

This is a mighty stumbling block with many. But to my mind the matter is extremely simple. The whole can be comprised in two simple rules. One is—"Be sure, in all your equipage, dress, and furniture, to show that you have no fellowship with the designs and principles of those who are aiming to set off themselves, and to gain the applause of men." The other is—"Let economy be first consulted, and then convenience. Follow Christian economy; that is, save all you can for Christ's service; and then, let things be as convenient as Christian economy will admit."

Objection. "Would you have us all to turn Quakers, and put on their plain dress?"

Who does not know that the plain dress of the Quakers has won for them the respect of all the thinking part of the ungodly in the community? Now, if they had coupled with this: zeal for God, weanedness from the world, contempt for riches, the self-denying labor for the conversion of sinners to Christ which the gospel enjoins, and the clear views of the

169

plan of salvation which the gospel inculcates, they would long since have converted the world. And if all Christians would imitate them in their plain dress (I do not mean the precise cut and fashion of their dress, but in a *plain* dress, throwing contempt upon the fashions of the world), who can doubt that the conversion of the world would hasten on apace?

Objection. "Would you make us all into Methodists?"

Who does not know that the Methodists, when they were noted for their plain dress and for renouncing the fashions and show of the world, used to have power with God in prayer—and that they had the universal respect of the world as sincere Christians? And who does not know that since they have laid aside this peculiarity, and conformed to the world in dress and other things, and seemed to be trying to lift themselves up as a denomination, and gain influence with the world, they are losing the power of prayer? Would to God they had never thrown down this wall. It was one of the leading excellences of Wesley's system to have his followers distinguished from others by a plain dress.

Objection. "We may be proud of a plain dress as well as of a fashionable dress. The Quakers are as proud as we are."

So may any good thing be abused. But that is no reason why it should not be used, if it can be shown to be good. I put it back to the objector: "Is that any reason why a Christian female, who fears God and loves the souls of men, should neglect the means which may make an impression that she is separated from the world, and pour contempt on the fashions of the ungodly in which they are dancing their way to hell?"

Objection. "This is a small thing, and ought not to take up so much of a minister's time in the pulpit."

This is an objection often heard from worldly professors. But the minister that fears God will not be deterred by it. He will pursue the subject until such professing Christians are cut off from their conformity to the world, or cut off from the church. It is not merely the dress, as dress, but it is the conformity to the world in dress and fashion that is the great stumbling block in the way of sinners. How can the world be converted, while professing Christians are conformed to the world? What good will it do to give money to send the gospel to the heathen, when Christians live so at home? Well might the heathen ask, "What profit will it be to become Christians, when those who are Christians are pursuing the world with all the hot haste of the ungodly?" The great thing necessary for the church is to break off from conformity to the world, and then they will have power with God in prayer, and the Holy Ghost will descend and bless their efforts, and the world will be converted.

Objection. "But if we dress so, we shall be called fanatics."

Whatever the ungodly may call you, fanatics, Methodists, or anything, you will be known as Christians, and in the secret consciences of men you will be acknowledged as such. It is not in the power of unbelievers to pour contempt on a holy church that is separated from the world. How was it with the early Christians? They lived separate from the world and it made such an impression that even infidel writers say of them, "These men win the hearts of the mass of the people, because they give themselves up to deeds of charity, and pour contempt on the world." Depend upon it, if Christians would live so now, the last effort of hell would soon be expended in vain to defeat the spread of the gospel. Wave after wave would flow abroad, till the highest mountain tops were covered with the waters of life.

3. In regard to *politics*:

Objection. "In this way, by acting on these principles, and refusing to unite with the world in politics, we could have no influence in government and national affairs."

I answer, first, "It is so now." Christians, as such, have no influence. There is not a Christian principle adopted because it is Christian, or because it is according to the law of God.

I answer, secondly, "If there is no other way for Christians to have an influence in the government, but by becoming conformed to the world in their habitual principles and parties, then let the ungodly take the government and manage it in their own way, and you go and serve God."

I answer, thirdly, "No such result will follow." Directly the reverse of this would be the fact. Only let it be known that Christian citizens will on no account assist bad men into office; only let it be known that the church will go only for men that will aim at the public good, and both parties will be sure to set up such men. And in this way, the church could legitimately exert an influence by compelling all parties to bring forward only men who are worthy of an honest man's support.

Objection. "In this way the church and the world will be arrayed against each other."

The world is too selfish for this. You cannot make parties so. Such a line can never be a permanent division. For one year the ungodly might unite against the church, and leave Christians in a small minority. But in the end, the others would form two parties, each courting the suffrages of Christians, by offering candidates such as Christians can conscientiously vote for.

Remarks

1. By non-conformity to the world, you may save much money for doing good.

In one year a greater fund might be saved by the church than has ever been raised for the spread of the gospel.

2. By non-conformity to the world, a great deal of time may be saved for doing good that is now consumed and wasted in following the fashions, and obeying the maxims, and joining in the pursuits of the world.

3. At the same time, Christians in this way would preserve their peace of conscience, would enjoy communion with God, would have the spirit of prayer, and would possess far greater usefulness.

Is it not time something was done? Is it not time that some church struck out a path that should not be conformed to the world, but should be according to the example and Spirit of Christ?

You profess that you want to have sinners converted. But what avails it if they sink right back again into conformity with the world? Brethren, I confess, I am filled with pain in view of the conduct of the church. Where are the proper results of the glorious revivals we have had? I believe they were genuine revivals of religion and outpourings of the Holy Ghost that the church has enjoyed the last ten years. I believe the converts of the last ten years are among the best Christians in the land. Yet after all, the great body of them are a disgrace to religion. Of what use would it be to have a thousand members added to the church, if it remains just as it is now? Would religion be any more honored by it in the estimation of ungodly men? One holy church, that is really crucified to the world, and the world to it, would do more to recommend Christianity, than all the churches in the country living as it now does. Oh, if I had strength of body to go through the churches again, instead of preaching to convert sinners I would preach to bring up the churches to the gospel standard of holy living. Of what use is it to convert sinners and make them such Christians as these? Of what use is it to try to convert sinners and make them feel there is something in religion, and then when they go to trade with you, or meet you in the street, have you contradict it all, and tell them by your conformity to the world that there is nothing in it?

Where shall I look, where shall the Lord look, for a church like the first church that will come out from the world, and be separate, and give themselves up to serve God? Oh, if this church would do so. But it is of little use to make Christians, if they are not better. Do not understand me as saying that the converts made in our revivals are spurious. But they live so as to be a disgrace to religion. They are so stumbled by old professors that many of them do more harm than good. The more there are of them, the more occasion infidelity seems to find for her jeers and scoffs.

Now, do you believe that God commands you not to be conformed to the world? Do you believe it? And dare you obey it, let people say what they will about you? Dare you now separate yourselves from the world, and never again be controlled by its maxims, and never again copy its practices, and never again will to be whiffled here and there by its fashions? I know a man that lives so, I could mention his name, he pays no attention to the customs of the world in this respect, and what is the result? Wherever that man goes, he leaves the impression behind that he is a Christian. Oh, if one church would do so, and would engage in it with all the energy that men of the world engage in their business, they would turn the world upside down. Will you do so? Will you break off from the world now, and enter into covenant with God, and declare that you will dare to be singular enough to be separate from the world, and from this time set your faces as a flint to obey God, let the world say what they will? Dare you do it? Will you do it?

14

LOVE IS THE WHOLE OF RELIGION*
Romans 13:10

"Love worketh no ill to his neighbor; therefore love is the fulfilling of the law."

In speaking from these words, I design:

   I. *To make some remarks on the nature of love.*
  II. *To show that love is the whole of religion.*
 III. *Some things that are not essential to perfect love.*
 IV. *Some things that are essential.*
  V. *Some of the effects of perfect love.*

I. *I am to make some remarks on the nature of love.*
1. The first remark I have to make is that there are various forms under which love may exist.

The two principal forms, so far as religion is concerned, are benevolence and complacency. Benevolence is an affection of the mind or an act of the will. It is willing good, or a desire to promote the happiness of its object. Complacency is esteem or approbation of the character of its object. Benevolence should be exercised towards all beings, irrespective of their moral character. Complacency is due only to the good and holy.

2. Love may exist either as an affection or as an emotion.

When love is an affection, it is voluntary, or consists in the act of the will. When it is an emotion, it is involuntary. What we call feelings, or emotions, are involuntary. They are not directly dependent on the will, or controlled by a direct act of will. The virtue of love is mostly when it is in the form of an affection. The happiness of love is mostly when it is in the form of an emotion. If the affection of love be very strong, it produces

---

Lectures to Professing Christians (1880), pp. 419-436.

a high degree of happiness, but the emotion of holy love is happiness itself.

I said that the emotion of love is involuntary. I do not mean that the will has nothing to do with it, but that it is not the result of a mere or direct act of the will. No man can exercise the emotion of love by merely willing it. And the emotion may often exist in spite of the will. Individuals often feel emotions rising in their minds, which they know to be improper, and they try by direct effort of will to banish them from their minds; and finding that impossible, therefore conclude that they have no control of these emotions. But they may always be controlled by the will in an indirect way. The mind can bring up any class of emotions it chooses by directing the attention sufficiently to the proper object. They will be certain to rise in proportion as the attention is fixed, provided the will is right in regard to the object of attention. So of those emotions which are improper or disagreeable; the mind may be rid of them by turning the attention entirely away from the object and not allowing the thoughts to dwell on it.

3. Ordinarily, the emotions of love towards God are experienced when we exercise love toward Him in the form of affection.

But this is not always the case. We may exercise good will towards any object, and yet at times feel no sensible emotions of love. It is not certain that even the Lord Jesus Christ exercised love towards God in the form of emotion at all times. So far as our acquaintance with the nature of the mind goes, we know that a person may exercise affection and be guided and be governed by it constantly, in all his actions, without any felt emotion of love towards its object at the time. Thus a husband and father may be engaged in laboring for the benefit of his family, and his very life controlled by affection for them, while his thoughts are not so engaged upon them as to make him feel any sensible emotions of love to them at the time. The things about which he is engaged may take up his mind so much that he has scarcely a thought of them; and so he may have no felt emotion towards them; and yet, he is all the time guided and governed by affection for them. Observe here, that I use the term, "affection," in the sense of President Edwards, as explained by him in his celebrated *Treatise on the Will.* An affection in his treatise is an act of the will or a volition.

4. Love to our neighbor naturally implies the existence of love to God, and love to God naturally implies love to our neighbor.

The same is declared in the 8th verse, "Owe no man anything, but to love one another: for he that loveth another hath fulfilled the law. For this, Thou shalt not commit adultery, Thou shalt not kill, Thou shalt not steal, Thou shalt not bear false witness, Thou shalt not covet; and if there be any other commandment, it is briefly comprehended in this saying, namely, Thou shalt love thy neighbor as thyself." Here it is taken for granted that love to our neighbor implies the existence of love to God; otherwise, it could not be said that "he that loveth another hath fulfilled the law." The apostle James recognizes the same principle, when he says, "If ye fulfill the royal law according to the scripture, Thou shalt love thy neighbor as thyself, ye do well." Here love to our neighbor is spoken of as constituting obedience to the whole law. Benevolence, that is, good will to our neighbor, naturally implies love to God. It is love to the happiness of being. So the love of complacency towards holy beings naturally implies love to God, as a being of infinite holiness.

II. *I am to show that love is the whole of religion.*

In other words, all that is required of man by God consists in love, in various modifications and results. Love is the sum total of all.

1. The first proof I shall offer is that the sentiment of love is taught in the text, and many other passages of Scripture.

The Scriptures fully teach that love is the sum total of all the requirements both of the law and gospel. Our Saviour declares that the great command, "Thou shalt love the Lord thy God with all thy heart, soul, mind and strength, and thy neighbor as thyself," is the sum total of all the law and the prophets, or implies and includes all that the whole Scriptures, the law and the gospel require.

2. God is love, and to love is to be like God, and to be perfect in love is to be perfect as God is perfect.

All God's moral attributes consist in love acting under certain circumstances and for certain ends. God's justice in punishing the wicked, His anger at sin, and the like, are only exercises of His love to the general happiness of His kingdom. So it is in man. All that is good in man is some modification of love. Hatred to sin is only love to virtue acting itself out in opposing whatever is opposed to virtue. So true faith implies and includes love, and faith which has no love in it, or that does not work by love, is no part of religion. The faith that belongs to religion is an affectionate confidence in God. There is a kind of faith in God which has no love in it. The devil has that kind of faith. The convicted sinner has it. But there is no religion in it. Faith might rise even to the faith of miracles, and yet if there is no love in it, it amounts to nothing. The apostle Paul in the 13th chapter of 1 Corinthians, says, "Though I have the gift of prophecy, and understand all mysteries, and all knowledge; and though I have all faith, so that I could remove mountains, and have not charity, I am nothing."

Just so it is with repentance. The repentance that does not include love is not "repentance towards God." True repentance implies obedience to the law of love, and consequent opposition to sin.

III. *I will mention some things that are not essential to perfect love.*

1. The highest degree of emotion is not essential to perfect love.

It is manifest that the Lord Jesus Christ very seldom had the highest degree of emotion of love, and yet He always had perfect love. He generally manifested very little emotion or excitement. Excitement is always proportioned to the strength of the emotions as it consists in them. The Saviour seemed generally remarkably calm. Sometimes His indignation was strong, or He had grief for the hardness of men's hearts; and sometimes we read that He rejoiced in spirit. But He was commonly calm, and manifested no high degree of emotion. And it is plainly not essential to perfect love that the emotion of love should exist in a high degree.

2. Perfect love does not exclude the idea of increase in love or growth in grace.

I suppose the growth of the mind in knowledge to all eternity naturally implies growth in love to all eternity. The Lord Jesus Christ, in His human nature, grew in stature and in favor with God and man. Doubtless, as a child, He grew in knowledge, and as He grew in knowledge, He grew in love toward God as well as in favor with God. His love was perfect when He was a child, but it was greater when He became a man. As a human being, He probably always continued to increase in love to God as long as He lived. From the nature of mind, we see that it may be so with all the saints in glory, that their love will increase to all eternity, and yet it is always perfect love.

3. It is not essential to perfect love that love should always be exercised towards all individuals alike.

We cannot think of all individuals at once. You cannot even think of every individual of your acquaintance at once. The degree of love towards an individual depends on the fact that the individual is present to the thoughts.

4. It is not essential to perfect love that there should be the same degree of the spirit of prayer for every individual, or for the same individual at all times.

The spirit of prayer is not always essential to pure and perfect love. The saints in heaven have pure and perfect love for all beings, yet we know not that they have the spirit of prayer for any. You may love any individual with a very strong degree of love, and yet not have the spirit of prayer for that individual. That is, the Spirit of God may not lead you to pray for the salvation of that individual. You do not pray for the wicked in hell. *The spirit of prayer depends on the influences of the Holy Ghost leading the mind to pray for things agreeable to the will of God.* You cannot pray in the Spirit with the same degree of fervor and faith for all mankind. Jesus Christ said expressly that He did not pray for all mankind: "I pray not for the world." Here has been a great mistake in regard to the spirit of prayer. Some suppose that Christians have not done all their duty when they have not prayed in faith for every individual, as long as there is a sinner on the earth. Then Jesus Christ never did all His duty, for He never did this. God has never told us He will save all mankind, and never gave us any reason to believe He will do it. How then can we pray in faith for the salvation of all? What has that faith to rest on?

5. Perfect love is not inconsistent with those feelings of languor or constitutional debility which are the necessary consequence of exhaustion or ill health.

We are so constituted that excitement naturally and necessarily exhausts our powers. But love may be perfect, notwithstanding. Though one may feel more disposed to lie down and sleep than to pray, yet his love may be perfect. The Lord Jesus Christ often felt this weariness and exhaustion, when the spirit was still willing, but the flesh was weak.

IV. *What is essential to perfect love.*

1. It implies that there is nothing in the mind inconsistent with love.

No hatred, malice, wrath, envy, or any other malignant emotions that are inconsistent with pure and perfect love are present.

2. That there is nothing in the life inconsistent with love.

All the actions, words, and thoughts are continually under the entire and perfect control of love.

3. That the love to God is supreme.

The love to God is completely supreme, and so entirely above all other objects that nothing else is loved in comparison with God.

4. That love to God is disinterested.

God is loved for what He is; not for His relation to us, but for the excellence of His character.

5. That love to our neighbor should be equal; i.e., that his interest and happiness should be regarded by us of equal value with our own, and he and his interests are to be treated accordingly by us.

V. *I am to mention some of the effects of perfect love.*

1. One effect of perfect love to God and man will certainly be delight in self-denial for the sake of promoting the interests of God's kingdom and the salvation of sinners.

See affectionate parents, how they delight in self-denial for the sake or promoting the happiness of their children. There is a father; he gives himself up to exhausting labor, day by day, and from year to year, through the whole of a long life, rising early, and eating the bread of carefulness continually, to promote the welfare of his family. And he counts all this self-denial and toil not a grief or a burden, but a delight, because of the love he bears to his family. See that mother; she wishes to educate her son at college. And now, instead of finding it painful, it is a joy to her to sit up late and labor incessantly to help him. That is because she really loves her son. Such parents rejoice more in conferring gifts on their children, than they would in enjoying the same things themselves. What parent does not enjoy a piece of fruit more in giving it to his little child than in eating it himself? The Lord Jesus Christ enjoyed more solid satisfaction in working out salvation for mankind than any of His saints can ever enjoy in receiving favors at His hands. He testified that it is more blessed to give than to receive. This was the joy set before Him, for which He endured the cross and despised the shame. His love was so great for mankind that it constrained Him to undertake this work, and sustained Him triumphantly through it. The apostle Paul did not count it a grief and a hardship to be hunted from place to place, imprisoned, scourged, stoned, and counted the offscouring of all things for the sake of spreading the gospel and saving souls. It was his joy. The love of Christ so constrained him; he had such a desire to do good that it was his highest delight to lay himself on that altar as a sacrifice to the cause. Other individuals have had the same mind with the apostle. They have been known who would be willing to live a thousand years, or to the end of time, if they could be employed in doing good, in promoting the kingdom of God, and saving the souls of men—willing to forego even sleep and food to benefit objects they so greatly love.

2. It delivers the soul from the power of legal motives.

Perfect love leads a person to obey God, not because he fears the wrath of God, or hopes to be rewarded for doing this or that, but because he loves God and loves to do the will of God. There are two extremes on this subject. One class makes virtue to consist in doing right, simply because it is right, without any reference to the will of God, or any influence from God. Another class makes virtue to consist in acting from love to the employment, but without reference to God's authority, as a Ruler and Lawgiver. Both of these are in error. To do a thing simply because he thinks it right, and not out of love to God is not virtue. Neither is it virtue to do a thing because he loves to do it, with no regard to God's will. A woman might do certain things because she knew it would please her husband, but if she did the same thing merely because she loved to do it, and with no regard to her husband it would be no virtue as it respects her husband. If a person loves God, as soon as he knows what is God's will, he will do it because it is God's will. Perfect love will lead to universal obedience to do God's will in all things, because it is the will of God.

3. The individual who exercises perfect love will be dead to the world.

I mean by this that he will be cut loose from the influence of worldly considerations. Perfect love will so annihilate his selfishness that he will have no will but the will of God, and no interest but God's glory. He will not be influenced by public sentiment, or what this and that man will say or think. See that woman! What is she not willing to do from natural affection for her husband? She is willing to cut loose from all her friends, as much as if she was dead to them, and not pay the least regard to what they say, and leave all the riches, and honors, and delights they can offer, to join the individual whom she loves, and live with him in poverty, in disgrace, and in exile. Her affection is so great that she does it joyfully, and is ready to go from a palace to any cottage or cave on earth, and be perfectly happy. And all that her friends can say against the man of her affection has not the least influence on her mind, except to make her cling the more closely to him. This one *all-absorbing* affection has actually killed all the influences that used to act on her. To attempt to influence her by such things is in vain. There is only one avenue of approach to her mind—only one class of motives move her—and that is through the object of her affection.

So far as the philosophy of mind is concerned, the perfect love of God operates in the same way. The mind that is filled with perfect love is impossible to divert from God, while love continues in exercise. Take away his worldly possessions, his friends, his good name, his children; send him to prison, beat him with stripes, bind him to the stake, fill his flesh full of pine knots and set them on fire; and then leave him his God, and he is happy. His strong affection can make him insensible to all things else. He is as if he were dead to all the world, except his God. Cases have been known of marytrs who, while their bodies were frying at the stake, were so perfectly happy in God, as to lose their sense of pain. Put such a one in hell, in the lake of fire and brimstone, and as long as he enjoys God, and the love of God fills his soul, he is happy.

Who has not witnessed or heard of cases of affection, approaching in degree to what I have described, where a person is in fact dead to all other things and lives only for the loved object. How often do you see fond parents, who live for an only child, and when that child dies, wish themselves dead. Sometimes a husband and wife have such an absorbing affection for each other that they live for nothing else; and if the husband dies, the wife pines away and dies also. The soul-absorbing object for which she lived is gone, and why should she live any longer? So, when an individual is filled with the perfect love of God, he wishes to live only to love and serve God. He is dead to the world, dead to his own reputation, and has no desire to live for any other reason, here, or in heaven, or anywhere else in the universe, but to glorify God. He is willing to live, here or anywhere else, and suffer and labor a thousand years, or to all eternity, if it will glorify God.

I recollect hearing a friend say, often, "I don't know that I have one thought of living a single moment for any other purpose than to glorify God, any more than I should think of leaping right into hell." This was said soberly and deliberately, and the whole life of that individual corresponded with the declaration. He was intelligent, sober-minded, and honest, and I have no doubt expressed what had been the fullest conviction of his mind for years. What was this but perfect love? What more does any angel in heaven do than this? His love may be greater in degree, because his strength is greater. But the highest angel could not love more perfectly than to be able to say in sincerity, "I should as soon think of leaping into hell as of living one moment for any other object but to glorify God." What could Jesus Christ himself say more than that?

4. It is hardly necessary to say that perfect joy and peace are the natural results of perfect love.

But I wish to turn your attention here to what the apostle says in the 13th chapter of 1 Corinthians, when speaking of charity, or love. You will observe that the word here translated "charity" is the same that is in other places rendered *love*. It means love. "Though I speak with the tongues of men and of angels, and have not charity, I am become as sounding brass, or a tinkling cymbal. And though I have the gift of prophecy, and understand all mysteries, and all knowledge; and though I have all faith so that I could remove mountains, and have not charity, I am nothing." He might have even the faith of miracles so strong that he could move mountains from their everlasting foundations, and yet have no love. "And though I bestow all my goods to feed the poor, and though I give my body to be burned, and have not charity, it profiteth me nothing." You see how far he supposes a man may go without love. "Charity suffereth long." Long-suffering is meekness under opposition or injury. This is one of the effects of love; to bear great provocations, and not retaliate or revile again. Love is kind, or affectionate in all intercourse with others; never harsh or rude, or needlessly giving pain to any. Love envieth not; never dislikes others because they are more thought of or noticed, more honored or useful, or make greater attainments in knowledge, happiness or piety. Is not puffed up with pride, but always humble and modest. Doth not behave itself unseemly, but naturally begets a pleasant and courteous deportment towards all. However unacquainted the individual may be with the ways of society, who is actuated by perfect love, he always appears well; it is natural to him to be so kind and gentle and courteous. Seeketh not her own, or has no selfishness. Is not easily provoked. This is always the effect of love. See that mother! How long she bears with her children, because she loves them. If you see an individual that is testy, or crusty, easily flying into a passion when anything goes wrong—he is by no means perfect in love, if he has any love. To be easily provoked is always a sign of pride. If a person is full of love, it is impossible to make him exercise sinful anger while love continues. He exercises such indignation as God exercises, and as holy angels feel at what is base and wrong, but he will not be provoked by it. Thinketh no evil. Show me a man that is always suspicious of the motives of others, and forever putting the worst construction on the words and actions of his fellowmen, and I will show you one who has the devil in him, not the Holy Ghost. He has that in his own mind which makes him think evil of others. If an individual is honest and simplehearted himself, he will be the last to think evil of others. He will not be always smelling heresy or mischief in others. On the contrary, such persons are often liable to be imposed on by designing men, not from any want of good sense, but from the effect of love. They do not suspect evil, where the exterior appears fair, nor without the strongest proof. Love rejoiceth not in iniquity, but rejoiceth in the truth. See a man who exults at his neighbor's fall, or cries out, "I told you so;" and I tell you, that man is far enough from being perfect in love. Beareth all things, all provocations and injuries, without revenge. Believeth all things, instead of being hard to be convinced of what is in favor of others, he is always ready to believe good wherever there is the least evidence of it. Hopeth all things; even where there is reason to suspect evil, as long as there is room for hope, by putting the best construction upon the thing which it will bear. Where you see an individual that has not this spirit, rest assured, he is by no means sincerely in love. Nay, he has no love at all.

I might pursue this course of thought farther, but have not time. Love worketh no ill to his neighbor. Mark that, *no ill*! Perfect love never overreaches, nor defrauds, nor oppresses, nor does any ill to a neighbor. Would a man under the influence of perfect love sell his neighbor rum? Never. Would a man that loved God with all his heart, perfectly, hold his neighbor as a slave? Love worketh no ill to his neighbor; slavery denies him the wages that he has earned, and perhaps sells him, and tears him away from his family, deprives him of the Bible, and endeavors as far as possible to make him a brute. There cannot be greater falsehood and hypocrisy than for a man who will do that to pretend that he loves God, now that light is shed upon this subject, and the attention of men has turned upon it. Will a man hate his own flesh? How can he love God when he hates or injures his neighbor?

I designed to remark on one other effect of perfect love. It uniformly shows itself in great efforts for the sanctification of the church and the salvation of souls. Where a person is negligent or deficient in either of these, he is by no means perfect in love, whatever may be his pretensions.

Remarks

1. You see why it is true, what the apostle James says, "If any man among you seem to be religious, and bridleth not his tongue, but deceiveth his own heart, this man's religion is vain."

The man that professes to be religious, and yet allows himself to speak against his neighbor with an unbridled tongue to injure his neighbor, deceives himself; if he thinks he loves his neighbor as himself. Strange love!

2. There may be much light in the mind concerning religion, without love.

You often see individuals, who understand a great deal intellectually about religion, and who can spread it out before others, while it is plain they are not actuated by the spirit of love. They have not the law of kindness on their lips.

3. Those individuals who have much religious knowledge and zeal, without love, are most unlovely and dangerous persons.

They are always censorious, proud, heady and high-minded. They may make a strong impression, but do not produce true religion. They zealously affect you, but not well.

4. The drift of a man's zeal will determine the character of his religion.

It will show whether the light in his mind is accompanied with love. If it is, his zeal will not be sectarian in its character. Show me a man full of jealousy towards all that do not belong to his sect or party, and there is a man far enough from perfect love.

True love is never denunciatory or harsh. If it has occasion to speak of the faults of others, it does it in kindness, and with sorrow. Perfect love cannot speak in a rough or abusive manner, either to or of others. It will not lay great stress on the mere circumstantials of religion, nor be sticklish for particular measures or forms. Many will contend fiercely either for or against certain things, as for or against new measures; but if they were full of love, they would not do it. The zeal that is governed by perfect love will not spend itself in contending for or against any forms in religion, nor attack minor errors and evils. Love leads to laying stress on the fundamentals in religion. It cleaves to warm-hearted Christians, no matter of what denomination they may be, and loves them, and delights to associate with them.

This zeal is never disputatious or full of controversy. Find a man who loves to attend ecclesiastical meetings, and enters into all the janglings of the day, and that man is not full of love. To a mind filled with holy love, it is exceedingly painful to go to such meetings and see ministers dividing into parties, and maneuvering, and caucussing, and pettifogging, and striving for mastery. Find an individual who loves controversy in the newspapers; he is not full of love. If he was, he would rather be abused, and reviled, and slandered, either in person or by the papers, than turn aside to defend himself or to reply. He would never return railing for railing, but contrariwise blessing. And as much as possible, he would live peaceably with all men.

5. How much that is called religion has no love.

How much of what passes for works of religion is constrained by outward causes and influences, and not by the inward power of love. It ought to be better understood than it is, that unless love is the mainspring, no matter what the outward action may be, whether praying, praising, giving, or anything else, there is no religion in it. How much excitement, that passes for religion, has no love. How much zeal has no religion in it. See that man always full of bitter zeal, and, if reproved for it, flying to the example of Paul, when he said, "Thou child of the devil." If he was under the influence of perfect love, he would see that his circumstances are so different as not to justify the exercise of such a spirit.

6. Those religious excitements which do not consist in the spirit of love are not revivals of religion.

Perhaps the church may be much excited, and bustle about with a great show of zeal, and boisterous noise, but have no tenderness of spirit. Perhaps those who go about may show a spirit of insolence, and rudeness, and pick a quarrel with every family they visit. I once knew a young man who acknowledged that he aimed at making people angry, and the reason he assigned was, that it often brought them under conviction, and so issued in conversion. And so it might if he should go in and utter horrid blasphemies in their presence until they were frightened into a consideration of their own character. But who would defend such conduct on the ground that such was now and then the result? And if this be the character of the excitement, it may be a revival of wrath, and malice, and all uncharitableness, but it is not a revival of religion. I do not mean that when some or many are filled with wrath, it is certain proof that there is no revival of religion; but that when the excitement has this prevailing character, it is not a true revival of religion. Some among them may have the spirit of love, but certainly those who are filled with a bitter disputatious zeal are not truly religious. Religion may be in some persons revived, but in the main, in such cases, it is a revival of irreligion.

7. When persons profess to be converted, if love is not the ruling feature in their character they are not truly converted.

However well they may appear in other respects, no matter how clear their views, or how deep their feelings, if they have not the spirit of love to God, and love to man, they are deceived. Let no such converts be trusted.

8. See what the world will be, when mankind are universally actuated by a spirit of love.

We learn that the time will come when there shall be nothing to hurt or destroy, and when the spirit of love will universally prevail. What a change in society! What a change in all the methods of doing business, and in all the intercourse of mankind, when each shall love his neighbor as himself, and seek the good of others as his own! Could one of the saints of the present day revisit the earth at that period, he would not know the world in which he had lived; all things would be so altered. Is it possible, he would exclaim, "that this is the earth; the same earth that used to be so full of jangling, and oppression, and fraud?"

9. The thing on which the Lord Jesus Christ is bent is to bring all mankind under the influence of love.

Is it not a worthy object? He came to destroy the works of the devil; and this is the way to do it. Suppose the world was full of such men as Jesus Christ was in His human nature—compare it with what it is now. Would not such a change be worthy of the Son of God? What a glorious end—to fill the earth with love.

10. It is easy to see what makes heaven.

It is love—perfect love. And it is easy to see what makes heaven begun on earth, in those who are full of love. How sweet their temper; what delightful companions; how blessed to live near them: so full of candor, so kind, so gentle, so careful to avoid offence, so divinely amiable in all things!

And is this to be attained by men? Can we love God in this world with all the heart, and soul, and strength, and mind? It is our privilege and our duty to possess the Spirit of Christ—shall we exhibit the spirit of the devil? Beloved, let our hearts be set on perfect love, and let us give God no rest till we feel our hearts full of love—till all our thoughts and all our lives are full of love to God and love to man. Oh, when will the church come up to this ground? Only let the church be full of love, and she will be fair as the moon, clear as the sun, and terrible to all wickedness in high places and low places as an army with banners.

15

DOUBTFUL ACTIONS ARE SINFUL*
Romans 14:23

"He that doubteth is damned if he eat, because he eateth not of faith; for whatsoever is not of faith is sin."

It was a custom among the idolatrous heathen to offer the bodies of slain beasts in sacrifice. A part of every beast that was offered belonged to the priest. The priests used to send their portion to market to sell, and it was sold in the shambles as any other meat. The Christian Jews that were scattered everywhere were very particular as to what meats they ate, so as not even to run the least danger of violating the Mosaic law; and they raised doubts, and created disputes and difficulties among the churches. This was one of the subjects about which the church of Corinth was divided and agitated, until they finally wrote to the apostle Paul for directions. A part of the First Epistle to the Corinthians was doubtless written as a reply to such inquiries. It seems there were some who carried their scruples so far that they thought it not proper to eat any meat; for if they went to market for it, they were continually in danger of buying that which was offered to idols. Others thought it made no difference; they had a right to eat meat, and they would buy it in the market as they found it, and give themselves no trouble about the matter. To quell the dispute they wrote to Paul, and in chapter 8 he takes up the subject and discusses it in full.

"Now, as touching things offered unto idols, we know that we all have knowledge. Knowledge puffeth up, but charity edifieth. And if any man think that he knoweth anything, he knoweth nothing yet as he ought to know. But if any man love God, the same is known of him. As

---

Lectures to Professing Christians (1880), pp. 36-58.

concerning therefore the eating of those things that are offered in sacrifice unto idols, we know that an idol is nothing in the world, and that there is none other God but one. For though there be that are called gods, whether in heaven or in earth, (as there be gods many, and lords many,) but to us there is but one God, the Father, of whom are all things, and we in him, and one Lord Jesus Christ, by whom are all things, and we by him. Howbeit there is not in every man that knowledge; for some with conscience of the idol unto this hour eat it as a thing offered unto an idol; and their conscience, being weak, is defiled."

"His conscience is defiled"; that is, he regards it as a meat offered to an idol, and is really practising idolatry. The eating of meat is a matter of total indifference, in itself.

"But meat commendeth us not to God; for neither if we eat are we the better; neither if we eat not, are we the worse. But take heed lest by any means this liberty of yours become a stumbling block to them that are weak. For if any man see thee, which hast knowledge, sit at meat in the idol's temple, shall not the conscience of him which is weak be emboldened to eat those things offered to idols; and through thy knowledge shall the weak brother perish for whom Christ died?"

Although they might have a sufficient knowledge on the subject to know that an idol is nothing, and cannot make any change in the meat itself, yet if they should be seen eating meat that was known to have been offered to an idol, those who were weak might be emboldened by it to eat the sacrifices as such, or as an act of worship to the idol, supposing all the while that they were but following the example of their more enlightened brethren.

But when you sin so against the brethren, and wound their weak conscience, you sin against Christ. "Wherefore, if meat make my brother to offend, I will eat no more flesh while the world standeth, lest I make my brother to offend."

This is his benevolent conclusion, that he would rather forego the use of flesh altogether than be the occasion of drawing a weak brother away into idolatry. For, in fact, to sin so against a weak brother is to sin against Christ.

In writing to the Romans he takes up the same subject—the same dispute had existed there. After laying down some general maxims and principles, he gives this rule:

"Him that is weak in faith receive ye, but not to doubtful disputation. For one believeth that he may eat all things; another who is weak, eateth herbs."

There were some among them who chose to live entirely on vegetables, rather than run the risk of buying in the shambles flesh which had been offered in sacrifice to idols. Others ate their flesh as usual, buying what was offered in market, asking no questions for the sake of conscience. Those who lived on vegetables charged the others with idolatry. And those that ate flesh accused the others of superstition and weakness. This was wrong.

"Let not him that eateth, despise him that eateth not; and let not him which eateth not, judge him that eateth; for God hath received him. Who art thou that judgest another man's servant? to his own master he standeth or falleth; yea, he shall be holden up; for God is able to make him stand."

There was also a controversy about observing the Jewish festival days and holy days. A part supposed that God required this, and therefore they observed them. The others neglected them because they supposed God did not require the observance.

"One man esteemeth one day above another; another esteemeth every day alike. Let every man be fully persuaded in his own mind. He that regardeth the day, regardeth it unto the Lord; and he that regardeth not the day, to the Lord he doth not regard it. He that eateth, eateth to the Lord, for he giveth God thanks; and he that eateth not, to the Lord he eateth not, and giveth God thanks. For none of us liveth to himself, and no man dieth to himself. For whether we live, we live unto the Lord; and whether we die, we die unto the Lord: whether we live therefore, or die, we are the Lord's. For to this end Christ both died, and rose, and revived, that he might be Lord both of the dead and living. But why dost thou judge thy brother? Or why dost thou set at nought thy brother? For we shall all stand before the judgment seat of Christ. For as it is written, As I live, saith the Lord, every knee shall bow to me, and every tongue shall confess to God. So then every one of us shall give account of himself to God. Let us not therefore, judge one another any more: but judge this rather, that no man put a stumbling block, or an occasion to fall in his brother's way."

Now mark what he says.

"But if thy brother be grieved with thy meat, now walkest thou not charitably: destroy not him with thy meat, for whom Christ died."

That is, I know that the distinction of meats into clean and unclean is not binding under Christ; but to him that believes in the distinction, it is a crime to eat indiscriminately, because he does what he believes to be contrary to the commands of God. "All things indeed are pure, but it is evil to him that eateth with offence." Every man should be persuaded in his own mind that what he is doing is right. If a man eat of meats called unclean, not being clear in his mind that it is right, he offends God.

"It is good neither to eat flesh, nor to drink wine, nor *any thing* whereby thy brother stumbleth, or is offended, or is made weak."

This is a very useful hint to those wine-bibbers and beer-guzzlers, who think the cause of temperance is not going to be ruined by their not giving up wine and beer, when it is notorious, to every person of the least observation, that these things are the greatest hindrance to the cause all over the country.

"Hast thou faith? Have it to thyself before God. Happy is he that condemneth not himself in THAT thing which he alloweth. And he that doubteth is damned if he eat, because he eateth not of faith; for whatsoever is not of faith is sin."

The word rendered damned means condemned, or adjudged guilty of breaking the law of God. If a man doubts whether it is lawful to do a thing, and while in that state of doubt he does it, he displeases God; he breaks the law and is condemned whether the thing be in itself right or wrong. I have been thus particular in explaining the text in its connection with the context, because I wished fully to satisfy your minds of the correctness of the principle laid down—*That if a man does that of which he doubts the lawfulness, he sins, and is condemned for it in the sight of God.*

Whether it is lawful in itself is not the question. If he doubts its lawfulness, it is wrong in him.

There is one exception which ought to be noticed here, and that is where a man as honestly and fully doubts the lawfulness of omitting to do it as he does the lawfulness of doing it. President Edwards meets this exactly in his 39th resolution:

"Resolved, never to do anything that I so much question the lawfulness of, as that I intend, at the same time, to consider and examine afterwards, whether it be lawful or not: except I as much question the lawfulness of the omission."

A man may have equal doubts whether he is bound to do a thing or not to do it. Then all that can be said is that he must act according to the best light he can get. But where he doubts the lawfulness of the act, but has no cause to doubt the lawfulness of the omission, and yet does it, he sins and is condemned before God, and must repent or be damned. In further examination of the subject, I propose:

I. *To show some reasons why a man is criminal for doing that of which he doubts the lawfulness.*

II. *To show its application to a number of specific cases.*

III. *Offer a few inferences and remarks, as time may allow.*

I. *I am to show some reasons for the correctness of the principle laid down in the text—that if a man does that of which he doubts the lawfulness, he is condemned.*

1. One reason why an individual is condemned if he does that of which he doubts the lawfulness, is—That *if God so far enlightens his mind as to make him doubt the lawfulness of an act, he is bound to stop there and examine the question and settle it to his satisfaction.*

To illustrate this: suppose your child is desirous of doing a certain thing, or suppose he is invited by his companions to go somewhere, and he doubts whether you would be willing, do you not see that it is his duty to ask you? If one of his schoolmates invites him home, and he doubts whether you would like it, and yet goes, is not this palpably wrong?

Or suppose a man cast away on a desolate island, where he finds no human being, and he takes up his abode in a solitary cave, considering himself as all alone and destitute of friends, or relief, or hope; but every morning he finds a supply of nutritious and wholesome food prepared for him, and set by the mouth of his cave, sufficient for his wants that day. What is his duty? Do you say, "He does not know that there is a being on the island, and therefore he is not under obligations to anyone?" Does not gratitude, on the other hand, require him to search and find out his unseen friend, and thank him for his kindness? He cannot say, "I doubt whether there is any being here, and therefore will do nothing but eat my allowance and take my ease, and care for nothing." His not searching for his benefactor would of itself convict him of as desperate wickedness of heart, as if he knew who it was, and refused to return thanks for the favors received.

Or suppose an Atheist opens his eyes on this blessed light of heaven, and breathes this air, sending health and vigor through his frame. Here is evidence enough of the being of God to set him on the inquiry after that Great Being who provides all these means of life and happiness. And if he does not inquire for further light, if he does not care, if he sets his heart against God, he shows that he has the heart as well as the intellect of an Atheist. He has, to say the least, evidence that there MAY BE a God. What then is his business? Plainly, it is to set himself honestly, and with a most child-like and reverent spirit, to inquire after Him and pay Him reverence. If, when he has so much light as to doubt whether there may not be a God, he still goes around as if there were none, and does not inquire for truth and obey it, he shows that his heart is wrong, and that it says let there be no God.

There is a Deist, and here a book claiming to be a revelation from God. Many good men have believed it to be so. The evidences are such as to have perfectly satisfied the most acute and upright minds of its truth. The evidences, both external and internal, are of great weight. To say there are NO evidences is itself enough to bring any man's soundness of mind into question, or his honesty. There is, to say the least that can be said, sufficient evidence to create a doubt whether it is a fable and an imposture. This is in fact but a small part, but we will take it on this ground. Now is it his duty to reject it? No Deist pretends that he can be so fully persuaded in his own mind, as to be free from all doubt. All he dares to attempt is to raise cavils and create doubts on the other side. Here, then, it is his duty to stop, and not oppose the Bible, until he can prove without a doubt that it is not from God.

So with the Unitarian. Granting (what is by no means true) that the evidence in the Bible is not sufficient to remove all doubts that Jesus Christ is God; yet it affords evidence enough to raise a doubt on the other side, and he has no right to reject the doctrine as untrue, but is bound humbly to search the Scriptures and satisfy himself. Now, no intelligent and honest man can say that the Scriptures afford "no evidence" of the divinity of Christ. They do afford evidence which has convinced and fully satisfied thousands of the most acute minds, and who have before been opposed to the doctrine. No man can reject the doctrine without a doubt, because here is evidence that it may be true. And if it may be true, and there is reason to doubt if it is not true, then he rejects it at his peril.

Then the Universalist. Where is one who can say he has not so much as a doubt whether there is not a hell, where sinners go after death into endless torment. He is bound to stop and inquire, and search the Scriptures. It is not enough for him to say he does not believe in a hell. It may be there is, and if he rejects it, and goes on reckless of the truth whether there is or not, that itself makes him a rebel against God. He doubts whether there is not a hell which he ought to avoid, and yet he acts as if he was certain and had no doubts. He is condemned. I once knew a physician who was a Universalist, and who has gone to eternity to try the reality of his speculations. He once told me that he had strong doubts of the truth of Universalism, and had mentioned his doubts to a minister, who confessed that he, too, doubted its truth, and he did not believe there was a Universalist in the world who did not.

2. For a man to do a thing when he doubts whether it is lawful shows that he is selfish, and has other objects besides doing the will of God.

It shows that he wants to do it to gratify himself. He doubts whether God will approve of it, and yet he does it. Is he not a rebel? If he honestly wished to serve God, when he doubted he would stop and inquire and examine until he was satisfied. But to go forward while he is in doubt, shows that he is selfish and wicked, and is willing to do it whether God is pleased or not, and that he wants to do it, whether it is right or wrong. He does it because he wants to do it, and not because it is right.

3. To act thus is an impeachment of the divine goodness.

He assumes it as uncertain whether God has given a sufficient revelation of His will, so that he might know his duty if he would. He virtually says that the path of duty is left so doubtful that he must decide at a venture.

4. It indicates slothfulness and stupidity of mind.

It shows that he had rather act wrongly than use the necessary diligence to learn and know the path of duty. It shows that he is either negligent or dishonest in his inquiries.

5. It manifests a reckless spirit.

It shows a want of conscience, an indifference to right, a setting aside of the authority of God, a disposition not to do God's will, and not to care whether He is pleased or displeased, a desperate recklessness and headlong temper that is the height of wickedness.

The principle, then, which is so clearly laid down in the text and context, and also in the chapter which I read from Corinthians, is fully sustained by examination—That for a man to do a thing, when he doubts the lawfulness of it, is sin, for which he is condemned before God, and must repent or be damned.

II. *I am now to show the application of this principle to a variety of particular cases in human life.*

1. I will mention some cases where a person may be equally in doubt with respect to the lawfulness of a thing, whether he is bound to do it or not to do it.

Take the subject of Wine at the Communion Table.

Since the temperance reformation has brought up the question about the use of wine, and various wines have been analyzed and the quantity of alcohol they contain has been disclosed; and since the difficulty has been shown of getting wines in this country that are not highly alcoholic, it has been seriously doubted by some whether it is right to use such wines as we can get here in celebrating the Lord's Supper. Some are strong in the belief that wine is an essential part of the ordinance, and that we ought to use the best wine we can get, and there leave the matter. Others say that we ought not to use alcoholic or intoxicating wine at all; and that, since wine is not in their view essential to the ordinance, it is better to use some other drink. Both these classes are undoubtedly equally conscientious and desirous to do what they have most reason to believe is agreeable to the will of God. And others, again, are in doubt on the matter. I can easily conceive that some conscientious persons may be very seriously in doubt which way to act. They are doubtful whether it is right to use alcoholic wine, and are doubtful whether it is right to use any other drink in the sacrament. Here is a case that comes under President Edwards' rule, "where it is doubtful in my mind, whether I ought to do it or not to do it," and which men must decide according to the best light they can get, honestly, and with a single desire to know and do what is most pleasing to God.

I do not intend to discuss this question of the use of wine at the communion, nor is this the proper place for a full examination of the subject. I introduced it now merely for the purpose of illustration. But since it is before us, I will make two or three remarks.

(1) I have never apprehended as much evil as some do from the use of common wine at the communion. I have not felt alarmed at the danger or evil of taking a sip of wine, a teaspoonful or so, once a month, or once in two months, or three months. I do not believe that the disease of intemperance (and intemperance, you know, is in reality a disease of the body) will be either created or continued by so slight a cause. Nor do I believe it is going to injure the temperance cause so much as some have supposed. And therefore, where a person uses wine as we have been accustomed to do, and is fully persuaded in his own mind, he does not sin.

(2) On the other hand, I do not think that the use of wine is any way essential to the ordinance. Very much has been said and written and printed on the subject which has darkened counsel by words without knowledge. To my mind there are stronger reasons than I have anywhere seen exhibited for supposing that wine is not essential to this ordinance. Great pains have been taken to prove that our Saviour used wine that was unfermented, when he instituted the supper, and which therefore contained no alcohol. Indeed, this has been the point chiefly in debate. But in fact it seems just as irrelevant as it would be to discuss the question of whether he used wheat or oaten bread, or whether it was leavened or unleavened. Why do we not hear *this* question vehemently discussed? Because all regard it as unessential.

In order to settle this question about the wine, we should ask, "What is the meaning of the ordinance of the Supper? What did our Saviour design to do?" It was to take the two staple articles for the support of life, food and drink, and use them to represent the necessity and virtue of the atonement.

It is plain that Christ had that view of it; for it corresponds with what He says, "My flesh is meat indeed, and my blood is drink indeed." So He poured out water in the temple, and said, "If any man thirst, let him come unto me and drink." He is called the "Bread of Life." thus it was customary to show the value of Christ's sufferings by food and drink. Why did He take bread instead of some other article of food? Those who know the history and usages of that country will see that He chose that article of food which was in most common use among the people. When I was in Malta, it seemed as if a great part of the people lived on bread alone. They would go in crowds to the market place, and buy each a piece of coarse bread, and stand and eat it. Thus the most common and the most universally wholesome article of diet is chosen by Christ to represent His flesh. Then why did He take wine to drink? For the same reason; wine is the common drink of the people, especially at their meals, in all those countries. It is sold there for about a cent a bottle, wine being cheaper than small beer is here. In Sicily I was informed that wine was sold for five cents a gallon, and I do not know but it was about as cheap as water. And you will observe that the Lord's Supper was first observed at the close of the Feast of the Passover, at which the Jews always used wine. The meaning of the Saviour's in this ordinance, then, is this: "As food and drink are essential to the life of the body, so His body and blood, or His atonement, are essential to the life of the soul." For myself, I am fully convinced that wine is not essential to the communion, and I should not hesitate to give water to any individual who conscientiously preferred it. Let it be the common food and drink of the country, the support of the life to the body, and it answers the end of the institution. If I was a missionary among the Esquimaux Indians, where they live on dried seal's flesh and snow-water, I would administrate the Supper in those substances. It would convey to their minds the idea that they cannot live without Christ.

I say, then, that if an individual is fully persuaded in his own mind, he does not sin in giving up the use of wine. Let this church be fully persuaded in their own minds, and I shall have no scruple to do either way, if they will substitute any other wholesome drink that is in common use, instead of the wine. And at the same time, I have no objection myself against going on in the old way.

Now, do not lose sight of the great principle that is under discussion. It is this: where a man doubts honestly, whether it is lawful to do a thing, and doubts equally, on the other hand whether it is lawful to omit doing it, he must pray over the matter, and search the Scriptures, and get the best light he can on the subject, and then act. And when he does this, he is by no means to be judged or censured by others for the course he takes. "Who are thou that judgest another man's servant?" And no man is authorized to make his own conscience the rule of his neighbor's conduct.

A similar case is where a minister is so situated that it is necessary for him to go a distance on the Sabbath to preach, as where he preaches to two congregations, and the like. Here he may honestly doubt what is his duty, on both hands. If he goes, he appears to strangers to disregard the Sabbath. If he does not go, the people will have no preaching. The direction is; let him search the Scriptures, get the best light he can, make it a subject of prayer, weigh it thoroughly, and act according to his best judgment.

So in the case of a Sabbath-school teacher. He may live at a distance from the school, and be obliged to travel to it on the Sabbath, or they will have no school. And he may honestly doubt which is his duty, to remain in his own church on the Sabbath, or to travel there, five, eight, or ten miles, to a destitute neighorhood to keep up the Sabbath school. Here he must decide for himself, according to the best light he can get. And let no man set himself up to judge over a humble and conscientious disciple of the Lord Jesus.

You see that in all these cases it is understood and is plain that the design is to honor God, and the sole ground of doubt is which course will really honor Him. Paul says, in reference to all laws of this kind, "He that regardeth the day, regardeth it unto the Lord; and he that regardeth not the day, to the Lord he doth not regard it." The design is to do right, and the doubt regards the means of doing it in the best manner.

2. I will mention some cases where the DESIGN is wrong; where the object is to gratify self, and the individual has doubts whether he may do it lawfully. I shall refer to cases concerning which there is a difference of opinion—to acts of which the least that can be said is that a man must have doubts of their being lawful.

(1) Take, for instance, the making and vending of alcoholic drinks.

After all that has been said on this subject, and all the light that has been thrown upon the question, is there a man living in this land who can say he sees no reason to doubt the lawfulness of this business? To say the least that can be said, there can be no honest mind but must be brought to doubt it. We suppose, indeed, that there is no honest mind but must know it is unlawful and criminal. But take the most charitable supposition possible for the distiller or the vender, and suppose he is not fully convinced of its unlawfulness. We say he must, at least, DOUBT its lawfulness. What is he to do then? Is he to shut his eyes to the light, and go on, regardless of truth; so long as he can keep from seeing it? No. He may cavil and raise objections as much as he pleases, but he knows that he has doubts about the lawfulness of his business; and if he doubts, and still persists in doing it, without taking the trouble to examine and see what is right, he is just as sure to be damned as if he went on in the face of knowledge. You hear these men say, "Why, I am not fully persuaded in my own mind that the Bible forbids making or vending ardent spirits." Well, suppose you are not fully convinced, suppose all your possible and conceivable objections and cavils are not removed, what then? You know you have doubts about its lawfulness. And it is not necessary to take such ground to convict you of doing wrong. If you doubt its lawfulness, and yet persist in doing it, you are on the way to hell.

(2) So where an individual is engaged in an employment that requires him to break the Sabbath.

As for instance, attending on a post-office that is opened on the Sabbath, or a turnpike gate, or in a steam-boat, or any other employment that is not work of necessity. There are always some things that must be done on the Sabbath; they are works of absolute necessity or of mercy.

But suppose a case in which the labor is not necessary, as in the transportation of the mail on the Sabbath, or the like. The least that can be said, the lowest ground that can be taken by charity itself, without turning fool, is, that the lawfulness of such employment is doubtful. And if they persist in doing it, they sin, and are on the way to hell. God has sent out the penalty of his law against them, and if they do not repent they must be damned.

(3) Owning stocks in steamboat and railroad companies, in stages, canal boats, etc., that break the Sabbath.

Can any such owner truly say he does not doubt the lawfulness of such an investment of capital? Can charity stoop lower than to say that man must strongly doubt whether such labor is a work of necessity or mercy? It is not necessary in the case to demonstrate that it is unlawful—though that can be done fully, but only to show so much light as to create a doubt of its lawfulness. Then, if he persists in doing it, with that doubt unsatisfied, he is condemned—and lost.

(4) The same remarks will apply to all sorts of lottery gambling. He doubts.

(5) Take the case of those indulgences of appetite which are subject of controversy, and which, to say the least, are of doubtful right.

(a) The drinking of wine, and beer, and other fermented intoxicating liquors. In the present aspect of the temperance cause, is it not questionable at least whether making use of these drinks is not transgressing the rule laid down by the apostle: "It is good neither to eat flesh nor drink wine, nor anything whereby thy brother stumbleth, or is offended, or made weak"? No man can make me believe he has no doubts of the lawfulness of doing it. There is no certain proof of its lawfulness, and there is strong proof of its unlawfulness, and every man who does it while he doubts the lawfulness is condemned, and if he persists is damned.

If there is any sophistry in all this, I should like to know it, for I do not wish to deceive others nor to be deceived myself. But I am entirely deceived if this is not a simple, direct, and necessary inference, from the sentiment of the text.

(b) Tobacco. Can any man pretend that he has no doubt that it is agreeable to the will of God for him to use tobacco? No man can pretend that he doubts the lawfulness of his OMISSION of these things. Does any man living think that he is bound in duty to make use of wine, or strong beer, or tobacco, as a luxury? No. The doubt is all on one side.

What shall we say then, of that man who doubts the lawfulness of it, and still fills his face with the poisonous weed? He is condemned.

(c) I might refer to tea and coffee. It is known generally, that these substances are not nutritious at all, and that nearly eight millions of dollars are spent annually for them in this country. Now, will any man pretend that he does not doubt the lawfulness of spending all this money for that which is of no use, and which are *well known* (to all who have examined the subject) to be positively injurious, intolerable to weak stomachs, and as much as the strongest can dispose of? And all this while the various benevolent societies of the age are loudly calling for *help* to send the gospel abroad and save a world from hell? To think of the church alone spending millions upon their tea tables—is there no doubt here?

(6) Apply this principle to various amusements.

(a) The theatre. There are vast multitudes of professors of religion who attend the theatre. And they contend that the Bible nowhere forbids it. Now mark. What Christian professor ever went to a theatre and did not doubt whether he was doing what was lawful. I by no means admit that it is a point which is only doubtful. I suppose it is a very plain case, and can be shown to be, that it is unlawful. But I am now only meeting those of you, if there are any here, who go to the theatre, and are trying to cover up yourselves in the refuge that the Bible nowhere expressly forbids it.

(b) Parties of pleasure, where they go and eat and drink to surfeiting. Is there no reason to doubt whether that is such a use of time and money as God requires? Look at the starving poor, and consider the effect of this gaiety and extravagance, and see if you will ever go to another such party or make one, without doubting its lawfulness. Where can you find a man, or a woman, that will go so far as to say they have no doubt? Probably there is not one honest mind who will say this. And if you doubt, and still do it, you are condemned.

You see that this principle touches a whole class of things about which there is a controversy, and where people attempt to parry off by saying it is not worse than to do so and so; and thus they seek to get away from the condemning sentence of God's law. But in fact, if there is a doubt, it is their duty to abstain.

(c) Take the case of balls, of novel reading, and other methods of wasting time. Is this God's way to spend your lives? Can you say you have no doubt of it?

(7) Making calls on the Sabbath. People will make a call, and then make an apology about it. "I did not know that it was quite right, but I thought I would venture it." He is a Sabbath-breaker in heart, at all events, because he doubts.

(8) Compliance with worldly customs on New Year's Day. Then the ladies are all at home, and the gentlemen are running all about town to call on them, and the ladies make their great preparations, and treat them with their cake, and their wine, and punch—enough to poison them almost to death—and all together are bowing down to the goddess

of fashion. Is there a lady here that does not doubt the lawfulness of all this? I say it can be demonstrated to be wicked, but I only ask the ladies of this city, "Is it not *doubtful* whether this is all lawful?" I should call in question the sanity of the man or woman that had no doubt of the lawfulness of such a custom, in the midst of such prevailing intemperance as exists in this ciy. Who among you will practice it again? Practice it if you dare—at the peril of your soul! If you do that which is merely doubtful, God frowns and condemns; and HIS voice must be regarded.

I know people try to excuse the matter, and say it is well to have a day appropriated to such calls, when every lady is at home and every gentleman freed from business, and all that. And all that is very well. But when it is seen to be so abused and to produce so much evil, I ask every Christian here, if you can help doubting its lawfulness? And if it be doubtful, it comes under the rule: "If meat make my brother to offend." If keeping New Year's leads to so much gluttony, and drunkenness, and wickedness, does it not bring the lawfulness of it into doubt? Yes, that is the least that can be said, and they who doubt and yet do it, sin against God.

(9) Compliance with the extravagant fashions of the day.

Christian lady! Have you never doubted, do you not now doubt, whether it be lawful for you to copy these fashions, brought from foreign countries, and from places which it were a shame even to name in this assembly? Have you no doubt about it? And if you doubt and do it, you are condemned, and must repent of your sin, or you will be lost forever!

(10) Intermarriages of Christians with impenitent sinners.

This question always comes up; "But after all you say, it is not *certain* that these marriages are not lawful." Supposing it be so, yet does not the Bible and the nature of the case make it at least doubtful whether they are right? It can be demonstrated, indeed, to be unlawful. But suppose it could not be reduced to demonstration; what Christian ever did it and did not doubt whether it was lawful? And he that doubteth is condemned. See that Christian man or woman that is about forming such a connection—doubting all the way whether it is right: trying to pray down conscience under pretext of praying for light: praying all around your duty, and yet pressing on. *Take care!* You know you doubt the lawfulness of what you propose, and remember that "he that doubteth is damned."

Thus you see, my hearers, that here is a principle that will stand by you when you attempt to rebuke sin, if the power of society be employed to face you down, or put you on the defensive, and demand absolute proof of the sinfulness of a cherished practice. Remember *the burden of proof does not lie on you* to show beyond a doubt the absolute unlawfulness of the thing. If you can show sufficient reason to question its lawfulness, and to create a valid doubt whether it is according to the will of God, you shift the burden of proof to the other side. And unless they can remove the doubt, and show that there is no room for doubt, they have no right to continue in the doubtful practice, and if they do, they sin against God.

Remarks

1. The knowledge of duty is not indispensable to moral obligation, but *the possession of the means of knowledge is sufficient to make a person responsible.*

If a man has the means of knowing whether it is right or wrong he is bound to use the means, and is bound to inquire and ascertain at his peril.

2. If those are condemned, and adjudged worthy of damnation, who do that of which they doubt the lawfulness, what shall we say of the multitudes who are doing continually that which they know and confess to be wrong?

Woe to that man who practises that which he condemns. And "happy is he that condemneth not himself in that thing which he alloweth."

3. Hypocrites often attempt to shelter themselves behind their doubts to get clear of their duty.

The hypocrite is unwilling to be enlightened; he does not wish to know the truth, because he does not wish to obey the Lord, and so he hides behind his doubts, and turns away his eye from the light, and will not look or examine to see what his duty is, and in this way he tries to shield himself from responsibility. But God will drag them out from behind this refuge of lies by the principle laid down in the text that their very doubts condemn them.

Many will not be enlightened on the subject of temperance, and still persist in drinking or selling rum, because they are not fully convinced it is wrong. And they will not read a tract or a paper, nor attend a temperance meeting, for fear they shall be convinced. Many are resolved to indulge in the use of wine and strong beer, and they will not listen to anything calculated to convince them of the wrong. It shows that they are determined to indulge in sin, and they hope to hide behind their doubts. What better evidence could they give that they are hypocrites?

Who, in all these United States, can say that he has no doubt of the lawfulness of slavery? Yet the great body of the people will not hear anything on the subject, and they go into a passion if you name it, and it is even seriously proposed (both at the north and at the south) to pass laws forbidding inquiry and discussion on the subject. Now suppose these laws should be passed for the purpose of enabling the nation to shelter itself behind its doubts whether slavery is a sin that ought to be abolished immediately—will that help the matter? Not at all. If they continue to hold their fellowmen as property, in slavery, while they doubt its lawfulness, then they are condemned before God; and we may be sure their sin will find them out, and God will let them know how He regards it.

It is amazing to see the foolishness of people on this subject; as if by refusing to get clear of their doubts, they could get clear of their sin. Think of the people of the south: Christians, and even ministers, refusing to read a paper on the subject of slavery, and perhaps sending it back with abusive or threatening words. Threatening! For what? For reasoning with them about their duty? It can be demonstrated absolutely that slavery is unlawful, and ought to be repented of, and given up, like any other sin. But suppose they only doubt the lawfulness of slavery, and do not mean to be enlightened; they are condemned of God. Let them know that they cannot put this thing down, then they cannot clear themselves of it. So long as they doubt its lawfulness, they cannot hold men in slavery without sin; and that they do doubt its lawfulness is demonstrated by this opposition to discussion.

We may suppose a case, and perhaps there may be some such in the southern country, where a man doubts the lawfulness of holding slaves, and equally doubts the lawfulness of emancipating them in their present state of ignorance and dependence. In that case he comes under Pres. Edward's rule, and it is his duty not to fly in a passion with those who would call his attention to it, not to send back newspapers and refuse to read, but to inquire on all hands for light, and examine the question honestly in the light of the Word of God, till his doubts are cleared up. The least he can do is to set himself with all his power to educate them and train them to take care of themselves as fast and as thoroughly as possible, and to put them in a state where they can be set at liberty.

4. It is manifest there is but very little conscience in the church.

See what multitudes are persisting to do what they strongly doubt the lawfulness of.

5. There is still less love to God than there is conscience.

It cannot be pretended that love to God is the cause of all this following of fashions, this practising indulgences, and the other things of which people doubt the lawfulness. They do not persist in these things because they love God so well. No, no, but they persist in it because they wish to do it, to gratify themselves, and they had rather run the risk of doing wrong than to have their doubts cleared up. It is because they have so little love for God, so little care for the honor of God.

6. Do not say in your prayers, "Oh Lord, if I have sinned in this thing, Oh Lord, forgive me the sin."

If you have done that of which you doubted the lawfulness, you have sinned; whether the thing itself be right or wrong. And you must repent and ask forgiveness.

And now, let me ask you all, "Are you convinced that to do what you doubt the lawfulness of, is sin?" If you are, I have one more question to ask you: "Will you from this time relinquish everything of which you doubt the lawfulness? Every amusement, every indulgence, every practice, every pursuit? Will you do it, or will you stand before the solemn judgment seat of Jesus Christ, condemned?" If you will not relinquish these things, you show that you are an impenitent sinner, and do not INTEND to obey God, and if you do not repent you bring down upon your head God's condemnation and wrath, forever.

BIBLIOGRAPHY

Lectures to Professing Christians, by Charles G. Finney, Oberlin, Ohio: E. J. Goodrich, 1880. The London: Milner and Company, 1837 edition contains an extra sermon "Why Sinners Hate God." The sermons in this book are taken from the Oberlin edition.

Sermons on Gospel Themes, by Charles G. Finney, New York: Fleming H. Revell Company, 1876.

Sermons on Important Subjects, by Charles G. Finney, New York: John S. Taylor, 1836.

Sermons on the Way of Salvation, by Charles G. Finney, Oberlin, Ohio: Edwin J. Goodrich, 1891. These sermons were collected and edited posthumously by Finney's biographer, G. F. Wright.

APPENDIX I

More Sermons on Romans

The following sermons on Romans were published over a number of years in *The Oberlin Evangelist.* If there is sufficient demand, the editor may publish them in a second volume of "Finney's Sermons on Romans." This volume of his sermons on Romans includes only those sermons and lectures found in the out-of-print volumes of his works.

1. Holding the Truth in Unrighteousness—Romans 1:18
      Vol. XXIII, August 14, 1861
      Vol. XXIII, August 28, 1861
2. The Foundation, Conditions, and Relations of Faith—
      Romans 4:1-5
      Vol. XII, February 13, 1850
3. Death to Sin—Romans 6:7
      Vol. II, July 15, 1840
4. (No title given)—Romans 6:11
      Vol. I, April 24, 1839*
5. (No title given)—Romans 7:9
      Vol. XV, July 6, 1853
6. Thanks for Gospel Victory—Romans 7:25
      Vol. XVIII, January 30, 1856
7. Justification—Romans 8:1
      Vol. V, July 19, 1843
8. Moral Depravity—Romans 8:7
      Vol. XXIV, March 12, 1862
      Vol. XXIV, March 26, 1862
9. License, Bondage, and Liberty—Romans 8:15
      Vol. XVI, May 24, 1854
10. All Events, Ruinous to the Sinner—Romans 8:28
      Vol. IX, January 20, 1847

*The three sermons from 1839 can be found in Charles G. Finney, *The Promise of the Spirit*, compiled and edited by Timothy L. Smith (Minneapolis: Bethany Fellowship, Inc., 1980). None of the others is currently in print.

APPENDIX II

Confession of Faith of the Congregational Church of Oberlin

We publish this document by special request. It was the intention of its framers that it should include only the fundamental doctrines of the gospel—those which all real Christians do in fact believe, because they are incorporated into the very flesh and blood of the Christian life. The 8th article respects the gospel ordinances and the Christian Sabbath. These institutions were thought to be of great, if not indispensable, value to the prosperity of the visible church, though the belief of them may not be essential to the evidences of personal piety. With this exception, it is held that a creed should aim to comprise precisely the fundamental doctrines of the gospel—all these and no others. We rest this position on the obvious ground that in no other way can we hope to prevent the manifold and great evils of sectarianism. A church on this ground opens its doors equally to all Christians, and shuts them against all others. All real Christians and none others believe, love, and practice the fundamental doctrines of the gospel system.

ED.

CONFESSION OF FAITH

Article 1. We believe that the Scriptures of the Old and New Testaments are given by inspiration of God, and are the only infallible rule of faith and practice.

Article 2. We believe in one God—the Creator and Ruler of the Universe, existing in a divine and incomprehensible Trinity—the Father, the Son Jesus Christ, and the Holy Ghost—each possessing all divine perfections.

Article 3. We believe in the fall of our first parents, and the consequent entire apostasy, depravity, and lost condition of the human race.

Article 4. We believe in the incarnation, death, and atonement, of the Son of God; and that salvation is attained only through repentance and faith in his blood.

Article 5. We believe in the necessity of a radical change of heart, and that this is effected through the truth, by the agency of the Holy Ghost.

Article 6. We believe that the moral law is binding on all mankind as the rule of life, and that obedience to it is the proper evidence of a saving change.

Article 7. We believe that credible evidence of a change of heart is an indispensable ground of admission to the privileges of the visible church.

Article 8. We believe that the ordinances of Baptism and the Lord's Supper, together with the Christian Sabbath, are of perpetual obligation in the church.

Article 9. We believe in a future judgment, the endless happiness of the righteous, and the endless misery of the wicked.*

---

*The Oberlin Evangelist, Vol. VII, May 7, 1845.

Finney served this congregation for 35 years, and he no doubt was a strong influence in the writing of this confession which emphasized Christian unity. Many articles were written in *The Oberlin Evangelist* promoting Christian unity and the overcoming of sectarianism. It should be observed that these sermons on Romans cover these articles of confession in various ways.

Further reading by Charles G. Finney available from
BETHANY HOUSE PUBLISHERS:

FINNEY ON REVIVAL—A condensation of Finney's famous "Revival Lectures."

FINNEY'S SYSTEMATIC THEOLOGY

THE HEART OF TRUTH—The major truths of God's revelation shared with Oberlin College students by Finney.

LOVE IS NOT A SPECIAL WAY OF FEELING— "The Attributes of Love" edited and updated for the modern reader.

THE AUTOBIOGRAPHY OF CHARLES G. FINNEY— Condensed and edited by Helen Wessel.

REFLECTIONS ON REVIVAL—Compiled by Donald W. Dayton.

PRINCIPLES OF PRAYER—Compiled and edited by Louis G. Parkhurst, Jr. Forty daily meditations on how to pray, gleaned from Finney's writings.

FINNEY LIVES ON—Written by V. Raymond Edman, a study of Finney's Bible methods and messages.

THE PROMISE OF THE SPIRIT—Compiled and edited by Timothy L. Smith from Finney's writings on the subject of Christian holiness.